Latino Politics

Latino Politics

Second edition

LISA GARCÍA BEDOLLA

polity

First edition published in 2009 by Polity Press
This edition published in 2014 by Polity Press

Polity Press
65 Bridge Street
Cambridge CB2 1UR, UK

Polity Press
350 Main Street
Malden, MA 02148, USA

ISBN-13: 978-0-7456-6499-6
ISBN-13: 978-0-7456-6500-9(pb)

A catalogue record for this book is available from the British Library.

Library of Congress Cataloging-in-Publication Data

García Bedolla, Lisa, 1969-
  Latino politics / Lisa García Bedolla. – Second edition.
    pages cm
  Includes bibliographical references.
  ISBN 978-0-7456-6499-6 (hardcover : alkaline paper) – ISBN 0-7456-
6499-7 (hardcover : alkaline paper) – ISBN 978-0-7456-6500-9 (paperback :
alkaline paper) – ISBN 0-7456-6500-4 (paperback : alkaline paper)
1. Hispanic Americans–Politics and government. 2. Hispanic Americans-
-Economic conditions. 3. Hispanic Americans–Social conditions.
4. Immigrants–United States. 5. Political participation–United States.
6. United States–Race relations–Political aspects. 7. United States–Ethnic
relations–Political aspects. 8. United States–Politics and government.
9. United States–Foreign relations. I. Title.
  E184.S75G369 2014
  305.868'073–dc23
                                            2014014640

Typeset in 9.5/13 Swift Light by
Servis Filmsetting Limited, Stockport, Cheshire
Printed and bound in the United Kingdom by Clays Ltd, St Ives PLC

For further information on Polity, visit our website:
www.politybooks.com

To Pepe:
Thank you for sharing your life with me

Contents

Plates, Figures, and Tables

Plates

Figures

Tables

Preface to the Second Edition

I completed the second edition in late summer 2013. This was an ambivalent time for Latinos in US politics. On the one hand, the November 2012 election led to unprecedented interest in and discussion about the Latino vote and its current and future impact on US elections. On the other, comprehensive immigration reform (CIR) had passed the Senate in early summer but was stalled in the House, with Republicans like Iowa representative Steve King saying, about border security options, "we could also electrify this wire [on the border] with the kind of current that would not kill somebody, but it would simply be a discouragement for them to be fooling around with it. We do that with livestock all the time."[1] Clearly, sectors of the Republican Party, reflecting nontrivial sectors of US society, barely see Latino immigrants as worthy of basic human dignity and respect. The CIR bill itself, while providing a pathway for citizenship for the estimated 11 million unauthorized immigrants in the United States (many of whom are Latino), also for the first time tied those immigrants' ability to regularize their status to the implementation of a set of border security policies by the Department of Homeland Security. No border security, no pathway. And the pathway provided can only be described as arduous, with a minimum 15-year wait to gain citizenship and a remarkable number of hoops to jump through before reaching that point. Most analysts believe only about two-thirds of undocumented immigrants would receive relief under this bill. Compared to the Immigration Reform and Control Act (IRCA) in 1986, this bill is far less generous, more punitive, and much more focused on border security.

So how do we explain the fact that Latino political power has only increased since 1986, yet the immigration policy climate has worsened significantly? Part of the explanation lies with that increase in power and demographic growth. Many Americans, alarmed by significant demographic change within their local communities, sometimes express their unease through anti-immigrant attitudes. Latinos were much less threatening when they weren't living next door, attending their children's schools, or representing them on the city council. This by no means is meant to imply that a majority of Americans feel this way. Rather, it speaks to the complex conscious and unconscious responses individuals have to rapid demographic, technological, and social change. It is easier to blame our anxiety on those who look different, or speak differently, in our local community than on the complex economic restructuring that has so deeply affected all Americans' opportunity structures over the past few decades. During periods of adjustment, things often get worse before they get better. I believe that is the moment we are in now.

I hope that this volume will help students to understand that process of change within US politics, how we got to this point, and what to expect in the future. The first volume was a labor of love, my attempt to historicize US Latino politics in order to better understand the community's experiences today. Since its publication, I have been honored and humbled to receive generous and positive feedback from readers from across the country. Many shared their family's migration and incorporation experiences with me. I would like to take this opportunity to thank all those who have picked up and enjoyed the book. It is incredibly gratifying to know that the product was of use to so many; it is my hope that this new volume will continue to speak to readers' interests and personal experiences.

With this second volume, Polity's editorial staff have again been wonderful. Louise Knight has been very supportive and patient, and all the support staff have been delightful to work with. I appreciate the commitment the people at Polity have shown to this volume and to the others in their minority politics series, as well as the resources they have dedicated to them. At the time they commissioned these works, few presses were publishing in the area of US minority politics. They should be commended for their foresight and their willingness to take that risk, as well as for the high quality of the final products.

In August 2013, my youngest child Micaela, with whom I was pregnant when completing the first volume, entered kindergarten. Her kindergarten classmates will be worlds different from the ones I shared a classroom with in September 1974. My class was all white (except for me). There were no language accommodations for me, nor any real understanding of the potential developmental issues I faced as a bilingual and bicultural student. Micaela's school has a range of supports available for its language learners, a commitment to celebrating the rich and varied cultural backgrounds of its student body, and a desire to educate students for the 21st-century global world. One can only imagine how this foundation will serve her in the future. This book is about children like Micaela and the ways in which they and their ancestors have transformed US politics since the nineteenth century. I am excited to see the world this new generation will be able to construct for all of us.

Acknowledgements

This book represents the coming together of two sets of interests that have driven my intellectual work: the politics of the domestic and of the international. Also, as an academic, I have always been interested in questioning how things came to be rather than accepting the conventional answers. Unfortunately, much of the study of US politics begins at the US border, with little reference to the broader world outside or focus on internal communities that do not hold power.

Consequently, when I began studying US politics I found little that described my experience or my history. Surely, I should not have been invisible to those who study "American" politics, given that Florida, Louisiana, and what is now the western United States were once Spanish-speaking polities and that the term "America" encompasses not only North America but also Central and South America and the Caribbean. Thus, on the domestic side, as a Latina growing up in the United States, I have had an ongoing concern with the political experiences of those of Latino origin residing there.

From an international perspective, as the daughter of Cuban immigrants, I have been faced with the geopolitical, historical, and social aspects of our family's experience at every Thanksgiving dinner where we add black beans, rice, and pork to the traditional menu of turkey and stuffing. Those meals were always served alongside often heated political debate. As a result of those spirited discussions, I have continually felt a strong desire to know better the history of my parents' country of origin and how and why my family ended up in the United States.

With this volume, I am finally able to bring together these two foci of experience. It is my hope that it helps readers to contextualize the US Latino experience beyond US borders, in order for them to understand more fully the factors influencing this community's migration, politics, and politicization in the United States. And, importantly, I hope that, through a greater knowledge of the history of US relations with the Americas and their inhabitants, readers will understand better how these relationships have influenced the trajectory of American democracy since the nineteenth century.

Such an enterprise cannot be undertaken without amassing considerable debts. This book would not have been possible without the support of my husband, José Luis Bedolla, who not only provided important intellectual encouragement but also balances his demanding career and our home life in a way that provides me the time and space necessary to do my work. I am continually humbled by the personal and professional support that he gives me. In my professional life, I also have had the good fortune of benefiting from the support and guidance of a broad intellectual community, all of whom have contributed in important ways to my thinking and sanity during this book's creation. This community includes, but is not limited to: Marisa Abrajano, Tony Affigne, Michael Alvarez, Cristina Beltrán, John Bretting, Amy Bridges, Daniel Brunstetter, Leo Chávez, María Chávez, Arlene Dávila, Heather Elliott, Cynthia Feliciano, Raúl Fernández, Paul Fymer, Gilbert González, Don Green, Michael Jones-Correa, Jane Junn, Claire Kim, Taeku Lee, Jessica Lavariega Monforti, Paula Mcclain, Melissa Michelson, Michael Montoya, Naomi Murakawa, Kevin Olson, Hector Perla, Karthick Ramakrishnan, Ray Rocco, Vicki Ruiz, Rubén Rumbaut, Kamal Sadiq, Mark Sawyer, Ronald Schmidt, Sr., Andrea Simpson, Rogers Smith, Dara Strolovitch, Jessica Trounstine, Deborah Vargas, Dorian Warren, and Janelle Wong. I am indebted to them for their generous support and cogent insights. Any errors that remain are my own.

CHAPTER ONE

Introduction: Latinos and US Politics

Objectives
- Understand the definitions of agency and structure
- Understand what it means for race to be a social construction
- Understand the historical meaning and privileges that have been attached to whiteness in the United States
- Understand how Latinos fit (or not) into the US racial structure
- Understand the political, social, and economic implications of how Latinos were categorized racially
- Understand the effect US foreign and economic policy has on Latin American countries, on Latinos' decisions to migrate, and on their treatment upon arrival

Latinos, Immigration, and Politics

Scholars studying Latinos in the United States focus a great deal on issues of immigration and of political participation. Interestingly, both these issues most often are conceptualized as individual acts. Immigration is seen as a personal decision made by an individual or family, with little consideration of the macroeconomic context that influences that decision. Similarly, political engagement is most often discussed as (by and large) an individual choice. Individuals choose to vote, contact their elected officials, or run for political office. If they do not do so, it is because of a lack of interest rather than because of any sort of larger, structural constraint.

Yet the fact of the matter is that none of us, as individuals, can act with complete freedom, or with *agency* – defined as "the capacity, condition, or state of acting or of exerting power."[1] In other words, agency is about how much we, as individuals, can accomplish on our own, about our ability to determine, by ourselves, the direction of our lives. Yet there are also institutional structures that may impede our ability to exercise that agency – to do exactly what we want, when we want

1

it, and the way we want it. On the most basic level, there are rules and laws which limit our freedom of action. But, more importantly, there are also other kinds of institutional structures, social, political, or economic, which may constrain an individual's ability to act. Those structures include, but are not limited to, the employment and the housing markets; the legal system, including immigration rules; the political system; the educational system; and so on. How these structures operate within an individual's life varies over time and by geographic location. They are not static, yet they are not always easy to change either. Thus structures have an important impact on an individual's ability to change their life for the better.

In this book I will explore the migration processes and political activity of the population of Latin American origin in the United States, placing an emphasis on the interaction between agency and structure. For example, during the Central American solidarity movement, the US government refused to characterize Central American migrants as political refugees, despite the violence and political upheaval that existed in their home countries. These migrants were able to exercise agency in deciding to leave their homelands, yet were structurally constrained by the US government when they attempted to regularize their migration status in the United States. Yet, as we will see in chapter 7, in coalition with other migrants and political organizations, they mobilized to change the US government's position and were partly successful, thus changing the institutional structure which future Central American migrants would face when arriving in the United States.

The Central American case is a good example of the interplay between agency and structure and of why it is important. When considering political activity and engagement, particularly that of minority groups, we must realize that there is a historical background and an institutional context which frame an individual's decision-making process. In order to decide to act politically, an individual must feel empowered to do so and must feel that her action can make a difference. If that person comes from a community or group which, historically, has not had much influence in the political system, it is less likely that she will feel that that is the best way to spend her time; or it is more likely that she will choose non-traditional forms of engagement (like protesting) in order to express her political views. Thus individuals do not make their political decisions in a vacuum.

The purpose of this book is to show the reader the historical and institutional context within which to situate US Latino political engagement.

Understanding that context will help the reader also to understand why Latinos make the political decisions they do and what structural factors influence these choices. Only to look at one or the other is to miss an important part of the story.

Defining Latino: What's in a Name?

This text examines the history, migration, and politics of different groups of Latin American origin living in the United States. To begin with, it is important to consider what these groups should be called. The title of my book uses the word "Latino," which is meant to describe all individuals, foreign and US-born, who have ancestry in any of the Spanish-speaking nations of Latin America.[2] The term "Hispanic" was adopted by the US government during the 1970s and has the same definition as "Latino." Scholars like Nicolas DeGenova and Ana Ramos-Zayos argue these pan-ethnic identifiers were designed by the US government to erase the particular histories of Latin American groups in the United States, such as Mexicans and Puerto Ricans.[3] In contrast, "Chicano" is meant to describe, specifically, individuals of Mexican origin in the United States. This term came directly out of the political organizing within the Mexican American community in the US southwest during the 1960s; hence its usage often presumes a certain political consciousness, in addition to being a national-origin identifier. "Boricua" is a term used to describe Puerto Ricans in the United States (it comes from the name of an indigenous group native to the island), and "Nuyorican," more specifically, is sometimes used to denote individuals of Puerto Rican origin living in New York City. "Quisqueya/o" is sometimes used to describe Dominicans (it is the indigenous word for the island of *Española*). Thus there are many terms which are used to describe individuals of Latin American origin; some of them are national-origin-specific, others spring directly from the political mobilization of the community or from the desire of group members to come up with new terms to describe themselves. For the sake of simplicity, this text uses the term "Latino" to refer to groups of Latin American origin generally, and national-origin-specific terms to describe the experiences of individuals from particular countries. But it is important to note that these labels can be politically or personally important. Many Latinos choose to use different words to describe their identities – terms that are grounded in their particular historical, personal, and political experiences.

Latinos' "Ethnicity" and "Race"

The fact that this book focuses on the experiences of Latinos in the United States also implies that Latinos constitute a social group, one that should be the focus of the present study. But what does it mean for something to be a social group? Political theorist Iris Young described a social group as "a collective of persons differentiated from others by cultural forms, practices, special needs or capacities, structure of power, or privilege."[4] According to Young, what makes a collection of people into a group is "less some set of attributes its members share than the relation in which they stand to others." In other words, defining Latinos as a social group does not mean that we need to assume that all Latinos are the same, share the same experiences, or have the same goals or aspirations. We will see in the next chapters that this is not the case. Latino national-origin groups have had very different experiences in the United States. They arrived at different points in American history, migrated for very different reasons, settled in different geographic settings, and have been treated in disparate ways by the US government. There are important experiential differences within Latino national-origin groups as well; these are due to geographic location, class status, nativity, generation, gender, sexual orientation, and other factors. Despite this heterogeneity, what is similar about the experiences of all US Latinos is where they were placed in the US racial hierarchy and how that placement has affected their social, political, and economic opportunities.

Given their differences of experience and background, if Latinos are a social group, are they a racial group or an ethnic one? The distinction between these two characterizations has been the source of ongoing debates among scholars – debates which will not be resolved here. The term "race" presupposes a common biological or genealogical ancestry among people. "Ethnicity" places more of an emphasis on culture than on common genetic traits. In an attempt to bring together both concepts, Michael Omi and Howard Winant define race as "a concept which signifies and symbolizes social conflicts and interests by referring to different types of human bodies."[5] They emphasize social conflicts in order to get us away from biological understandings of what race is. There is no biological foundation for separate "races" of humans. As recent DNA tests have proven, many individuals whom we see as "Black" are in fact more European than African in terms of their DNA. For example, Henry Louis Gates, a prominent African American intellectual, found he has as much European DNA as West African DNA (most African Americans are about 20 percent European). This kind of testing forces us to reconsider what "race" means and to see how these categorizations have more to do with society than with biology.

Feminist philosopher Linda Alcoff suggests using the term "ethnorace" to describe the Latino experience in the United States. For her, ethnorace is a concept which combines the experiences of both ethnicity and race. She argues that "using only ethnicity belies the reality of most Latinos' everyday experiences, as well as obscures our own awareness about how ethnic identifications often do the work of race while seeming to be theoretically correct and politically advanced. Race dogs our steps; let us not run from it else we cause it to increase its determination."[6] The term ethnorace is meant to describe the ways in which factors often attributed to culture, such as language, can be racialized. In other words, ascriptive attributions can be based on linguistic or cultural practices that are not "racial" (or biological), but still can have racialized consequences. Because I believe the lived experiences of Latinos in the United States include both racialized and ethnic/cultural traits, I describe them as an ethnoracial group. Scholars like Omi, Winant, and Alcoff are attempting to find ways to define a social phenomenon which has historical roots and important material consequences but which is nevertheless artificial in that its underlying reality is fluid and changes over time.

In order to describe race in a way that recognizes this fluidity, scholars explain racial processes as social constructions. Social construction means that the values attached to particular external attributes, such as skin color, are defined, or constructed, by society. Put another way, the problem is not that of the recognition of ethnoracial differences among people, but rather that of the values, or hierarchies, attached to those differences. For the bulk of United States history, being defined as "white" gave members of that group access to social, legal, economic, and political privileges which were closed to those not defined as "white." For example, one of the first laws passed by the United States Congress in 1790 was a citizenship law which stipulated that no non-white person could become a naturalized citizen of the United States. This restriction remained in force until 1943, when individuals of Chinese origin were allowed to be naturalized for the very first time. This racial restriction on naturalization was finally removed completely for all groups in 1952, with the McCarran Walter Act. In addition, many states made it illegal for a non-white to testify in court against a white, to serve on juries, to live where they wanted to live, or to work in the most skilled jobs. These restrictions limited non-whites' access to the protection of the legal system and their possibilities for social, political, and economic mobility. Thus racial constructs have been directly related to access to fundamental items like resources, citizenship rights, and the protection of the state (that is, to having a criminal justice system which actually defends your person and/or your property). Therefore race may be constructed, but which category an individual belongs to has had, and continues to have, significant material and political implications for their life chances.

Because racial categorizations determined access to resources, US federal and state governments had to come up with schemes in order to determine the "race" to which individuals belonged. Often referred to as the "one-drop rule," these schemes attempted to define who was white and who was not. The "one drop" refers to the fact that, in much of the country and particularly in the south, having one drop of Black blood made it impossible by law to claim "whiteness." For example in California, in 1849, having half or more of "Indian" blood would lead to one's being considered not "white," and half or more of Black blood made a person *mulatto*. In 1851, the law was changed so that only one quarter of Indian blood would make a person not "white." Yet many of these laws were challenged, leading the courts to have to determine what constituted being "white." An especially good example is that of the pre-requisite cases. These were cases brought by individuals who wanted to contest the 1790 law barring non-whites from being naturalized in the United States.[7] Looking at petitions by Asian Indians from 1909 to 1923, we see that in 1909 the court in *Balsara* ruled that Asian Indians were *probably* not white, because the people on the jury thought it unlikely that Congress intended for Asian Indians to be considered white under the 1790 law. Yet in 1910 the court ruled in two cases that Asian Indians were white, on the basis of the petitioner's skin color and of scientific evidence regarding the origins of the Caucasian race. This ruling was reaffirmed in 1913, with appeal to legal precedent. Yet in 1917 the court ruled that Asian Indians were *not* white, on the basis of common knowledge and congressional intent. The same court reversed this position in 1919 and 1920, deciding again that the Asian Indians involved in those cases were white. Then in 1923 the Supreme Court ruled again, on the basis of common knowledge, that Asian Indians were not white. From that point on, on the basis of the 1923 legal precedent, the court ruled that Asian Indians are not white and therefore ineligible for naturalization. The Asian Indian case shows how difficult it was for the courts to maintain these kinds of racial categorizations in the face of any sort of systematic scrutiny. Yet that is exactly what the US government did; and its actions had important consequences for those US groups which were considered non-white. Latinos were one of those groups.

When Latinos became part of the United States, either through immigration or through conquest (as in the case of Puerto Ricans, or of Mexican Americans in the nineteenth-century southwest), they were inserted into this established racial order. Even though many Latinos are recent immigrants, it is important to realize that this historical racial hierarchy continues to influence the playing field upon which their community sits today. For example, one complication for Latinos was that one-drop rules presupposed a strict, biological understanding of what race is. Under those regimes, a person was Black, white, or Indian, and there was no legal representation for intermediate categories like *mulattos* (people of Black and white ancestry). Latinos, on the other hand, come from a variety of racial backgrounds. When the Spaniards arrived in Latin America, that continent had an indigenous population which numbered millions of inhabitants. Although a large proportion of this native population perished through disease and wars of conquest, a significant part survived, particularly in Mexico, Central America, Colombia, Perú, and Bolívia. The Spanish mixed with these groups, as did the Africans, creating what are called *mestizos* – individuals of mixed European, African, and indigenous descent. In the Caribbean, little of the indigenous population remained, which made it necessary for Spaniards to import African slaves to use as the bulk of the labor force. Those Africans mixed with the Spaniards and with the indigenous groups who remained on the islands, creating a new racial admixture; this is often called "*mulatto*." After the end of slavery, Caribbean plantation-owners imported hundreds of thousands of Chinese laborers to work in the fields. In the nineteenth and twentieth centuries, large numbers of Asians from other countries, including Japan, settled in other parts of Latin America, adding to its racial mixture. This is why, in the early twentieth century, José Vasconcelos called Latin Americans *la raza cósmica* (the cosmic race) – one made up of the blood of all the world's races.

During the colonial period, the Spaniards developed a complex *casta* system which laid out the racial hierarchy according to how much European, Black, or indigenous blood a particular individual had. Like the American system, the Spanish system placed the white Europeans on top; but the remainder included many more racial options than were available in the United States at that time. Most Latin American countries abolished the Spanish system after independence. But they still maintained the racial hierarchies. The difference was that their understanding of race included mixed race as a possibility, which was not true in most parts of the United States after the late nineteenth century.[8]

Thus, when Latinos arrived in the United States, they had to fit into a relatively rigid racial hierarchy, where it was very important whether a person was defined as "Black" or "white." Yet many Latinos are of mixed race. Those of Mexican or Central American origin tend to be of mixed indigenous background and those from the Caribbean are more likely to have African origins. But are they "Indian?" Or are they "Black?" Or something else? The problem with people of mixed race is that often there can be significant differences in skin color even within the same family. One sibling can be quite dark-skinned, another one quite light-skinned. Since the US racial structure did not allow for the possibility of admixture, what often happened was that the lighter-skinned sibling would be treated as "white," the darker as "Black." At the height of segregation, this meant that they would go to separate schools, get to use separate bathroom facilities, and in general would have a very different set of opportunities, simply because one was seen as white and the other was not. Latinos, then, complicated the US racial structure and did not fit neatly into any of its racial categories. This racial ambiguity meant that the place they chose to settle in, and the particular racial history in that place, had an important impact on the kinds of opportunities open to them. There was no one uniform response to, or treatment of, Latinos as a "race."

For example, there were large numbers of Latinos, mostly of Mexican origin, living in the state of Texas during the nineteenth century. Many had been there originally when Texas was part of Mexico. Texas turned into a slave state once it became part of the United States, and after emancipation it developed and enforced strict Jim Crow laws, requiring racial segregation in neighborhoods, schools, and public facilities. Like the rest of the south, Texas also passed laws to keep Blacks from voting. Yet in Texas, African Americans were not the only large minority group; there were Mexican Americans as well. Jim Crow laws were applied to the Mexican population because they too were seen as non-white, despite their legal categorization as white under the Treaty of Guadalupe Hidalgo. This was not true in New Mexico, however, where Latinos of Mexican origin remained in the majority until the twentieth century: in New Mexico segregation was not as extreme as in Texas. Mexican Americans were allowed voting rights there. Moreover, they held public office positions and much of the political power until the mid twentieth century. Thus local context had an important impact on racial definitions and racial restrictions, even in the case of the same national-origin group. These differences were possible because of Latino racial ambiguity.

Thus race is not "real" in a biological sense, but racial categories still have important implications for the opportunities which various groups have in our society. Without an understanding of the historical legacy of race, it is difficult to understand the current distribution of resources and opportunities within American society. Being white gave individuals access to citizenship; access to land under the Homestead Act in the nineteenth century (which was restricted to whites); access to legal protection and the right to organize unions, which significantly increased unionized workers' wages and benefits (many unions prohibited non-white membership, and many people of color worked in industries not covered under the National Labor Relations Act); access to subsidized federal home loans (the Federal Housing Administration [FHA] program redlined and excluded African American, Mexican American, and mixed race neighborhoods); and access to public education of adequate quality.[9] Recent studies have shown that whites and African Americans with similar levels of income and education still have very different levels of total wealth because whites are much more likely to inherit real estate and other funds from their parents.[10] That inheritance is the fruit of a highly exclusionary racial history. Because of this history, "color-blindness" will not erase the inequality which has accumulated from racial categorizations. It is only by looking at race that we can begin to address its negative legacy.

Gender: Seeing Latino Politics Intersectionally

Gender also interacts with ethnoracial categories in ways that affect Latino incorporation patterns. Appreciating intersectionality – the idea that human beings possess multiple identifications simultaneously and that the intersection of those identities has important implications for their beliefs, attitudes, and experiences – is important for understanding Latino political engagement. Studies have shown that Latino men and women migrate for different reasons, and that women now make up a growing proportion of Latino migration streams. In the early twentieth century, Latin-American-origin migration was quite male-dominated; by the early twenty-first century, that trend had shifted, with growing numbers of Latin-American-origin women choosing to migrate to the United States. Gender ratios among the foreign-born vary in important ways by national origin and by legal status.[11] The majority of Dominican migrants, for example, are female, while there are more male than female Mexican migrants. Unauthorized migration flows, in addition, tend to be heavily male and more than three-quarters of the United States' unauthorized migrants come from Mexico and Central America. These gender differences have their roots in social and economic forces within the home countries and have an effect on immigrants' integration experiences in the United States.

One key aspect of those experiences is how males and females are treated by US immigration policy. Studies suggest that immigration policies that, on the surface, seem gender-neutral, in practice have very different consequences for male and female migrants.[12] In 2004, 73.2 percent of women applying for employment-based visas did so as a dependent of a visa holder; only 26.8 percent were primary visa holders. Similarly, under family reunification, women often must apply for sponsorship by male family members, requiring long waits before they are allowed to migrate to the United States and making them dependent on male family members for their migration status. These differences, in turn, affect women's ability to settle and work in the United States.

In response to their particular structural position, female migrants engage in social network activity differently from male migrants and experience socioeconomic trajectories that vary from those of men.[13] Those differences in terms of labor market structures and network relationships have a direct impact on how female migrants engage with the political system. Of course, these gender differences are not only present among immigrants: native-born Latinos also vary in terms of gender roles, social network relationships, and economic opportunity structures. Therefore, it is important to consider the role gender differences play in helping to frame how male and female Latinos choose to engage in political activity. Using an intersectional lens is important, then, for understanding the complexity of Latino political experiences in the United States.

Latino Political Incorporation

But how do racialization and gender relate to Latino politics? Racialization processes and gender differences are important because they have shaped the way Latinos are seen by non-Latinos, the opportunities Latinos have been afforded, and the kinds of restrictions which have been placed on their incorporation into political life. Some Latinos living in the United States have been present in their communities since before they became part of the United States. We will see in the following chapters the significance of that long-term relationship. Yet a very large proportion of Latinos in the United States have arrived there since 1970. So, even though not all Latinos are immigrants or recent immigrants, the community contains sufficient numbers of immigrants for thinking about how immigrant politics varies from non-immigrant politics to be an important part of learning about the Latino political experience in the United States. Immigrant political incorporation is different from non-immigrant political incorporation because of two factors:

1 Immigrants choose to be part of the United States, and therefore must overcome important structural hurdles before they can even consider engaging politically.
2 Immigrant inclusion is about defining the boundaries of the US polity, and therefore speaks in important ways to issues of race, inequality, and power within American society, in ways that are some-what different from (but related to) what is happening with US-born racialized groups.

Immigrants do not arrive in their new country as a clean slate. They bring a set of resources and a historical experience that shape their decision to migrate and their opportunity structure once they arrive. Thus the study of Latino immigrant incorporation needs to begin with the international structural context which embeds the decision to migrate. Immigrants' decisions to migrate are rooted in macro-geopolitical processes over which their subjects have little control, such as economic recession or dislocation, war, or natural disaster. Once immigrants arrive in the United States, they must deal with an immigration bureaucracy which, as we will see in the following chapters, does not treat them all the same. The country an immigrant comes from, and the relationship the US government has with that country at the time of migration, strongly affect how easy or difficult the legal aspects of the migration process are going to be. Hence, not only the immigrants' legal and economic status upon their arrival, but even their tendency to come from particular countries and their choice to migrate to the United States, are intimately related with US foreign and economic policy.

US Foreign and Economic Policy and Latino Politics

The United States' relations with Latin America have been deeply affected by two important US principles: manifest destiny and the Monroe doctrine. The idea of manifest destiny – that the United States was "destined" to be an Anglo-Saxon Protestant nation that stretched from coast to coast – had its roots in colonial political thought. In a letter to his father in 1811, John Quincy Adams wrote:

> The whole continent of North America appears to be destined by Divine Providence to be peopled by one nation, speaking one language, professing one general system of religious and political principles, and accustomed to one general tenor of social usages and customs. For the common happiness of them all, for their peace and prosperity, I believe it is indispensable that they should be associated in one federal Union.[14]

Like Adams, many Americans believed that it was God's will that the United States should control the North American territory, and that the nation needed to be based on a common set of political ideals, religious beliefs, and cultural practices. This creed was one of the main justifications underlying US territorial expansion through the US–Mexico War. We will see that it also had important consequences for how the US dealt with the incorporation of the Mexican population present in those territories when they were annexed into the United States. Over time, this idea that it was the United States' destiny to control a particular geographic sphere would expand beyond the North American continent and extend across the western hemisphere through the Monroe doctrine.

John Quincy Adams developed the Monroe doctrine in 1823, when he was President James Monroe's Secretary of State. The main thrust of the doctrine was that, as countries in the Americas were becoming independent from the imperial European powers, the United States did not want Europe to re-colonize the western hemisphere. In his State of the Union message in December of that year, President Monroe declared that the United States would not interfere in European wars or internal affairs and expected Europe to stay out of the affairs of the new world. European attempts to influence the new world would be interpreted by the United States as threats to its "peace and safety."

President James Polk invoked the principle of manifest destiny and the Monroe doctrine in an 1845 address to Congress in support of westward expansion into Mexican territory. In 1904, President Theodore Roosevelt added the "Roosevelt corollary" to the Monroe doctrine, which defined US intervention in Latin American domestic affairs as necessary for US national security:

> All that this country [the United States] desires is to see the neighboring countries stable, orderly, and prosperous. Any country whose people conduct themselves well can count upon our hearty friendship. If a nation shows that it knows how to act with reasonable efficiency and decency in social and political matters, if it keeps order and pays its obligations, it need fear no interference from the United

States. Chronic wrongdoing, or an impotence which results in a general loosening of the ties of civilized society, may in America, as elsewhere, ultimately require intervention by some civilized nation, and in the Western Hemisphere the adherence of the United States to the Monroe Doctrine may force the United States, however reluctantly, in flagrant cases of such wrongdoing or impotence, to the exercise of an international police power.[15]

This corollary was used to justify US intervention in Cuba, Haiti, Nicaragua, and the Dominican Republic. It was officially reversed in 1934 with the advent of Franklin D. Roosevelt's "good neighbor" policy toward Latin America. Yet the principle that the United States' political and economic interests are intimately related to those of Latin America remained. Throughout the twentieth century, the United States' economic interests played a central role in the development of Latin American banking, infrastructure, and industry. Similarly, the US government, particularly after the start of the Cold War, continually intervened in Latin American internal governmental and military affairs.

This US involvement is critically important for understanding Latino migration flows to the United States. Many Latin American migrants worked for US companies in their home countries. Many were directly recruited by those companies to come to the United States, and those companies often lobbied the US Congress to ensure that these migration flows would continue. The economic development policies pursued by Latin American governments, and therefore the economic opportunities available to their populations, particularly employment, often were strongly influenced by the US financial sector and by the US government. After the advent of the Cold War, US strategic concerns and levels of military aid often affected the success or failure of social movements to redistribute wealth in these countries. Thus, the way the United States expressed its political and economic interests in the region affected the Latin Americans' economic and political situation on the ground, the facility with which they were able to migrate to the United States, and the legal terms under which they were accepted (or not) under US immigration policy.

Conclusion

We will see in the following chapters that there were important domestic and international political reasons why the US government involved itself in the politics of Latin American countries and encouraged or discouraged migration from them. For different reasons, the US government has made immigrant settlement much easier for some national-origin groups than for others. This, in turn, has affected how quickly and under what terms Latino immigrants have been allowed to join the polity. These decisions also have affected the immigrants' choice of places to settle, the kinds of transnational and co-ethnic social networks available to them in those places, and what political and economic opportunity structures were present in those communities. It follows that that experience has had an important impact on these immigrants' trust in government, feelings of personal efficacy, and willingness to become engaged politically. These opportunity structures also affect their socioeconomic mobility; immigrants of higher SES are more likely to engage politically. This means that having more economic opportunities also affects political incorporation. This is a good example of how agency and structure interact. A particular immigrant brings a set of skills (education, funding, personal drive) which affect her ability to succeed in her new country. But that success is also affected by the institutions she must interact with on the ground. How open those institutions are, and how much they will enable her to take advantage of their resources, is outside of her control.

What this interaction looks like for immigrants from each national-origin group also varies over time. Each national-origin group discussed in this volume has faced particular challenges, has organized so as to improve their position, and all have achieved important successes. That mobilization, in turn, has changed the structural context for new immigrants. Therefore nothing in these stories is "static"; there is constant movement across historical time. It is only by looking at the historical trajectory of each national-origin group that we may understand fully the Latino political incorporation process today. This is what we will be doing in the following chapters.

QUESTIONS FOR DISCUSSION

1 What are two examples of how agency and structure affect Latino political engagement?
2 Do Latinos comprise a social group in the United States? Why or why not?
3 How did Latinos' racial ambiguity affect their treatment under US law?
4 Why is it important to look at the Latino experience intersectionally?
5 How did manifest destiny and the Monroe Doctrine affect Latino migration patterns and political incorporation in the United States?

CHAPTER TWO

Latina/o Participation: Individual Activity and Institutional Context

Objectives
- Understand Latino demographics, particularly national-origin differences in socioeconomic status, age, and nativity
- Understand Latino participation patterns, including national-origin differences and differences in the types of activities Latinos engage in
- Understand the political institutional context in the United States, its majoritarian nature, and what that means for the participation and representation of minority groups

Latino Political Engagement

In the 2000 presidential election, for the first time the Republican candidate, George W. Bush, exceeded his Democratic rival, Al Gore, in the amount his campaign spent on Spanish-language advertising targeting Latino voters. The Bush campaign hired veteran political strategist Lionel Sosa to develop a sophisticated and well-run Spanish-language outreach campaign. This effort is credited with significantly increasing Latino support for Bush in comparison to support for the 1996 Republican candidate, Bob Dole. In 2007, candidates competing for the Democratic presidential nomination participated, for the first time ever, in a bilingual presidential debate televized on the most popular Spanish-language channel, Univisión. Similarly, during the 2012 presidential campaign, both major-party presidential candidates – Barack Obama and Mitt Romney – appeared in presidential forums on Univisión. In addition, actress Eva Longoria and wealthy San Antonio businessman Henry Muñoz founded the Futuro Fund, a Latino-focused fundraising effort for the Obama campaign that raised $32 million to help Obama woo the Latino vote.[1] Due to the fund's success, in 2013 Muñoz became the first Latino to be selected as Finance Chairman of the Democratic National Committee. Why are we seeing increased attention being paid to Latino voters by both political parties at the national level? The answer is simple: demographics.

Demographics

According to the US census, in 2012 there were just over 53 million Latinos currently living in the United States, making Latinos 16.9 percent of the total US population and the nation's largest minority group.[2] From 2000 to 2010, the Latino population grew 48 percent.[3] Much of this population growth has been among US-born Latinos, who made up 64 percent of the Latino population in 2011. Future estimates of population growth in the US suggest that the Latino population will double by 2060; that year, an estimated one in three Americans will be of Latino origin. In terms of the national-origin distribution of the US Latino population in 2011, individuals of Mexican origin constituted by far the largest group, at 65 percent. They were followed by Puerto Ricans (9.3 percent), Central Americans (8.4 percent), South Americans (5.7 percent), Cubans (3.6 percent), and Dominicans (3 percent).[4] Thus, although there is substantial national-origin diversity within the Latino population in the United States, it is important to keep in mind that almost two-thirds of US Latinos are of Mexican origin.

The Latino community varies from the US population at large along a number of parameters which include age, income, and education, and which, we will see below, are important when considering the factors driving their participation patterns. Table 2.1 compares Latinos to the American population along several dimensions. We can see that the Latino population is significantly younger than the US population overall. Relative to Americans in general, more Latinos are under the age of 18 and fewer are over the age of 65. Latinos earn significantly less than other Americans, although, interestingly, there is less of a gender gap in earnings among Latinos than there is among the total US population. The poverty rate among Latinos is more than twice that of the general population, and is particularly high among children (those under 18). Latino households also tend to be larger, which means that household income for the Latino population is expected to support a larger number of people than income for the rest of the population. Latino educational attainment is also lower on average: many more Latinos than other Americans have less than a 9th-grade education, and the number of Latinos with a college degree is less than half of that found in the general population.

Table 2.1 Age, Nativity, Income, Household, and Education for Latinos and Total US Population

	Latinos	Total US population
Age		
median age	27	37
population under 18	35.1%	22.4%
population aged 65 and over	5.7%	14.2%
Nativity		
foreign population	36%	7.9%
Income and poverty		
median annual earnings for men 25 and older	$26,497	$37,653
median annual earnings for women 25 and older	$18,765	$23,395
percentage of overall population living in poverty	26.6%	12.9%
population under 18 living in poverty	35%	18%
Household size		
population living in household with 2 people or fewer	39.2%	64%
population living in household with 5 people or more	22.7%	8.3%
Educational attainment		
population with less than a 9th-grade education	20.7%	2.7%
population with a high school diploma or more	64.3%	91.1%
population with a college degree or more	14.1%	32.9%

Source: American Community Survey, 2011.

This demographic information is important not only in terms of getting a snapshot of the community, but also in terms of how it may affect Latino public policy preferences. Given the relative youth of the community, one can imagine educational attainment and educational quality being very important issues, along with policies aimed at decreasing poverty rates among children. On the other hand, given the small number of Latinos over the age of 65, issues such as social security and retirement may not be as immediate. Because of these demographic differences, it is unlikely that voters from the general US population will have the same political concerns and policy preferences as Latinos. That is why it is important that Latinos have a voice in the political process which is equal to their demographic numbers. As we will see below, there are a number of reasons why that has yet to be established.

Not only do Latinos differ from the general US population, they also differ on a number of important parameters across national-origin groups. Table 2.2 summarizes age, nativity, income, and educational attainment across the Latino national-origin groups we will be studying in this book. In terms of age, Cubans stand out as the oldest national-origin group, with a median age of 40, more than 10 years higher than any other national-origin group. Mexicans have the largest under-18 population and Salvadorans and Guatemalans the smallest over-65 group. More than two-thirds of Guatemalans and over 60 percent of Salvadorans are foreign born. Among the foreign-born populations, Mexicans, Salvadorans, and Guatemalans have the highest rates of non-citizenship. In terms of income, Puerto Ricans and Cubans have the highest median incomes, and Salvadorans and Guatemalans the lowest. This is likely a reflection of low levels of educational attainment among Salvadorans and Guatemalans – over half of individuals over the age of 25 from these two countries have less than a high school diploma. Salvadorans and Guatemalans also have much lower levels of college degree attainment than the other national-origin groups.

An awareness of these differences is important because they demonstrate that the Latino community is not monolithic, but rather is made up of disparate national-origin groups that are situated within varied economic and social opportunity structures. As we will see in the following chapters, each of those groups has a unique history and a distinct set of social, political, and economic challenges. Those differences can and do affect the kinds of public policies each group supports, their partisan attachments, and their political engagement.

Table 2.2 Age, Nativity, Income, and Education by Country of Origin

	Mexican	Puerto Rican	Cuban	Dominican	Salvadoran	Guatemalan
POPULATION SIZE	33,557,922	4,885,294	1,891,014	1,554,819	1,977,657	1,214,076
Female	48.6%	51%	49.3%	53.3%	49.6%	43.3%
Male	51.4%	49%	50.6%	46.7%	50.4%	56.7%
AGE						
Median age	25	27	40	29	29	27
Population under 18	36.6%	33.3%	21.2%	29%	29.5%	29.2%
Population 65 and over	4.4%	6.6%	16.7%	6.3%	3.2%	2.6%
NATIVITY						
Percent foreign born	35.6%	NA[a]	58.8%	56.5%	62.4%	67%
Entered US before 1990 (% of foreign-born)	34.8%	NA[a]	48.3%	36.9%	35.5%	27.1%
Entered US 2000 or later (% of foreign-born)	34.5%	NA[a]	32.3%	33.5%	36.2%	48.7%
Non-citizen (% of foreign-born)	77%	NA[b]	45%	53.1%	72.7%	76%

Table 2.2 *continued*

	Mexican	Puerto Rican	Cuban	Dominican	Salvadoran	Guatemalan
INCOME						
Median income (year-round full-time workers)	$27,000	$35,100	$33,300	$28,000	$25,000	$23,000
EDUCATIONAL ATTAINMENT						
Pop. over 25 with < high-school diploma	43.4%	25.5%	24%	34.5%	53.1%	54.4%
Pop. over 25 with high-school diploma	26.2%	30%	28.7%	26.5%	24.1%	22.1%
Pop. over 25 with college degree or more	9.4%	16.3%	23.7%	15%	7.3%	8.5%

a Since Puerto Rico is a US territory, no Puerto Rican is "foreign-born," although those born on the mainland have a different legal status from those born on the island (see ch. 4)

b All Puerto Ricans are US citizens

Sources: 2011 American Community Survey, 1-year estimates, and Pew Hispanic Center's National-Origin Statistical Summaries, 2010.

Understanding Political Participation

Since the 1960s, political scientists have been studying American political behavior – which factors explain why individuals turn out and vote, or why they engage in other kinds of political activity such as contacting elected officials, contributing to campaigns, engaging in political protest, and so on. This work, which has focused mainly on the general US population, has found that a person's socioeconomic status (SES) – their education, income, and occupation – is the best predictor of their likelihood to vote. In other words, those who are more educated, have higher incomes, and come from professional occupations (versus more blue-collar jobs) are more likely to vote than those who are less educated, poorer, or do manual labor. This is intuitively logical. Higher SES individuals have more resources in terms of personal capacity, time, and flexibility they can use to help toward paying the "cost" of engaging in politics.

Yet when this work has been extended to minority communities, it seems not to be able to explain all the aspects of their engagement. Political scientist Katherine Tate finds that education and income are only occasionally related to African American participation, and studies of Latinos have found that SES can explain only part of the gap between Latino and Anglo electoral and nonelectoral participation.[5] Scholars attempting to find other explanations have turned to psychological resources – feelings of efficacy, trust in government, and civic duty – as the explanatory factors. Studies using these approaches have found that levels of political interest and efficacy have a significant effect on participation. These models center around the idea that feelings of "linked fate," "political alienation," "group identity," and "group conflict" have an impact on minority groups' political attitudes and behavior.[6] In other words, individuals feel (or do not feel) connections to particular groups, and their political attitudes and levels of participation are influenced in important ways by those feelings.

But, the fact that feelings of group attachment are important to participation does not mean we can assume that Latinos automatically feel a particular attachment to "Latinos" as a social group. As political scientist Cristina Beltrán points out in *The Trouble with Unity*, Latino-oriented collective engagement in the United States is a *political* product, rather than something that simply exists outside the realm of politics and history.[7] We will see in the subsequent chapters that the varied national-origin groups discussed in this volume have engaged in a variety of political movements, campaigns, and other collective organizing efforts. Each of those efforts was a product of a particular moment in historical time, a unique set of political circumstances, and the specific experiences of that local community. Therefore, we cannot assume that a common "Latino" political identity exists. Instead, to understand Latino politics, we need to consider where, historically, a "Latino" (or national-origin-focused) identity might come from and under what circumstances that identity can (or cannot) translate into political action.

It is also important to consider how nativity can affect ethnoracial groups' participation within US electoral politics. Figures 2.1 to 2.5 summarize Latino registration and voting rates from 1978 to 2012 in comparison to those of other US ethnoracial groups. What is clear from these figures is that nativity is a big issue for the two largest immigrant groups in the United States: Latinos and Asian Americans. If one looks only at the citizen population, their registration and voting rates are somewhat similar to those of whites and Blacks, albeit still lower. Yet when these rates are compared to those of the general population, we see that the proportion of individuals over 18 who are registered and voting within these groups represents a significantly lower percentage than for the US population as a whole. In figure 2.2, we see that, in presidential elections, which are the highest turnout elections in the United States, only about 30 percent of the Latino population overall actually votes. That is compared to about 60 percent for whites and Blacks. Compared to other advanced industrialized nations, those numbers are low across the board. For Latinos, it means that only a very small proportion of the overall population is able to have an electoral voice during even the most high turnout elections. Figure 2.4 shows that, in midterm elections, the proportion of the total Latino population voting goes down to about 20 percent, while for whites it remains at about 50 percent. This means that, relative to whites, Latinos have even less electoral influence in low turnout elections (a summary of registration and turnout from 1978 to 2012 may be found in the appendix).

These differences are due to the fact that Latinos have lower registration rates than whites or Blacks, combined with the fact that about 40 percent of the community consists of non-citizens, which means that they are ineligible to vote. As we saw in table 2.2 above, Mexican, Salvadoran, and Guatemalan immigrants have low rates of naturalization among their foreign-born populations.[8] Latinos also are, on average, younger than other US ethnoracial groups, meaning that fewer Latinos are over age 18, as a proportion of the population, than is true for other

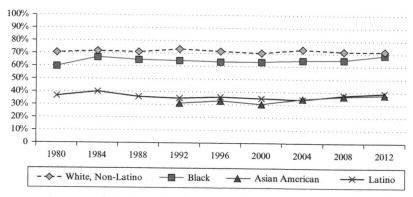

Figure 2.1 *Registration in Presidential Elections as Percentage of Total Population, 1980–2012*

Source: *US Department of the Census, Current Population Survey, November 2012 and earlier reports.*

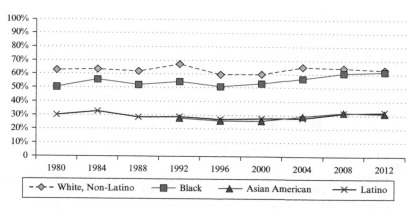

Figure 2.2 *Voting in Presidential Elections as Percentage of Total Population, 1980–2012*

Source: *US Department of the Census, Current Population Survey, November 2012 and earlier reports.*

groups. Thus a smaller segment of the population is eligible to vote than in other populations. Only about 43.9 percent of Latinos are eligible to vote, and a smaller proportion of that eligible group chooses to register and vote than is true among whites or Blacks. The result is that Latino voters do not come close to representing the demographic power of the Latino population as a whole. In the rest of this book, we will explore the historical and institutional reasons why this is the case, focusing

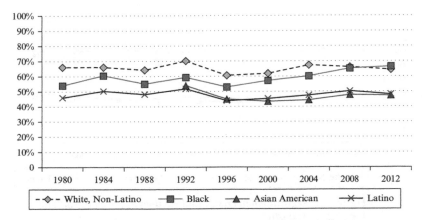

Figure 2.3 *Voting in Presidential Elections as Percentage of Citizen Population, 1980–2012*

Source: *US Department of the Census, Current Population Survey, November 2012 and earlier reports.*

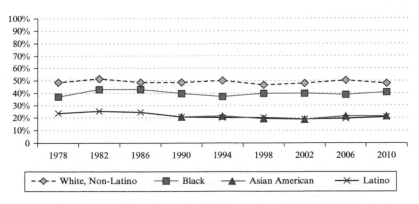

Figure 2.4 *Voting in Midterm Elections as Percentage of Total Population, 1978–2010*

Source: *US Department of the Census, Current Population Survey, November 2012 and earlier reports.*

specifically on the six largest Latino national-origin groups: Mexicans, Puerto Ricans, Cubans, Dominicans, Salvadorans, and Guatemalans.

These national-origin groups vary in terms of their group histories and of the kinds of political activity they have chosen to engage in. According to the 2012 Current Population Survey, 11.2 million Latinos voted in the presidential election in November 2012, comprising about 48 percent of

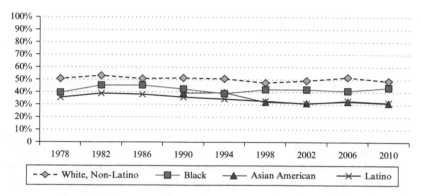

Figure 2.5 *Voting in Midterm Elections as Percentage of Citizen Population, 1978–2010*

Source: *US Department of the Census, Current Population Survey, November 2012 and earlier reports.*

Latino eligible voters. The highest rate of turnout was among Cubans (at 67.2 percent) and the lowest among Mexicans (at 42.2 percent). Puerto Ricans fell somewhere in the middle, at 52.8 percent turnout. Although some of this variation is attributable to differences in SES among the groups, it also highlights important differences in the kinds of political activities each national-origin group chooses to engage in. Historically, Mexicans and Puerto Ricans have been more likely to engage in protests than Cubans. Cubans, in turn, tend to engage in voting more than other types of political activities. These differences are due to history, geography, and the US institutional context. When thinking about the Latino electorate, we also need to keep in mind that Latina women register and vote at higher rates than Latino men across all national-origin groups. Nationally, Latina registration rates are about 10 points higher than those of men; turnout rates vary in similar ways. Therefore there are many cross-cutting factors that affect Latinos' propensity to go to the ballot box on Election Day.

Institutional Context

When Latinos decide to incorporate themselves into the US political system, they must do so within the context of a specific set of electoral and legislative rules which affect how much power a minority group will be able to muster within that system. These rules fall into two broad categories: *electoral rules* and *legislative rules*. We will explore each in turn.

Electoral Rules

Electoral rules are the rules which underlie the American electoral system. The most important rules with regard to Latinos are: majority rule; rules surrounding voting rights; and citizenship requirements for voting.

Majority rule   The most basic electoral rule underlying the American political system is the idea of *majority rule*: if you can get more than 50 percent of the vote, you win the election. That is why scholars describe the American political system as *majoritarian* – you must have a majority in order to win. Other democracies around the world are not organized this way. Some have proportional representational rules which guarantee a certain number of parliamentary seats, for example, to a particular minority group or party. Others have quota systems to ensure the representation of women or minority groups. The fact that the United States' electoral rules are majoritarian places important structural constraints on the electoral participation of minority groups like Latinos.

Since Latinos constitute a minority community within the United States, majority rule significantly affects their ability to express their interests through voting. Nationally, Latinos make up about 17 percent of the total US population. Yet, because of the demographic issues discussed above – namely the community's significant non-citizen population, large under-18 population, and low registration and voting rates – the 2012 Current Population Survey estimates that Latinos made up only about 8.4 percent of the voters in the 2012 presidential election. The story is similar at the state level. In California, for example, Latinos make up 38 percent of the state's population, yet only about 16 percent of likely voters. Similarly, in New Mexico – the state with the largest Latino population, 46.3 percent of the state total – Latinos make up 35 percent of voters. Of course, at the municipal level, in cities with a population over 75 percent Latino, Latinos can and often do make up the majority of voters. But that is rare. In most places and in most electoral races, for Latino voters to meet the 50 percent threshold they must build coalitions with like-minded groups in order to ensure the success of their chosen candidate or of their preferred policy proposal. This means that, in the electoral arena, Latinos are not in complete control of their destiny. As a minority group within a majoritarian system, they can win elections only if they join coalitions large enough to surpass the 50 percent threshold. This, of course, means that they must compromise with those groups regarding their policy preferences and their choice of candidate. Thus majority rule makes it difficult for US minority groups like Latinos to win elections.

The Voting Rights Act   Voting rights are important because, within a republican democracy, voting is the main way citizens may express their political preferences. Voting is also substantively important because it has *instrumental* value: it is an instrument that citizens use in order to determine who gets to make the laws and what kinds of public policies are put into place. For most of American history, the majority of the country's population – women and people of color – was denied the right to vote. This is why achieving the ability to exercise that right was a centerpiece of the civil rights movement. One of the greatest successes of the civil rights movement was the passage of the Voting Rights Act (VRA) in 1965. This Act was designed to outlaw the mechanisms – direct intimidation, poll taxes, literacy tests – which had been used to suppress African American voting in the south (we will see in chapter 3 that these methods were also used to disenfranchise Mexican Americans). The VRA, although originally conceived to address the African American case, positively affected the Latino community's ability to exercise the right to vote and to elect Latino candidates to public office.

In addition to outlawing the voting restrictions listed above, the VRA also made a number of counties with histories of excluding minority voters subject to federal electoral supervision. That supervision included "preclearance" of county districting rules and other electoral logistics. Initially, these rules targeted largely African American jurisdictions. Yet when Congress renewed the VRA in 1970, the number of counties subject to federal supervision expanded. As a result, for the first time, counties with significant Latino populations were included under the preclearance rules, which provided important protections to Latino voting rights. In 1975 the VRA was renewed again, and this marked the first time when Latinos were included directly under its provisions. From 1975 forward, the VRA was expanded so as to cover the protection of "language minorities," which included Latinos, Asian Americans, Alaska natives, and Native Americans. Under the 1975 rules, jurisdictions with a language-minority population of 5 percent or more were eligible to request federal election observers. The law also required that jurisdictions meeting this population threshold provide bilingual ballots to language-minority voters. Latinos were not included under the law by accident – these changes were the direct result of political organizing on the part of Mexican Americans and Puerto Ricans in the late 1960s and early 1970s, which is discussed in chapters 3 and 4.

The VRA has had an important impact on Latino political activity and representation. First, it removed the most overt structural barriers to voting. It outlawed things like direct intimidation of voters, capricious changes in voting rules and/or polling places, English-language requirements for registration and voting, lengthy residential requirements for voter registration, the manipulation or control of the Latino vote by economic elites, and the drawing of district lines so that they diluted the minority vote – a practice known as racial gerrymandering. Requirements of long-time residence for voter registration were especially detrimental to migrant workers, many of whom are Latino, because of their need to move regularly for their employment. Most of these barriers existed for Mexican Americans in Texas, but variants of them were used also to exclude Puerto Ricans from voting in New York City.

Second, the VRA significantly increased the number of Latino elected officials across the country. Although Latinos, unlike African Americans, were never excluded from public office entirely, because of racial gerrymandering Latino officeholders were relatively rare before 1975. In 1973 there were 1,280 Latino elected officials serving in the six most heavily Latino states: Arizona, California, Florida, New Mexico, New York, and Texas. By 2013, there were 5,263 Latino elected officials serving in those states – more than four times the number in 1973. Across all states in 2013, there were 6,011 Latinos serving as elected officials at the national, state, and local levels; 95 percent of those serve at the local level where it is easier for minority candidates to meet the majoritarian threshold necessary for election.[9] This dramatic growth in the number of Latino elected officials in the United States was largely due to legal changes in districting practices that occurred under the VRA. By 1982, the federal courts and Congress had established that states and localities with large and concentrated minority populations had an affirmative responsibility to create districts from which minority groups could elect the candidates of their choice. The VRA urged the creation, when possible, of majority–minority districts, which in practice guaranteed the election of minority representatives from a particular area. The downside to this move, however, was that it only allowed for minority representation from areas with high levels of racial segregation. That being said, even though African American candidates still find it difficult to be elected in majority white districts, Latino candidates generally need over

35 percent of the majority party's voters to be Latino in order to have a strong chance of taking that seat. This is a big change, which is due in large measure to the VRA.

In June 2013, the US Supreme Court, in *Shelby County* v. *Holder*, fundamentally changed the VRA. Section 5 of the VRA laid out the preclearance requirements for covered jurisdictions. Section 4(a) laid out the formula that would be used to determine which jurisdictions would be covered under Section 5.[10] In 1965, the formula standard under Section 4 had two parts: (1) if a jurisdiction, on November 1, 1964, had a "test or device" (such as literacy tests, moral character requirements to register, etc.) in place to restrict voting access; and (2) if fewer than 50 percent of eligible voters were registered to vote, and/or less than 50 percent of eligible voters had voted in the 1964 presidential election. If both items were found to be true, the jurisdiction was made subject to Section 5. In 1970, the formula was adjusted to reference the 1968 election. In 1975 the relevant election date was changed to 1972 and the definition of "test or device" was expanded to include the practice of providing any election information, including ballots, only in English in states or political subdivisions where members of a single language minority constituted more than 5 percent of the citizens of voting age. The 1975 change resulted in many Latino-heavy jurisdictions now being covered by the VRA.

In the *Shelby* decision, the Supreme Court ruled that the Section 4 formula, because it was based on 1972 electoral information, was too old and therefore not reflective of current practice. Subjecting covered jurisdictions to preclearance under that formula was thus deemed unconstitutional. The Supreme Court left open the possibility that Section 4 could be made constitutional by updating the VRA formula. Given the current make-up of Congress, however, it is highly unlikely that Congress will act in the near term to make this change. The result is that Section 5 is moot; no jurisdictions in the United States will be subject to preclearance under the old rules.

This constitutes a huge change in the power behind the VRA. Jurisdictions are still, after *Shelby*, subject to Section 2 requirements not to discriminate against ethnoracial and language-minority voters. But Section 2 challenges must occur *after* the election, and, even in cases where the plaintiffs win, they do not change the outcome in that election. Some legal analysts believe that it may be possible to make jurisdictions subject to preclearance under the VRA by "bailing in" jurisdictions under Section 3, rather than Section 5, under specific conditions of demonstrated intentional discrimination. Legal scholars call this a "pocket trigger" that would create a dynamic preclearance regime that could pass constitutional muster because it would be based on evidence from current practices.[11]

This is what many are considering attempting with the state of Texas. Since 1975, the Justice Department has found the state of Texas and its jurisdictions in violation of the VRA 207 times.[12] Within hours of the *Shelby* ruling, Texas Attorney General Greg Abbott announced that its voter identification law would take effect immediately, as would the state's 2012 redistricting plan, despite the fact that both had been struck down by the courts based on evidence of the state's discriminatory intent. Texas' current voter identification law is expected to affect the over 600,000 registered Texas voters who do not possess valid identification, a large proportion of whom are Latino. Similarly, the redistricting plan was shown to significantly dilute Latino voting strength in the areas of the state with the highest rates of Latino population growth. Emails from state officials, which were made public during the trial, showed that Latino vote dilution was a specific goal in how the maps were drawn. The Texas Attorney General contended that the *Shelby* ruling freed the state to do what it wished in both these instances because it was no longer subject to Section 5 preclearance. In July 2013, US Attorney General Eric Holder announced the federal government's plan to "bail in" Texas under Section 3's pocket trigger based on this evidence of discriminatory intent. At the time of this writing, the outcome of this move is still unclear.

After *Shelby*, it remains to be seen whether the progress that occurred under the VRA will be reversed or Section 3 will be used to create a dynamic preclearance system that can satisfy the current Supreme Court. What is clear is that legal changes under the VRA were an important structural change which had a positive impact on Latinos' ability to exercise the right to vote and to be represented by Latino elected officials. How the VRA is interpreted after *Shelby* will have an important impact on the kinds of structural obstacles Latinos face at the voting booth in years to come.

Citizenship and voting rights   About 40 percent of the Latino population in the United States is foreign born. This means that the Latino community continually has a large percentage of non-citizens. Since citizenship is, in most places in the United States, a requirement for voting, this means in turn that a large proportion of the population has no formal say in the US political system. Yet, for much of US history, citizenship was not a requirement for voting; this is a fairly recent phenomenon. During the nineteenth century, over twenty states and territories had alien voting rights. During the colonial era, non-citizens voted and held public office throughout the colonies. These policies were maintained after independence. Instead of citizenship, the key criteria for granting voting rights were race, gender, property, and residence. As the country expanded westward, states used non-citizen voting rights to encourage white immigrants to settle in their areas. For example, Congress approved non-citizen voting in Illinois, Indiana, Kansas, Kentucky, Michigan, Minnesota, Missouri, Nebraska, Nevada, North Dakota, Ohio, Oklahoma, Oregon, South Dakota, Washington, Wisconsin, and Wyoming. The year 1875 marked the height of non-citizen suffrage in the United States, with twenty-two states and territories granting white immigrants the right to vote. Most of these states only required that voters be white, male, and express an intent to naturalize. States saw the provision of non-citizen voting rights as a way to teach civic ideals to future citizens.

Around the end of the nineteenth century, concerns arose regarding the power and influence exercised by immigrant groups. As anti-immigrant sentiment grew, states began to retract their support of non-citizen suffrage. Many states passed constitutional amendments limiting the franchise to United States citizens. By the late 1920s, most states required that individuals must be citizens in order to vote. But non-citizen voting is not illegal. Currently a number of municipalities allow non-citizen voting. One of the most liberal statutes exists in Takoma Park, Maryland, where, since 1992, non-citizens have been allowed to vote in local elections and hold municipal office regardless of their migration status.

For the Latino community, the issue of non-citizen voting is not simply an academic one. Because non-citizens tend to be concentrated in particular geographic areas, their formal exclusion from the political process raises questions about democracy and representation in the United States. For example, the state of California has at least twelve municipalities where the non-citizen population makes up more than 50 percent of the adults living there.[13] These individuals work, pay taxes, have children in school, and yet have no formal say in who represents them in government. This is why many scholars and activists have called for non-citizen voting to be allowed at the local level, particularly in school board and municipal elections. They argue that this helps to teach non-citizens about participation and democracy and ensures that their voices are heard in matters which affect them or their children directly. Given that Latinos make up such a large share of the non-citizen population in the United States, any changes in this direction would have an important impact on their participation rates and ability to influence the political process.

Nonelectoral participation   Yet political participation is not solely about voting. There are many other ways in which individuals and groups can engage in the political process. These form what is called *nonelectoral participation*, which can include activities such as engaging in political protest, working for a community-based organization, contacting elected officials, signing petitions, boycotting a particular company or product, and so on. Any sort of collective activity aimed at addressing a political problem can be defined as nonelectoral activity. Other than giving contributions to elected officials (which may only be done by US citizens or permanent residents), non-citizens can engage in any of these types of activities. Thus nonelectoral participation is an important way through which non-citizen Latinos can express their political views. Nevertheless, the factors which determine who engages in nonelectoral participation have been found to be the same as for electoral participation: those who have higher incomes, higher levels of education, and are older are more likely to participate in these kinds of activities than those who are young, less educated, and have lower income levels. Since the Latino community in the United States is younger and less affluent than non-Latino whites, Latinos are less likely than whites to engage in these kinds of political activities, even though there are no legal barriers (such as citizenship status) to their participation.

Table 2.3 summarizes Latino political interest and engagement in some nonelectoral activities. As we have seen with electoral participation, there are differences among Latino national-origin groups in terms of their preferred forms of engagement. Salvadorans are the least likely to report interest in politics in general, while about two-thirds of Mexicans and Puerto Ricans say they find politics interesting. Cubans seem to be the group most interested in politics. Puerto Ricans are the most likely to report contacting an elected official and Guatemalans are the least likely. Just under a third of the respondents from all the groups prefer to use existing organizations to solve problems. All the group members seem slightly more likely to prefer to resolve problems informally, except for Salvadorans and Guatemalans. Thus, not all Latinos are the same in terms of their attitudes toward politics and the kinds of activities they

Table 2.3 Latino Political Engagement by National Origin

	Mexican	Puerto Rican	Cuban	Dominican	Salvadoran	Guatemalan
Somewhat interested to very interested in politics	66.2%	68.6%	73.3%	63.9%	47.7%	51.0%
Have contacted public official to express concerns	30.3%	45.1%	38.8%	29.0%	22.9%	17.4%
Prefer to resolve problems through existing organizations	27.5%	28.6%	24.0%	28.1%	30.2%	28.2%
Prefer to resolve problems informally	31.1%	29.4%	30.0%	32.5%	26.3%	21.5%
Total Number	5,704	822	420	335	407	149

Source: 2006 Latino National Survey.

choose to engage in. These differences reflect individual-level preferences combined with structural factors such as organizational density, local electoral rules, and the group's political history.

Therefore, the US political system operates under a set of electoral rules which either limit or facilitate minority participation and representation. When considering the political incorporation of a minority group like Latinos, it is important to keep these rules in mind and to understand the consequences they may have on the strategies groups choose to employ in order to express their political interests and on the chances that these tactics may enjoy success.

Legislative Rules

Legislative rules are the rules which govern decision-making within legislative institutions such as the United States Congress or the state legislatures. As with electoral participation, the emphasis on majority rule is very important within legislatures and dictates how decisions are made at the committee and floor vote levels. Party agendas and leadership are much more important within legislatures than they are within

American politics at large, and they affect elected officials' abilities to serve their constituents' interests.

Committee rules   Most legislative bodies rule through committees. This means that the responsibilities of a body in terms of policymaking are divided up across a number of standing committees. Each legislator serves on a few committees which are in charge of issues under its jurisdiction. For example, at the federal level, the Education and Workforce Committee is responsible for all legislation related to educational and workplace issues. Those legislators who serve on that committee have more of an impact on drafting legislation related to such issues than do legislative members who do not serve on that committee. The committee system is meant to streamline the law-making process. If all the members were able to have a say on every piece of legislation, the law-making process would be unmanageable. Instead, the proposed law is brought before the relevant committee, amended as the committee members see fit, and then voted on by the committee, which has to determine whether or not the revised legislation should be subject to a vote by the entire legislative body.

The committee system is an important part of the legislative process and is what makes law-making possible. However, for representatives of minority communities, it does have some important negative effects on their ability to pursue their political agenda. As we have seen with the electoral system in general, majority rule makes it difficult for minority communities to cross the 50 percent threshold necessary to win elections. This limitation is only compounded when majority rule is applied within the legislature itself. For example, in the 113th Congress (2013–15), there were 28 Latinos serving in the US House of Representatives, which contains a total of 435 members. In order to get any legislation passed, a Latino member first has to obtain the support of the majority of the relevant committee. Then they have to persuade 217 other representatives to support their proposal for the floor vote. We saw above how majority rule in the electoral system often makes coalition-building necessary for being elected. Once representatives are elected, coalitions become an absolute requirement in order to get legislation passed. Thus crossing the majority threshold in an election is only the very first step in the multiple levels of majority rule which affect the policymaking abilities of Latino elected officials.

Party influence and agendas   Majority rule is important not only within legislative bodies, but also within the two major political parties. For most Americans, political parties and their platforms have little relevance to their day-to-day lives. Within legislatures, however, parties are very important. In the United States, the political party system was created within Congress during the eighteenth century in order to help politicians to muster the number of votes necessary to pass legislation. This imperative remains valid today. To be successful, parties need their members to stick together and support the bills which the party leadership wants passed. Thus party loyalty is very important within legislatures, and this is something that party leaders spend a great deal of time working to develop. They do it through carrots and sticks – incentives and disincentives for following the party line.

On the side of incentives, the strongest one which party leaders have at their disposal is committee assignments. Who gets to sit on what committee is determined by the leaders of each party. And some committee assignments are much more popular than others. For example, within the US House of Representatives, the Appropriations Committee is responsible for all the appropriations (that is, spending) that go through the House. For obvious reasons, this is a very powerful committee and one that members want to join. If a member does what the leadership asks and votes with the party, the party leaders can reward him or her with a seat on a coveted committee. Conversely, if a member does not vote with the party on an important issue, their leadership can punish them by removing them from a particular committee or by denying them the committee assignment they want. Another incentive the parties can muster is support for a particular member when the time comes for reelection. Both political parties have national and statewide committees whose job is to raise money for the party's candidates. A loyal party member is more likely to receive this kind of financial support than a disloyal member. This is another way parties can encourage their members' support in legislative voting. Conversely, party leaders can deny these benefits to uncooperative members to discourage them from voting against the party line.

The question then arises: what are the members actually supporting? Individual representatives are focused on responding to the needs of their particular district or constituency. Party leaders, on the other hand, represent their districts but also have to consider the needs of the party in general. Because of the majoritarian electoral requirements both in electing representatives and in the legislatures themselves, party leaders need to develop policy proposals which appeal to the broadest possible number of people. Remember, any proposal must get over 50 percent of the vote. This often makes parties reluctant to take positions which can be seen as targeting the needs of a specific group. They would rather be seen as being as broad and inclusive as possible. The kinds of proposals that have this sort of broad appeal tend to represent the ideological center – to be not too extreme either in the liberal or in the conservative direction. Yet, from a political ideology standpoint, Latinos in general, and Latino elected officials in particular, tend to hold policy positions which are more liberal than those of Americans generally. For example, Latinos are more likely than other Americans to say they support increased government programs, particularly for education and health-related services. Thus, from a policy standpoint, the kinds of proposals Latino representatives are likely to advocate often fall to the left of the political center in the United States. Since party leaders want to put forward proposals that will be successful, the kinds of policy proposals advocated by Latino representatives will often not be included in the final legislation, or will be watered down so as to appeal to a broader number of people. In other words, the ability of Latino representatives to influence the party's agenda depends on the degree to which their policy preferences coincide with what will appeal to the party leadership and to a majority of the legislative members as a whole. Again, we see how having political influence can be difficult for minority group members within majoritarian legislative bodies.

Representation

The issue of party leaders, elected officials, and their policy agendas raises the question of representation. When the founders were writing the US Constitution, the only democracies they had as models were those of ancient Greece and Rome. Both of those systems allowed all citizens to engage in decision-making.[14] Yet, in a country the size of the United States this approach was not feasible. Instead, our founders developed a representative system of government – one in which citizens choose representatives to uphold their interests in the decision-making process. If the citizens do not agree with their elected representatives, they can remove them in the next election. Yet the founders never truly answered the question of what representation means within a majoritarian context. James Madison in *Federalist 10* argued that the tyranny of the majority – the tendency of the majority to impose their will on the minority – could be avoided if the majority shifted continually.[15] In other words, a particular individual may be in the majority on religious issues, but in the minority on economics; and, as long as the majority is made to shift across issues, this form of tyranny can be avoided.

Yet this formulation does not address the question of what a democratic system might do in a situation where a particular population, like Latinos, could potentially have different economic or educational preferences from the majority population. How can such a minority have its interests represented? And, more importantly, what happens if those interests can never be represented? Does that affect the legitimacy of the system? The VRA is meant to address this question by ensuring a minimal level of *descriptive representation* for minority groups – representation by an individual who shares the same race, gender, class, or national origin as the voter. But is this all that matters? Can we assume that a poor female representative can represent the interests of all poor females? The fact of the matter is that, at the state and federal levels, our elected representatives are predominantly male and much richer than the general population. Does that mean that they cannot represent the majority's interests?

This remains an open question – which is why some scholars argue for the idea of *substantive representation*: representation by someone who agrees with the voter ideologically and in terms of their public policy interests. The idea is that the voters have a representative with congruent policy views acting as their advocate. Yet how do we know what a voter's policy views are? And which voters should have their policy views represented? Any representative at any level of government will have constituents with opposing views. How should that representative decide which views "matter?" Also, is an elected official's job simply to echo her constituents' opinions, or should she vote according to her own judgement? These are important, and to a large extent unanswerable, questions. Yet they go to the heart of the problem of defining and measuring "representation." It is likely that most voters want their representative to represent their substantive interest, and they use descriptive representation as shorthand, on the basis of the assumption that, if an individual has had similar life experiences, they probably have similar policy preferences. But it is important to point out that this is not always the case and that continually questioning representation and what it means is crucial within the context of a representative democracy.

For minority groups, the issue of representation also raises a number of other questions, in particular about authenticity and accountability. In terms of authenticity, the pertinent question is: how often do minority voters get represented by the people they want (that is, how often does the candidate they support win?)? If the minority group votes as a bloc and continually loses, this threatens democratic legitimacy. As Madison pointed out, avoiding the tyranny of the majority requires that everyone should win every once in a while. This is why one of the factors taken into consideration in VRA litigation is the presence of racial bloc voting in a particular jurisdiction. This reflects authenticity; but accountability is equally important. If a politician has a very "safe" seat, how driven will he be to protect his constituents' interests? This is a growing problem in American politics in general, as the political parties regularly draw district lines which ensure very little party competition within legislative districts. For example, of the 435 seats up for election every two years in the US House of Representatives, only about 40 are truly competitive. This issue is only exacerbated in majority-minority seats. Since most of the minority groups subject to VRA scrutiny (African Americans, Latinos, Asian Americans, and Native Americans) vote overwhelmingly for the Democratic Party, creating a majority-minority seat often means creating a safe Democratic Party seat. This means, further, that those representatives are elected easily and have little competition for reelection. In addition, many of their constituents, for important historical reasons, are not as engaged politically as the general population. Within this context, who ensures that those representatives truly are accountable to the people that they represent? This remains one of the major challenges within US democracy and a particular problem for members of minority groups.

Minority representation also raises the problem of institutional compromise. To get their issues on their party agenda, minority representatives often need to make compromises in order to build coalitions. Yet many Americans, in the majority and in the minority alike, complain that their representatives forget them, or forget their promises, when they achieve political office. How much should minority representatives be willing to compromise? Democracy is built on the principle of compromise; yet is there a point, if they compromise too much, at which elected leaders cease to be "representative?" This too is an open question, and one which applies to all US representatives. But in the case of individuals who represent groups which have continually been the "losers" in terms of their public policy agendas, like Latinos, these questions take on additional salience.

Levels of Government and Regional Differences

The previous discussion was not meant to imply that all government is created equal. The scale required for election, funding, and success at the national level is exponentially greater than at the local level. This is one of the reasons why the majority of Latino elected officials is found at the local level. In general, it is easier for minority groups to be represented at the local level because it takes a smaller number of people to surpass the 50 percent threshold. From a districting standpoint, the creation of majority-minority districts at the local level still encourages segregation, but the size of the overall community can be smaller and yet still have representation. Thus it is much easier for minority groups to be represented, and have political influence, at the local level. Local governments, in turn, through their provision of basic services like putting up Stop signs, fixing sidewalks, picking up trash, and establishing zoning rules, can have huge direct effects on individuals' lives. For minority groups, the municipal level is the level where they are most likely to have a direct influence on political decision-making. Yet, ironically, most Americans, including Latinos, do not vote in their municipal elections.

In addition, not all governments across the United States are organized the same way. The structure of state and local governments in the United States varies significantly by region. The regional distribution of Latino populations varies as well. According to the 2010 census, 41 percent of Latinos in the United States live in the west, 36 percent live in the south, 14 percent in the northeast, and 9 percent in the midwest. National origin concentrations vary by region as well, and are summarized in table 2.4. About two-fifths of Salvadorans and Guatemalans live in the west. Over half of Mexicans live in California and Texas. More than three-quarters of Cubans live in the south; 68 percent of those are concentrated in Florida. About half of Dominicans live in New York state, as do just under a quarter of Puerto Ricans. Most of the western Latinos live in the southwest, which, by and large, is made up of "post-reform" cities – cities whose government structures were reorganized after the progressive movement in the early twentieth century. The progressive movement arose out of concerns about the corruption that characterized many of the party machines which ran cities in the northeast, such as Tammany Hall in New York City. Progressives wanted to reduce the power of those machines and of the immigrants who ran them. To do so, they advocated the bureaucratization of city government; this included the use of civil servants instead of political appointees, the enlargement

Table 2.4 Top Five States of Residence for Latino National-Origin Groups, 2010

National origin	Total		Rank			
		First	Second	Third	Fourth	Fifth
Mexican						
Area	US	California	Texas	Arizona	Illinois	Colorado
Population	31,798,258	11,423,146	7,951,193	1,657,668	1,602,403	757,181
Percent of total	100%	35.9%	25%	5.2%	5%	2.4%
Puerto Rican						
Area	US	New York	Florida	New Jersey	Pennsylvania	Massachusetts
Population	4,623,716	1,070,558	847,550	434,092	366,082	266,125
Percent of total	100%	23.2%	18.3%	9.4%	7.9%	5.8%
Cuban						
Area	US	Florida	California	New Jersey	New York	Texas
Population	1,785,547	1,213,438	88,607	83,362	70,803	46,541
Percent of total	100%	68%	5%	4.7%	4%	2.6%

Dominican

Area	US	New York	New Jersey	Florida	Massachusetts	Pennsylvania
Population	1,414,703	674,787	197,922	172,451	103,292	62,348
Percent of total	100%	47.7%	14%	12.2%	7.3%	4.4%

Salvadoran

Area	US	California	Texas	New York	Virginia	Maryland
Population	1,648,968	573,956	222,599	152,130	123,800	123,789
Percent of total	100%	34.8%	13.5%	9.2%	7.5%	7.5%

Guatemalan

Area	US	California	Florida	New York	Texas	New Jersey
Population	1,044,209	332,737	83,882	73,806	66,244	48,869
Percent of total	100%	31.9%	8%	7.1%	6.3%	4.7%

Source: Sharon R. Ennis, Merarys Ríos-Vargas, and Nora G. Albert, "The Hispanic Population: 2010," *Census Brief* (Washington, DC: US Census Bureau, 2010) tab. 4. Percentages calculated by author.

of city council districts, and the weakening of city mayors (so they could not use the office to appoint their friends, or use city resources to support their pet projects).

The progressives were highly successful, and most local governments in the southwest remain organized according to their ideals. Their reforms did diminish political corruption. But they had other consequences as well. Having larger districts means that candidates need to raise more money to run for public office and to have larger numbers of people supporting them. This situation has some negative effects. First, it makes it very difficult for a candidate to be successful without personal wealth, party backing, or corporate support. Second, voters are more distant from their representatives because they represent a larger number of people, which makes it nearly impossible for elected officials to have personal contact with a significant proportion of their constituents. For example, each Los Angeles County Supervisor represents about 2 million people, and it costs more than $5 million to run for a seat on the board. This clearly makes it difficult for constituents to feel connected to their government or to have any personal contact with their supervisor. It also puts the cost of running for a supervisorial seat outside of the reach of most people. The need to raise large amounts of money to run for office and to have large-scale name recognition also privileges incumbents. This makes turnover for elected officials very low, which decreases representational accountability.

Another local-level factor of importance is whether or not a locality has at-large or single-member districts. At-large districts mean that a city is defined as one large district, and a certain number of individuals are elected "at large" to serve on the city council. In an at-large election, all qualified voters within a particular district are able to vote. The exact mechanisms for choice can vary, but in general the candidate(s) who receive the highest number of votes win the election. A single-member district system means that the jurisdiction is broken up into a set number of districts, with non-overlapping geographic boundaries. Voters from that geographic area then select one representative to serve that representational unit. Studies have shown that cities with single-member districts are much more likely to elect minority representatives, because it is easier for the latter to surpass the 50 percent threshold within a small district than to do it within the city at large. As a result, under the VRA, courts have often ordered cities to adopt single-member districting when there is a geographically concentrated minority community which consistently supports candidates who lose under an at-large districting system. That being said, this remedy again requires residential segregation in order to ensure minority representation.

Conclusion

We have seen in this chapter that the Latino community in the United States is not monolithic in terms of its socioeconomic status, age, nativity, or political propensities. We have also seen that Latino registration and voting rates are lower than those of other groups even after controlling for nativity and age. When looking at the total population, only a very small portion of Latinos (about 30 percent in presidential elections) regularly engages in the electoral process. In the following chapters, we will explore the historical and structural reasons why Latinos of different national origins might, or might not, choose to vote.

Latinos' limited electoral voice has consequences. Voting is important because this is how we choose our representatives. Those representatives, in turn, make public policy. Electoral rules have a significant effect on which groups are able to win elections and therefore on which groups are able to have the representatives (and thus policies) of their choice. Once in office, legislative rules affect those representatives' ability to represent their constituents' interests. But how do we know if these representatives are doing a good job? "Representation" is one of the most difficult ideas to define or to measure. What exactly does it mean to be represented? It is likely that all members of the polity feel that their elected representatives reflect their interests on some issues but not on others. Looking from the outside, how can elected officials know what a particular constituency favors in terms of public policy? We cannot have ongoing surveys of every community in the United States. And, even if we did, the ranking of issues in order of importance would probably vary from month to month. In any case, even if representatives have perfect information about their constituents' preferences, they may choose to vote in a different way, according to their conscience. Are these representatives supposed simply to echo the beliefs of their constituency or to take principled positions based on their own political preferences? Is a representative still "representing" her community if she supports a minority position on the basis of a moral principle? These are very difficult questions to answer. Given that fact, many analysts use descriptive representation as a proxy for substantive representation, on the basis of the assumption that individuals with similar life experiences are better able to represent one another. On the descriptive side, Latinos remain significantly underrepresented at all levels of government, relative to their population. This is due to the fact that US institutional structures, with their majoritarian rules and historical exclusion of people of color and women, make it difficult for minorities to get elected. It is unlikely that the situation will change in the future. The question is: to what extent does the US political system represent Latino substantive interests? We will see in the following chapters that the answer to this question varies across time, national-origin group, and geographic context.

QUESTIONS FOR DISCUSSION

1 Does a "Latino" political identity exist? Why or why not?
2 How might Latino demographics affect Latino public policy preferences, in comparison with those of other ethnoracial groups in the United States?
3 In what ways do electoral and legislative rules affect Latino political representation and incorporation?
4 How does nativity affect Latinos' ability to have a political voice? Does that impact vary at the local, state, and national levels?
5 How can minority groups ensure fair and accountable representation within a majoritarian political system?

CHAPTER THREE

Mexican Americans:
Conquest, Migration, and Adaptation

Objectives
- Understand the unique relationship Mexico has had with the United States
- Understand how that relationship affected Mexican politics, including the United States' annexation of half of Mexico's territory
- Understand how development policies in Mexico and the United States encourage Mexican migration to the United States
- Understand how the Mexican population was integrated into the US racial hierarchy and how this affected its economic and political opportunities
- Understand the many ways in which the Mexican-origin population in the United States has engaged in politics

Introduction

On February 2, 1848, the United States and Mexico signed the Treaty of Guadalupe Hidalgo, which is the oldest treaty still in force between Mexico and the United States. As a result of that treaty, the US–Mexico War was officially ended and Mexico ceded over half of its territory (California, Nevada, Utah, and parts of Arizona, Colorado, New Mexico, and Wyoming) to the United States for a sum of $15 million. At that time, about 100,000 citizens of Mexico lived in the ceded territories. They were given a choice between returning to Mexico, becoming US citizens, or remaining Mexican citizens living on the lands which had become part of the United States. From this point forward, Mexican Americans have had to be incorporated into US society. This process of incorporation has been strongly influenced by the justifications underlying the Mexican War, the proximity of Mexico to the United States, and US economic and political interests in Mexico and in the United States.

Mexico and the United States are unique insofar as they share a 2,000-mile border. It is one of the largest contiguous land borders in the world, and the only place in the world where a developing country exists directly next to an advanced industrialized nation. The asymmetry in power between the two countries, economically as well as politically and, since the United States' defeat of Mexico in 1848, militarily, has had important effects on Mexicans' migration patterns and on their political incorporation in the United States.

Mexican Independence and the Early Republic

Like all of Latin America except Brazil, Mexico was a colony of Spain. Mexico achieved independence from Spain in 1821. The Mexican war for independence lasted 11 years, from 1810 to 1821. It began on the morning of September 16, 1810, when Father Miguel Hidalgo, a parish priest in the town of Dolores, rang the church bell calling all who heard it to fight for their independence. The initial insurgency was made up mostly of peasants fighting for ideals of political and economic equality. They quickly took control of Zacatecas, San Luis Potosí, and Valladolid. Their frontward momentum stopped when they attempted to march on Mexico City. In March 1811, the insurgents were ambushed in Monclova, and many, including Hidalgo, were taken prisoner. Hidalgo was executed in Chihuahua in July of that year. After his death, the war remained at a stalemate for some time. Small guerrilla bands organized raids around the countryside but neither they nor the Spaniards could claim victory. Independence was not secured until many powerful *criollos* (members of the Mexican elite), concerned about political instability in Spain, joined the fight. The newly created Mexican state was based on three guarantees: (1) the establishment of one national religion, Roman Catholicism; (2) the proclamation of Mexico as an independent nation; and (3) social equality for all groups within the new nation. In August 1821, Spain signed the Treaty of Córdoba, making Mexico an independent nation.

The length of the war, however, left the Mexican economy in disarray, and the new Mexican state was very weak. Elites were split between liberals and conservatives, and they staged numerous political *coups* in order to achieve their political and economic goals. Between 1821 and 1860, Mexico had 50 separate presidencies, 35 of which were held by army officers after *coups*. The other powerful force in Mexican politics was the Catholic church. Because the church missions held all indigenous lands in trust for the native peoples, at the time of independence it is estimated that the church owned one-third of all the land in Mexico.

The newly independent government in Mexico, in the midst of all this turmoil, realized that it needed to shore up its control over its northern territories. It began to grant tracts of land to individuals who were willing to live in these areas. Grantees did not have to be Mexican citizens when they received these grants. They simply had to be committed to living in the territories, learning Spanish, converting to Catholicism, and abiding by the laws of Mexico. Many American citizens took advantage of this opportunity and settled lands in northern Mexico, particularly in Texas. At the beginning, most of these settlers integrated themselves into Mexican society, often marrying into Mexican families. Yet by the 1820s the number of American settlers had grown, and many of these new arrivals wanted to engage in slavery. The 1824 Mexican Constitution had abolished slavery, which meant that the new slaveholders were violating Mexican law. When Mexican authorities attempted to enforce the law, American settlers and some native Tejanos revolted. This was the start of the Texas revolution of 1835.

At that time Andrew Jackson was President of the United States. A southern slaveholder, Jackson agreed with many of the pro-slavery Americans in Texas who thought that the territory should be annexed to the United States. During his first term of office, Jackson offered to purchase Texas from Mexico, but Mexico refused. The Texans won independence during Jackson's second term, but he did not push for Texas' annexation because of northern resistance to the addition of another slave state into the Union. Instead, he showed his support by recognizing Texas' independence and by establishing diplomatic relations with the Republic of Texas. In 1845, James Polk became President of the United States. He ran for office on a platform of expansionism, saying he supported the annexation of Texas and Oregon. Carrying through on his platform, soon after Polk's election the US Congress offered Texas annexation. This led Mexico to sever diplomatic relations with the United States. Polk also supported the acquisition of California, and to that end he sent an envoy to Mexico empowered to offer up to $20 million, plus the forgiveness of US damage claims from the Texas war, in exchange for California and New Mexico. Mexican President José Joaquín de Herrera decided to meet with Polk's envoy to discuss the Texas situation. His act was so unpopular that he was accused of treason and deposed from office. Thus Mexico did not entertain Polk's offer.

Polk, however, remained committed to the idea of US expansion (based on the idea of manifest destiny), and in 1846 he sent a military force to occupy a disputed territory in Texas between the Nueces River and the Río Grande. Mexico saw this as military aggression on the part of the

United States and attacked US General Zachary Taylor's forces. The US Congress then declared war on Mexico, officially commencing the US–Mexico War in 1846. The war lasted for two years and resulted in an overwhelming US victory over Mexico. It ended on February 2, 1848, with the signing of the Treaty of Guadalupe Hidalgo. The treaty was named after the city where the Mexican government had fled after the United States military captured Mexico City.

Under the terms of the treaty, Mexico ceded over half of its territory, over 500,000 square miles, to the United States. This area included California, Nevada, and Utah, and parts of Arizona, Colorado, Wyoming, and New Mexico. In return, the United States paid Mexico $15 million. Initially, there was a great deal of debate in the United States about how much of Mexico to annex. Some thought the entire country should be taken. Others, such as US Senator John C. Calhoun, worried about incorporating a "mongrel" race into the Union. In a speech on the Senate floor, Calhoun laid out his concerns as follows:

> I know further, sir, that we have never dreamt of incorporating into our Union any but the Caucasian race – the free white race. To incorporate Mexico would be the very first instance of the kind of incorporating an Indian race; for more than half of the Mexicans are Indians, and the other is composed chiefly of mixed tribes. I protest against such a union as that! Ours, sir, is the Government of a white race. The greatest misfortunes of Spanish America are to be traced to the fatal error of placing these colored races on an equality with the white race. That error destroyed the social arrangement which formed the basis of society . . . And yet it is professed and talked about to erect these Mexicans into a Territorial Government, and place them on an equality with the people of the United States. I protest utterly against such a project.
>
> Sir, it is a remarkable fact, that in the whole history of man, as far as my knowledge extends, there is no instance whatever of any civilized colored races being found equal to the establishment of free popular government, although by far the largest portion of the human family is composed of these races. And even in the savage state we scarcely find them anywhere with such government, except it be our noble savages . . . Are we to overlook this fact? Are we to associate with ourselves as equals, companions, and fellow-citizens, the Indians and mixed race of Mexico? Sir, I should consider such a thing as fatal to our institutions . . .
>
> We make a great mistake, sir, when we suppose that all people are capable of self-government. We are anxious to force free government on all; and I see that it has been urged in a very respectable quarter, that it is the mission of this country to spread civil and religious liberty over all the world, and especially over this continent. It is a great mistake. None but people advanced to a very high state of moral and intellectual improvement are capable, in a civilized state, of maintaining free government; and amongst those who are so purified, very few, indeed, have had the good fortune of forming a constitution capable of endurance.

Calhoun's concerns were shared by many. In the end, the United States decided to annex the least populated of the Mexican territories, in the hope that the individuals living there would either choose to return to Mexico or, because of their small numbers, would be more easily incorporated into American society.

The treaty itself was meant to lay out the terms of that incorporation. One of the stipulations that the Mexican negotiators insisted upon was that Mexican citizens remaining in the ceded territories be given all the rights and privileges of United States' citizens. The treaty explicitly stated that Mexicans who lived within the newly annexed territories would be "incorporated into the Union of the United States" with the "enjoyment of all the rights of citizens." We need to remember that slavery was legal at that point in the United States. In most states an individual had to be proven "white" in order to vote. And the 1790 naturalization law still made it illegal for a non-white person to become a naturalized citizen of the United States. Therefore, to enjoy the rights of a United States citizen, an individual needed to be classified as "white." As a result, the terms of the treaty made it necessary for all former Mexican citizens in the annexed territories to be legally defined as white. However, this classification was not applied to Mexicans of indigenous backgrounds. Even though Native Americans were full citizens of Mexico, the United States refused to grant citizenship to Mexicans of Native American descent until the 1930s.

Another key aspect of the treaty was its treatment of property rights in the conquered territories. In Article VIII, the treaty gave individuals in the annexed territories the right to keep their land, whether remaining in the United States or returning to Mexico, or to sell their land if they so chose, without having to pay any tax or contribution to the US government. Article X, as signed, stated explicitly that the United States would recognize all Mexican land grants. But the United States Senate, when ratifying the treaty, refused to ratify that article. This did not mean that land grants would not be honored, but rather that all grant claims would have to be proven in a US court before they would be recognized by American authorities. Thus the only land-related provision that remained in force after treaty ratification was that written in Article VIII, which only provided a very general right for individuals to remain on the land they owned and to dispose of that land in whatever manner they chose, without penalty.

These two provisions of the treaty – the classification of Mexicans as racially white and the need to prove Mexican and Spanish land grants in court – would have far-reaching effects on the social, political, and economic status of individuals of Mexican origin in the conquered territories.

Mexican Citizenship Status after Annexation

Mexicans, then, became part of the United States as a result of territorial conquest. As we saw in the Calhoun quotation above, they were commonly considered to be non-white and therefore incapable of self-government. Yet they were brought into the Union at the height of slavery in the United States, a period when whiteness was key to exercising the rights of US citizenship. The degree to which Mexicans were able to exercise those citizenship rights depended on where they were located (each state dealt with the Mexican population a bit differently); on their class status (wealthier Mexicans often were accorded greater rights); and on their phenotype (darker-skinned Mexicans often were categorized as "Indian," which severely limited their rights). Three important areas of citizenship are the exercise of formal voting rights, access to the protection of the criminal justice system, and the protection of private property. We will examine each in turn.

Formal Voting Rights

The Treaty of Guadalupe Hidalgo specifically stated that the Mexicans in the annexed territories should enjoy all the rights of citizens; but it also stated that that should occur "at the proper time," according to the wishes of the United States Congress. Within a year of the treaty's ratification, Congress gave the legislators of the ceded territories and states the right to determine the Mexicans' citizenship status. This right, which is provided to states by Article II of the US Constitution, gives states the right to determine who is eligible for citizenship and on what grounds. The courts at this point in US history also recognized that there were two levels of citizenship in the United States – state citizenship and federal citizenship. Thus, even though by ratifying the treaty the federal government implicitly recognized the Mexicans as "whites" and therefore subject to the full exercise of federal citizenship, the state governments did not need to recognize them as such. In practice, and often depending on their class status, Mexicans were treated very differently by state and territorial governments throughout the southwest. For example, the 1849 California Constitution gave the right of suffrage only to white males of Mexican descent. In New Mexico, the 1850 constitution gave the vote to all whites and to the Pueblo Indians, but in 1853 the US Congress rescinded the Pueblos' voting rights. Arizona was originally under the laws of New Mexico and later, in 1863, adopted a constitution similar to that of California, which only granted voting rights to white Mexicans. Texas limited citizenship status to whites and to Mexicans who were not Black or Indian.

Thus the state and territorial governments, in their granting of voting rights in the annexed territories, did not assume that all Mexicans were "white." In addition, these laws did not lay out any clear criteria for what constituted a "white." Many Mexicans in the annexed territories did not look "white." Most were what is called *mestizos*, "mixtures" of European, indigenous, and African ancestry – the kind of compound which Vasconcelos described as *la raza cósmica*. Again, thinking about race as a social construction, the interpretation of an individual's physical characteristics was often in the eye of the beholder, and, at least during the initial period after annexation, it was related in important ways to class. Those Mexican citizens who were *hacendados* (or landowners) and therefore dressed in European fashion, were educated, and considered of the upper class, were more likely to be granted their voting rights regardless of their physical appearance. One good example of this is Manuel Domínguez, a prominent California *hacendado* who, despite his dark complexion, was one of the signatories of the California State Constitution. His social status in Californian society was high enough to allow people to overlook his skin color, at least in some instances. But there were exceptions. For example, in April 1857, despite being a former Los Angeles county supervisor and signatory to the state constitution, he was not allowed to testify on behalf of a defendant in a San Francisco court because the Anglo lawyer for the plaintiff argued that his Indian blood legally barred him from testifying in a court case. The judge agreed and dismissed Domínguez from the stand. Another example is Pablo de la Guerra, a very prominent landholding *Californio* from Santa Barbara, who was prosecuted in 1870 for trying to exercise the rights of a white person.

The annexed territories were brought into the United States before the civil war, and most adopted voting rules similar to those of other states. Thus exercising the right to vote required that an individual be categorized as white and not as African, Indian, or Asian. This left many Mexicans without the ability to exercise this basic right of citizenship.

Protection of the Criminal Justice System

The protection both of individual liberties and of property rights relates to an essential function of government: maintaining social order. This relates to the principle of reciprocity, which lies at the heart of the relationship between citizen and government – the citizen gives up certain freedoms, and in return the government provides that citizen with a basic level of protection. Yet for Mexicans in the conquered territories this reciprocity did not hold in the same way for all group members. The degree to which the government (either federal or of the state) could be expected to protect your life or property depended in large part on the way your citizenship (and therefore rights) were defined by those governments and by the court system.

Under any governmental system, individuals agree to give up certain freedoms (for example the right to run a red light, to play music loudly at night, and the like) in return for protection from the government. If someone breaks into your house and causes you harm, you expect your local police or sheriff to come to your aid, and, in an ideal world, arrest and prosecute the perpetrators. This legal protection from the state requires that an individual be recognized by law enforcement in important ways. For Mexicans in the annexed territories, the rights of particular concern were the right to testify in court against whites and the right to serve on juries. The first right is important because, returning to the home robbery example, if a white person were to come into a Mexican home and the Mexican in question had the right to identify and bring charges against the white person, it would be very likely that their actions would have legal consequences. On the other hand, if that white person were to know that the Mexican could not give evidence in court, that person could literally murder his entire family before his very eyes and the victim would have no legal recourse. The issue of jury service is similar. The American justice system is based upon the principle of being judged by an unbiased group of your peers. Since Mexican Americans were excluded from juries throughout the southwest until the 1960s, they were not being tried by their peers. This made it much less likely that they would receive a fair trial. In 1939, the Supreme Court agreed, ruling in *Pierre v. the State of Louisiana*, that the exclusion of individuals from jury service on the basis of their race or color is a violation of the Fourteenth Amendment guarantee of equal protection. Despite this ruling, however, Mexican Americans and African Americans continued to be excluded from jury service throughout the south and southwestern United States until the 1960s. Both these exclusions, from testifying in court and from serving on juries, made it difficult for Mexicans to benefit from the protection of, or have a fair relationship with, the US criminal justice system.

Protection of Property

By 1890, almost all Mexicans in the annexed territories had lost their land. There were two main factors that led to this result. The first was the US system of taxation. Under the Mexican and Spanish systems, landowners paid taxes only on what was produced within a given year. Since the southwest is subject to highly variable weather conditions, such as recurring periods of drought and flood, this taxation system made it easier for Mexicans in the southwest to cope with these changes. Under the American system, however, taxes are paid on the land owned, regardless of its production in any given year. A large portion of Mexican landholders were ranchers. They owned a great deal of land, but only earned money during those years when enough of their livestock survived for them to be able to slaughter some of it and bring it to market. The period after annexation brought a great deal of extreme weather. For example in 1861 California experienced extreme flooding, which waterlogged many crops and drowned livestock. It is estimated that a quarter of the state's taxable wealth was destroyed. The floods were followed by two years of extreme drought, high winds, and a locust infestation, all of which made it difficult for livestock to find pasturage. As a result, in 1865, the *Sacramento Union* newspaper estimated that at least half of the 800,000 cattle in southern California had died. This made it very difficult for *hacendados* to raise the money needed to pay the taxes on their land.

The second factor affecting Mexican land ownership was the need to prove their land claims in an American court. Article X of the original Treaty of Guadalupe Hidalgo provided for the recognition of all Spanish and Mexican land grants in the annexed territories. The US Senate deleted that article when it ratified the treaty. But Article VIII, as it was approved, read: "In the said territories, property of every kind, now belonging to Mexicans not established there, shall be inviolably respected. The present owners, the heirs of these, and all Mexicans who may hereafter acquire said property by contract, shall enjoy, with respect to it, guarantees equally ample as if the same belonged to citizens of the United States."[2]

Yet all Mexican landowners had to get their land deeds honored and recognized by an American court. Until those claims were approved, the land did not "officially" belong to the *hacendado*. As a result, it was perfectly legal for squatters to take control of portions of the *hacendado*'s land while the claims were being resolved in court. The landowner could do nothing to make these individuals leave their property. Quite the opposite – in many cases the squatters committed violence against the landowner's family or livestock, and the owner had no recourse because the local law enforcement officials refused to bring charges against the squatters. Many state governments, in fact, actually encouraged squatting on Mexican-owned lands. For example, one of the early acts of the California state legislature was to pass a "Squatters' Law" which, among other things, made squatting legal; barred the landowner from taking action against the squatters as long as his or her land claim was not confirmed; and, in cases where the original landowner's claim was approved, required that they compensate the squatters for any "improvements" (dwellings, fencing, and so on) they made to the land while occupying it.[3]

In addition to having to deal with squatters, the *hacendados* also had to negotiate a new legal system (the Mexican system is based on Roman law, and therefore has very different rules of evidence and procedure), in a new language, and to engage in protracted legal fights in order to prove their claims. Even though about 75 percent of the land claims were eventually upheld for the original owner, it took an average of 17 years to resolve them. The Mexican landowners had to pay legal fees throughout that period; face squatters killing livestock and destroying crops; and also deal with the natural disasters mentioned above. In order to raise cash, many had to take out short-term mortgages, with interest rates as high as 4 to 7 percent a month. Some also had to resort to selling off portions of their land. Since there were few individuals in these territories with sufficient resources to purchase land, they often colluded to drive down the selling price. The end result was that, within 40 years of annexation, very few of the large landholders from the Mexican period still owned their original tracts of land.

Thus, even though the Treaty of Guadalupe Hidalgo guaranteed Mexicans in the annexed territories the full rights of US citizens, in practice the situation was very different. The ability of Mexicans to exercise their citizenship rights depended on where they were located, and often on their class status. As Mexicans lost their land, their class status eroded. This led to a decrease in their political power. Even though

Mexicans had held high political office in many states during the first two decades after annexation, by the turn of the twentieth century few of them held political office (except in New Mexico[4]), and voting rates were down across the board. At the turn of the twentieth century, the Mexican-origin community was left in a status subordinate to that of the Anglo population. As a result of racial segregation, Mexicans at the turn of the twentieth century lived and worked largely in separation from the Anglos. The population was relatively stable and there was little immigration from Mexico.

The Porfiriato and the Beginning of Mass Mexican Migration to the United States

Mexico's defeat in the US–Mexico War led to even greater political upheaval in Mexico: from 1850 to 1876, the country was in civil war. Political instability ended in 1876, when General Porfirio Díaz, a former associate of the Mexican independence hero Benito Juárez, seized power. He held office for 35 years and dramatically transformed the Mexican economy. Under Díaz, the United States began to play a dominant role in the Mexican economy, a role it maintains to the present day.

When Díaz took office, the United States and Britain were in the midst of the industrial revolution. Díaz' goal was to follow suit, bringing Mexico into the modern age. To do that, he fundamentally restructured the economy, particularly in agriculture and landownership. During the colonial period, the Catholic church had held indigenous tribal lands in trust for the Native American populations. Some of these corporate titles were broken up when the newly independent Mexican government secularized the mission system in 1844. At that time, the lands attached to the missions were put up for sale individually and formed the basis of much of the *hacienda* economy in what is now the southwestern United States. In central Mexico, however, many of these corporate land-holdings were not tied to a mission, but rather attached to indigenous villages which were held in trust for future generations. Díaz abolished these systems, opening up the lands for private use. The result was a significant increase in landlessness among the Mexican peasantry. Those who, until then, had been subsistence farmers now had to move to urban areas in order to find wage labor.

The availability of this labor force was an important part of Díaz' modernization plan: workers were needed to provide labor for new export industries. His government strongly encouraged foreign investment, the bulk of which came from the United States. Railroads were the corner-stone of this economic strategy. The United States invested in building railroads in northern Mexico that would link with growing rail lines across the southwestern United States. By 1902, US railroad investment in Mexico totaled $281 million; fully 80 percent of all railroad invest-ment in Mexico came from the United States.[5] The railroads were used to develop three main industries in Mexico: mining, export agriculture, and oil production. Mexico used the new rail lines to export their raw materials and to import the tools, machinery, and other products they needed to develop these economic sectors. But these sectors were heavily dependent on foreign capital, and largely owned by foreign firms. It is estimated that by 1910 half of Mexico's national wealth was owned by foreigners. American interests, in particular, owned three-quarters of all mining production and half of the oil fields, which gave them significant influence over the direction of the Mexican economy and its politics.[6]

Newly landless Mexican peasants, with the help of these new railroads, left their tribal lands to move north, in search of work. It is estimated that 300,000 Mexicans moved from southern to northern Mexico during the Porfiriato. This internal Mexican migration could be seen as the first step toward Mexican migration to the United States. The railroads and American companies investing in Mexico would serve as a conduit for the continued northward migration.

Many scholars argue that it was the social upheaval caused by the Mexican revolution, a bloody conflict which occurred from 1910 to 1920, that led to the first major wave of Mexican migration to the United

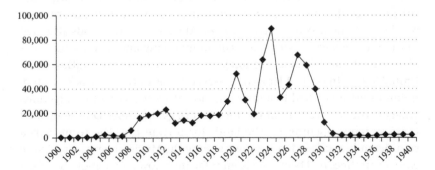

Figure 3.1 *Mexican Migration to the United States, 1900–1940*

Source: Susan B. Carter, Scott Sigmund Gartner, Michael R. Haines, Alan L. Olmsted, Richard Sutch, and Gavin Wright, eds., Historical Statistics of the United States, Millennial Edition Online. New York: Cambridge University Press 2006, Series Ad162–172, available at: http://hsus.cambridge.org/HSUSweb/HSUSEntryServlet.

States. Figure 3.1 summarizes Mexican migration to the United States from 1900 to 1940. A closer examination of the number of yearly arrivals from Mexico after the turn of the century reveals that significant increases in Mexican migration to the United States began in 1908 and grew dramatically in 1909 and 1910, before the revolution had taken root. Similarly, migration levels continued to grow throughout the 1920s, despite there being an end to most political violence in Mexico. Thus Mexican migration flows to the United States are better explained by Mexican economic restructuring and by US involvement in Mexican economic development policy starting in the late nineteenth century. These factors initiated an internal migration process in Mexico that led to an increasing movement from Mexico into the United States. US business interests and the US government facilitated this movement. US companies regularly sent recruiters to Mexico to bring back workers, often paying for their transportation costs. The US government and Congress, in response to strong lobbying from these business interests, supported Mexican migration by setting no limitations on the numbers of migrants who could enter the United States from the western hemisphere. This happened in spite of the fact that the US Congress severely limited European-origin migration through the 1924 National Origins Act. The US–Mexico border, as we understand it today, did not exist until 1925, when the United States created the Border Patrol to enforce the 1924 National Origins Act. Many in Congress were concerned that southern Europeans would use the Mexican border to cross into the United States. The Border Patrol was not meant to impede Mexican migration. Many Mexicans had family or other connections on the opposite side of the border and regularly traveled back and forth. Mexican workers were encouraged by US companies to harvest in the fields of California or to work in the steel mills of Indiana. Their work in the US helped them to support their families in Mexico, taking pressure off the Mexican government and providing cheap labor to a variety of business interests in the United States.

Deportations and US Immigration Policy

There were no numeric restrictions on migration from the western hemisphere to the United States until 1965. This is not to say that Mexican immigration was unrestricted. Starting in 1929, the State Department began limiting Mexican immigration through administrative means. Consular officials would deny Mexicans visas based on the ban on contract labor (if they were being sponsored by an employer), by applying a head tax and/or literacy tests, or on the grounds that they were deemed likely to become a public charge. During the first ten months of fiscal year 1930, the United States issued only 11,023 visas to Mexicans, estimating that the total for the year would be 13,000. This was a drastic decrease from the almost 60,000 visas that had been awarded to Mexicans annually, on average, over the previous five years. This reduction, of course, only applied to legal immigration. Mexicans, often in order to avoid paying the head tax and being subject to an intrusive physical exam, chose to cross the border in locations where they would not be subject to inspection by US immigration officials.[7]

The exclusion of Mexicans from the National Origins quota system was the result of heavy lobbying from southwestern agribusiness. They argued that Mexican labor was needed because Mexicans were physically better suited than whites to working long hours under the hot sun and that Mexican labor was safe because Mexicans would behave like "homing pigeons" and return home once the work was done. The Mexican government, on the other hand, supported Mexican migrants traveling to the United States to work throughout the harvest season because that gave them access to wages which would allow them to subsist even though their plots of land in Mexico were too small to sustain their families.

So even those who argued in favor of Mexican migration to the United States did it on the assumption that Mexicans would eventually go back home. The intention was not to create a permanent Mexican population in the United States. This position was supported by periodic deportation programs undertaken by the US government. During the Great Depression in the 1930s, many in the media began to blame the country's economic problems on Mexican migration. The government started a deportation campaign, requiring that Mexicans about to receive any kind of government aid "volunteer" to return to Mexico before receiving that aid. The largest deportation campaign was in Los Angeles: it is estimated that 500,000 Mexicans living there were deported with the assistance of the Los Angeles Police Department, although most of them (an estimated 60 percent) were US citizens. Another economic recession occurred after the Korean War in the 1950s. Again, the United States' economic problems were blamed on Mexican migrants. The US government began "Operation Wetback," which resulted in 1.3 million Mexicans being removed from the United States.

Ironically, Operation Wetback occurred less than a decade after the start of the Bracero Program, a contract labor program begun in 1942 to provide temporary Mexican workers for US agriculture during the Second World War. It is estimated that over 500,000 Mexican contract workers were imported into the United States through this program.[8] The Bracero Program remained in effect until 1964 – which meant that, as the United States was paying to deport Mexicans under Operation Wetback, it was also paying to bring Mexicans into the United States to work as contract laborers. This obvious contradiction highlights the complexity, and the mixed sets of economic interests, that lie at the heart of US immigration policy and underlie many of the United States' immigration problems in the present day.

Another US policy which would affect Mexican migration patterns was the US government's support for the development of *maquiladora* assembly plants (border-zone assembly plants) along the US–Mexico border. One of the concerns the Mexican government had in 1964, when the Bracero Program came to an end, was how they could provide employment to the affected labor force. Working in concert with the US government, the Mexican government developed the *Maquiladora* Program in order to create jobs for workers in Mexico. Companies were allowed to import unfinished components into Mexico without paying tariffs, as long as the finished products were re-exported into the United States. Most of the companies taking advantage of this program were American. They were able to benefit from paying lower wages for final assembly. Mexico benefited too, because the plants created jobs and provided the government with a much needed source of foreign exchange.

The *maquiladora* assembly plants did create many problems, however. The first was that they failed to provide jobs for former *braceros* (contract laborers brought to the US under the Bracero Program). In practice, US companies preferred to hire Mexican women for these jobs because they were seen as more malleable and less likely to form unions than Mexican men. This preference caused friction within Mexican households, because men had fewer economic opportunities in the *maquiladora* areas than the women, and some argue that this change in the gender dynamics within families has led to increases in violence against women in these border towns.[9] The plants also did little to help the Mexican economy. Since the parts were produced outside Mexico and the final products were immediately exported, the plants provided few backward or forward linkages to the Mexican economy. They did not lead to the development of new industries or to any significant technology transfer between the production companies and their Mexican counterparts.

They simply provided low-paid jobs. Those job opportunities afforded by the *maquiladoras* also led to even greater increases in northward internal migration within Mexico. Many Mexicans from the southern provinces traveled to the border areas in order to seek work in these plants. The result was an exponential increase in population across many border towns. This phenomenon put great stress on the area's infrastructure, leading to increases in disease, crime, and pollution in the border region. Nor would the northward movement of the Mexican workers stop at the border. Once *maquila* workers gained factory skills, many chose to continue their migration into the United States in order to seek opportunities there.

The problems surrounding the *Maquiladora* Program reflect deeper issues related to economic development in Mexico. Since the end of the Mexican revolution, the Mexican government has pursued an industrialization strategy which has done little to equalize the country's distribution of wealth or to decrease poverty substantially within the Mexican population. The United States, in its capacity as Mexico's largest trading partner, has played an important role in maintaining these development policies, particularly in terms of allowing Mexican migration to the United States to serve as a "safety valve" for the Mexican regime. Migration to the United States provides economic opportunities to Mexicans which make it possible for their families and communities to survive in Mexico, in particular through the remittances Mexican workers send home. For example, in 2012 Mexico received nearly $22.5 billion in remittances, an amount equivalent to over 170 percent of what Mexico received in foreign direct investment that year, and 28 percent of the total revenue of PEMEX (Petróleos Mexicanos – Mexico's national oil company).[10] Also, the Mexican elite has benefited greatly from these policies and from its relationship with the United States. Thus the economic links between the two countries, in terms of the movement of labor and capital, are important to both of them and help to explain why Mexicans constitute the largest immigrant group in the United States.

US policy toward Mexican migration changed significantly in 1965. The Immigration and Nationality Act of 1965 placed limits on Mexican immigration for the first time in US history. But it also emphasized family reunification as a key policy goal of American immigration policy. Since there was already a significant number of individuals of Mexican origin in the United States, Mexican migrants made up a large proportion of the visas awarded for family reunification. There are limits on the number of these visas that may be granted annually, based on

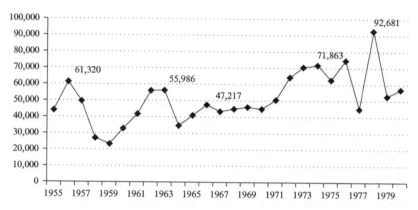

Figure 3.2 *Mexican Migration to the United States, 1955–1980*
Source: *Carter et al., 2006, Series. Ad162–172.*

country of origin and the visa preference category. As a result, family members applying for reunification often wait more than a decade to receive their visas. In addition, after the end of the Bracero Program, US companies, particularly in agriculture, continued to lobby the US government to establish temporary guestworker programs to provide them with needed labor. Many of these companies continued to recruit these guest workers from Mexico. Thus, as a result of US government policy, of the lack of income redistribution in Mexico, and of direct recruitment of Mexican workers by US companies, immigrants of Mexican origin continue to make up a large proportion of immigrants to the United States, even after the 1965 changes.

These changes in US immigration policy were critically important because, until 1965, Mexican migration had included resident-visa recipients and guestworkers (including *braceros*) numbering in the hundreds of thousands each year. In terms of resident visas, figure 3.2 shows that by 1965 there was an established pattern of Mexican migrant entries to the United States. During the decade before 1965, the numbers had averaged between about 40,000 and 50,000 annually. Under the 1965 immigration act, Mexican guestworker programs were eliminated and, for the first time, the US government placed a cap of 20,000 resident-visas per year on Mexican migration. This was despite the fact that flows from Mexico were usually three times that number, without the guestworker programs. This speaks to the role of the state in defining "legality" and "illegality" in different ways. Before 1965, the US government used administrative rules to deny Mexican immigrants the right to enter the

United States. So it was never the case that Mexican immigration was open and unrestricted. Mexican immigrants could also be deported, for various reasons, as noted above. After 1965, Mexican immigrants who fell beyond the 20,000-per-year cap were now seen as undocumented, even though they formed part of an established migratory flow that had been ongoing between the two countries since 1900. It was unrealistic for the US government to assume that these established patterns would change overnight as a result of the 1965 law. Not surprisingly, they did not. That discrepancy – between the migration levels already in place and the quota allowed to Mexico under the 1965 law – is a big part of why there was such dramatic growth in unauthorized migration (much of which is of Mexican origin) to the United States after 1965.

Thus, US immigration policy played an important role in defining the status Mexican immigrants would have when they arrived in the United States. Because the 1965 immigration law did not acknowledge the established migratory flows between Mexico and the United States, migrants who a decade earlier would have been granted legal entry now exceeded the quota limit and became "illegal." Despite this, during the second half of the twentieth century Mexico continued to be a significant source of migrants to the United States. About 30 percent of all current US immigrants were born in Mexico.[11] The next-largest sending country – China – accounts for only about 5 percent of the United States' current 40 million immigrants. But, because of these changes in US immigration policy, about half of current Mexican migrants are unauthorized. Since Mexico and the United States have a unique and long-term relationship, some scholars have argued that Mexico should be treated differently from other countries under US immigration policy.[12] We will see in the chapter on Cuban Americans that such special treatment is not without precedent. To date, however, no such policy has been considered by the US government.

Understanding the relationship between Mexican migration and US and Mexican economic and political interests is important because it not only affects the magnitude of the migration flows, but also determines the areas of Mexico where migrants originate from, the skills they bring with them, the parts of the United States where they end up settling, and, to some extent, the way they are treated by US political and economic institutions upon their arrival. Thus, the decisions of individual migrants to leave are not simply the product of their particular preferences, but rather the result of structural constraints on their economic opportunities – constraints which make them decide to leave their country of origin. In addition, their legal status upon arrival has depended on various changes in US immigration policy. These migrants' choices, therefore, are embedded within a set of very powerful interests, which have an impact on the opportunities and difficulties they face in the United States.

Mexican Settlement in the United States during the Twentieth Century

The Mexican community in the United States is diverse in terms of its generational status, indigenous identification, and location of settlement. It consists partly of the descendants of those who lived in the southwest when it became part of the United States. The community also includes recent immigrants and second-, third-, fourth-, or fifth-generation descendants of immigrants who settled in the United States for – most commonly – economic reasons. Mexican immigrants who arrived in the United States after the turn of the twentieth century tended to settle in the areas which had formerly been part of Mexico. This was the height of Jim Crow segregation in the United States, and Mexicans – consistent with the way they had been racially constructed after annexation – were seen as non-white. Even in those areas which were not part of the "south" (California, Arizona, New Mexico, Utah, Colorado), Mexicans were legally restricted in the choice of places they could live in, the kinds of jobs they could do, and the schools their children could attend.

During the first half of the twentieth century, Mexican residential segregation was carried out through the use of restrictive covenants. These were codicils added to home deeds which explicitly stated that the owner could not sell the home to anyone of African, Asian, or Mexican origin. These covenants were enforceable by law. In other words, if a landowner chose to ignore the restriction and sold their home to someone with the prohibited racial background, the neighbors could take that landowner to court and bar the sale, or sue the new homeowners.[13] US courts upheld the legality of these restrictions until the US Supreme Court ruled that they were unconstitutional in 1948. In addition to housing, sports facilities, particularly pools and playgrounds, were often segregated across the southwest. For example, in many places Mexicans had access to public swimming pools only on the day before the pools were cleaned, because Mexican swimmers were seen as "dirty." In terms of employment, many skilled trades were closed to non-whites, as were

Plate 3.1 *"Whites Only": Poster from the 1930s, Texas.*
Source: © League of United Latin American Citizens.

some labor unions, limiting Mexican Americans' access to well-paid jobs. Schools throughout the southwest were also segregated. Mexican students were placed in one classroom and often tracked toward home economics (for the females) and vocational training (for the males). In most school districts, Mexican students were strongly discouraged from attending high school.

Jim Crow laws, particularly in Texas, also had an important impact on Mexican Americans' ability to participate politically.[14] Throughout the south, a number of laws created to limit the Black franchise also served effectively to disenfranchise Mexican Americans. The first one concerned poll taxes. These were taxes an individual had to pay in order to vote. Given the low SES of many Mexicans, these taxes often put voting out of their economic reach. The second one consisted of literacy tests. These tests were ostensibly designed to ensure that voters were educated and therefore able to make informed electoral choices. In practice, there were no uniform standards for what constituted "literacy" – it was up to the particular poll worker to determine it, and often Mexican Americans were found to be "illiterate" just so as to be prevented from voting. The last law was the so-called "white man's primary." After the civil war, the south was universally Democratic. The Republican Party had little support in the south because Abraham Lincoln had been a Republican. This meant that Republican candidates had little (if any) chance of actually winning an election. Thus the actual electoral competition occurred at the primary level, because whichever candidate was chosen to represent the Democratic Party would, in fact, win the general election. States throughout the south, including Texas, restricted voting in the primary election to whites only. The courts found these restrictions to be legal because parties were considered private organizations and the restriction did not apply to the general election. In practice, the result was that African Americans and Mexican Americans were prohibited from having any meaningful impact on the electoral outcomes of these states.

In Texas as well as across the south, the Jim Crow system was sustained by continual violence. Mexican Americans in Texas were often victims of lynchings, deportations, and other kinds of harassment. The Texas Rangers often were involved. The legendary Ranger King Fisher is said to have once been asked by a boy how many men he had killed. He answered: "Seven." The boy said, "I thought it must be more than that," and Fisher replied: "I don't count Mexicans."[15] Vigilante justice was also common. For example, Jesus Romo was being held in custody by officers in California when he was taken by a group of masked men and hanged. The majority of the Mexican Americans lynched between 1848 and 1870 were already in police custody when they were taken and killed.[16] This kind of violence was so customary that in 1921 the *New York Times* reported that in Texas "the killing of Mexicans without provocation is so common as to pass unnoticed."[17]

Although there was less overt violence against Mexican Americans outside of Texas, Mexican Americans did not have full access to, or the full protection of, the legal system. They often were victims of police harassment and differential treatment. One example is provided by the "zoot suit riots" in Los Angeles. "Zoot suit" is a phrase which describes a popular style of dress employed by youth of all races during the 1940s.[18] In Los

Letter from Youth Committee for the Defense of Mexican American Youth, 1942

YOUTH COMMITTEE
for the
DEFENSE OF MEXICAN AMERICAN YOUTH
1700 East 22nd Street, Los Angeles (in care of Mrs. Telles)

Reginald Garcia, Chairman
Dora Baca, Vice Chairman
Frank Hermosillo, Secretary
Roger Cordona, Treasurer

Hon. Henry A. Wallace,
Vice President of the United States,
Washington, D.C.

Dear Mr. Wallace:

We are writing you this letter because we heard you speak on the 16th of September here in Los Angeles, and we feel you should know about the bad situation facing us Mexican boys and girls and our whole Spanish-speaking community.

What you said on that day was the truth, and you made us all think and wonder why everything around us was different than it should be.

On the very day you spoke there were 24 Mexican American boys accused of first degree murder. These 24 boys come from our neighborhood. In our neighborhood there are no recreation centers and the nearest movie is about a mile away. We have no place to play so the Police are always arresting us. That's why most of the boys on trial now have a record with the Police, from suspicion even up to robbery. A lot of the boys worked in Defense plants and have brothers in Australia fighting under Gen. MacArthur. Our folks work in some defense plants if they are citizens, but if they are not citizens they don't get jobs even though Mexico is in the war too. Our mothers and fathers would like to help in the Red Cross and Civilian Defense but they cannot because it's all in English. There is still a lot of discrimination in theaters and swimming pools and the Police are always arresting us and searching us by the hundreds when all we want to do is go into a dance or go swimming or just stand around and not bother anybody. They treat us like we are criminals just by being Mexicans or of Mexican descent. The newspapers have made us look like criminals too. They make fun of zoot suits and use the word "Mexicans" like it was a dirty word.

We have talked about all this in our club and we think it is very bad for the war because it is against unity and divides us from the rest of the people. Also some Mexican Nazi papers are saying that we are not satisfied and that we are sabotaging the war. Also there are some people around here that use these things to say that Uncle Sam is no good.

We know that is not true and we also know that us Mexican-American boys and girls can do a lot of things to win the war if someone will give us a chance. We have got a Defense Club to help the 24 boys on trial and the way we are raising money for that is to collect scrap iron. That way we help the boys and also help the war and also prove that we are not any help to the Fifth Column.

Mr. Wallace, we know that you can help us. Please go and see Mr. Rockefeller and ask him to help us too. He can tell them to give us radio programs in Spanish to tell us how we can help. Also if the Government would print up the speeches of you and President Roosevelt and President Avila Camacho we would distribute them, if they are in Spanish so our folks could read them. There are a lot of things we could do and we will talk about them in our meetings.

Discrimination is what hurts the most, so help us with that particularly because discrimination is the thing that makes the other Americans divide from us. Maybe also you can ask the city to give us places to play. The other thing is to ask the Police to stop arresting us all the time and treat us like criminals because we are Mexican or of Mexican descent.

Mr. Wallace, you helped us very much with your speech on the 16th of September and we need your help more so we can grow up to be good American citizens and win the war.

We don't like Hitler or the Japanese either.

We thank you very much.

Respectfully
(signed)

Source: www.pbs.org/wgbh/amex/zoot/eng_filmmore/ps_youth.html (last accessed December 14, 2008).

Angeles, the zoot suits became associated with Mexican Americans, who were called "gangsters" or *pachucos* in the popular press and were seen as "loafers" who were not contributing to the war effort. For this reason, in late 1942, clashes between white US servicemen stationed in Los Angeles and Mexican American youths became an almost daily occurrence. The violence intensified in June of that year, when 50 navy soldiers left the Naval Reserve Armory to seek out *pachuco* youths. They attacked anyone they saw as a zoot suiter, beating them, stripping them of their clothes, and sometimes lighting the suits on fire. The Los Angeles police were unwilling to step in and protect civilians from the marauding soldiers.[19]

The rioting intensified over the next few days.[20] A mob of 5,000 people, soldiers and civilians alike, gathered in downtown Los Angeles to engage in the violence. Finally, senior military officials brought the riots under control by declaring Los Angeles off-limits to all sailors, soldiers, and marines. The Los Angeles City Council then passed a resolution banning the wearing of zoot suits in public, which became an offense punishable by a 30-day jail term. After several days of rioting, more than 150

Mexican Americans had been injured and police had arrested and charged more than 500 Latino youths for "rioting" or "vagrancy," even though most had been victims rather than instigators. No white servicemen were charged. The zoot suit riots are a good example of the differential treatment the Mexican-origin community experienced through law enforcement.

School Segregation

While some school districts in the southwest did not segregate Mexican youths, residential and educational segregation frequently went hand in hand. Restrictive real estate covenants made school districts based on neighborhood composition unlikely to be racially integrated. In places like Fort Stockton, Texas, the street that divided the "white" area from the "Mexican" area was called Division Street. In the 1930s, Phoenix Arizona had the Washington Carver High School for Black students, the Phoenix Indian School for Native Americans, and a number of elementary schools, including the Tempe Eighth Street School, for "Spanish American" youth.[21] In California, the segregation of school children on the basis of race and nationality dated to California's first School Law passed in 1851, which explicitly stated that the state's "negro, Mongolian, and Indian" students could not attend school with white children. The state's largest minority group, Mexican Americans, was not explicitly referenced in the law, nor in its subsequent iterations, yet segregated classrooms and schools for Mexican children were the norm.

It was often argued by school and government officials that segregated schools were necessary in order to "Americanize" their Mexican American students. These beliefs were supported by educational theories of the time, which emphasized the exclusive use of English and the adoption of American values and work habits. Systems like this were backed by laws such as Arizona's Title XIX. Passed in 1899, the law stipulated English as the language of instruction in Arizona public schools. In the 1920s and 1930s, this law would be used to justify the segregation of Spanish-speaking students. This separation of Mexican students from whites was also supported by social prejudices that viewed Mexicans as a threat to the health and morals of the rest of the community.

Yet even under these circumstances, Mexican parents across the southwest sought educational equity for their children. In Lemon Grove, California, white and Mexican American students had always attended the same schools. But in January 1931 the local school board decided to build a separate facility for the Mexican American pupils. The new facility consisted of a two-room barn containing second-hand equipment, supplies, and books. For many of the students, the new school was much further away from their homes than the old one. The Mexican parents formed *El Comité de Vecinos de Lemon Grove* (the Committee of Lemon Grove Neighbors) and decided to boycott the school. Every family except one kept their children home. With the assistance of the Mexican consul, the Comité hired attorneys on behalf of the 85 children affected and filed suit. During the trial, the Lemon Grove school-board members justified their actions on the grounds that a separate facility was necessary to meet the needs of non-English-speaking children. To counter this argument, the students took the stand in order to prove their knowledge of English. In *Alvarez* v. *Lemon Grove School District*, Judge Claude Chambers ruled in favor of the parents and ordered the "immediate reinstatement" of the Mexican children to their old school. In bringing forward one of the first successful efforts supporting school desegregation in the United States, this case shows the ability of Mexican immigrants to challenge their second-class status. In this instance they used the Mexican consul's office to secure the resources to challenge a policy which, they believed, hurt their US-born children. This was possible despite the fact that the 1930s was a period of heightened animosity toward Mexican immigrants, as is shown by the ongoing deportation and repatriation campaigns.

In the 1940s, southern California was the site of another significant school desegregation case: *Méndez* v. *Westminster*. The *Méndez* v. *Westminster* ruling led to the desegregation of schools in the State of California and is widely believed to have laid the groundwork for the historical 1954 Supreme Court ruling in *Brown* v. *Board of Education*. The case began in 1944, when Soledad Vidaurri took her children and those of her brother, Gonzalo Méndez, to enroll them at the 17th Street School in Westminster, California. Although they were cousins, the Méndez and Vidaurri children looked quite different: Sylvia, Gonzalo Jr. and Gerónimo Méndez had dark skin, hair and eyes, while Alice and Virginia Vidaurri had fair complexions and features. An administrator looked at the five children. He said that Alice and Virginia could stay. But their dark-skinned cousins would have to register at the Hoover School, the town's "Mexican school," which was located a few blocks away. Furious at such blatant discrimination, Vidaurri returned home without registering any of the children in either school.

After their children were turned away, the Méndezes organized other

Mexican parents and together they persuaded the school board to propose a bond issue for the construction of a new, integrated school. When voters failed to support the measure, the school board refused to take further action. In 1945, with the help of the League of United Latin American Citizens (LULAC), the parents, acting on behalf of their own children and of 5,000 others, filed suit against the Westminster, Garden Grove, Santa Ana, and El Modena school districts in Orange County.

The plaintiffs sought desegregation of California's schools on the grounds that perpetuation of school admissions on the basis of race or nationality violated the Fifth and Fourteenth Amendments of the US Constitution. The school districts argued that the federal court did not have jurisdiction over school issues, and that in any case student segregation was necessary so that Mexican students could become "Americanized," which they deemed necessary because the Mexican students could not speak English. Yet the racial bias underlying these "Americanization" programs became apparent when Garden Grove School District Superintendent James L. Kent testified under oath that he believed people of Mexican descent to be intellectually, culturally, and morally inferior to Europeans and Americans. In his testimony, Kent also said he believed Mexicans were inferior in personal hygiene, in ability, and in their economic outlook, and he stated that even if a Mexican child had the same academic qualifications as a white child, he would never allow the Mexican child to enroll in an Anglo school.

Federal Judge Paul McCormick ruled in favor of Méndez and his co-plaintiffs on February 18, 1946. His opinion was stated as follows:

> The common segregation attitudes and practices of the school authorities in the defendant school districts in Orange County pertain solely to children of Mexican ancestry and parentage. They are singled out as a class for segregation . . . The equal protection of the laws pertaining to the public school system in California is not provided by furnishing in separate schools the same technical facilities, text books and courses of instruction to children of Mexican ancestry that are available to the other public school children regardless of their ancestry. A paramount requisite in the American system of public education is social equality. It must be open to all children by unified school association regardless of lineage.[22]

The school boards appealed against the decision, which attracted national attention. The American Civil Liberties Union, National Association for the Advancement of Colored People (NAACP), the American Jewish Congress, and the Japanese American Citizens League filed briefs in support of desegregation. The case is seen as a precursor to *Brown* v. *Board of Education* because Judge McCormick based his ruling not only on legal precedent but also on social science research, as the Supreme Court would later do in the *Brown* case. The case also marked the first time that a federal court concluded that the segregation of Mexican Americans in public schools was a violation of state law and was unconstitutional under the Fourteenth Amendment. The case led directly to the passage of the Anderson Bill in 1947, which repealed all California school codes mandating segregation and was signed into law by then California Governor Earl Warren – who seven years later would preside as Chief Justice over the *Brown* case.

Méndez v. *Westminster* established precedent for important cases in other states as well. In Texas, again with the aid of LULAC, Mexican American parents, led by Minerva Franco, successfully overturned the segregationist policies of the local schools. In *Minerva Franco v. Bastrop Independent School District* (1947), Federal District Judge Ben Rice cited the *Méndez* case in his own decision. Moving beyond the California ruling, Rice specifically declared unconstitutional even the segregation of Mexican Americans into separate classrooms within otherwise integrated schools. Another federal district court followed suit by striking down school segregation in Arizona in 1950.

These rulings, of course, only outlawed the legally based segregation of Mexican students. In practice, residential segregation resulted in continued *de facto* segregation of Mexicans across the southwest, a phenomenon which led scholars to estimate that, by 1973, in Los Angeles a larger proportion of Mexican children attended segregated schools than had in 1947.

Mexican American Political Organizing

As the organizing around these school desegregation cases shows, Mexican Americans did not simply accept their second-class status; the community organized itself and worked to defend itself from the beginning. From the nineteenth century on, they organized groups called *mutualistas* – mutual aid societies – who helped Mexican Americans deal with economic uncertainty. Many of these organizations emphasized economic protection, education, and community service. They provided sickness and burial insurance, loans, legal aid, social and cultural activities, libraries, classes, leadership opportunities, and locations to house *barrio* ("neighborhood") events. *Mutualista* membership tended to be restricted to men, but many had a separate "ladies' auxiliary" which the women could join; this allowed the men and women to work together in parallel, if separate, organizations.[23]

In California, Mexican Americans also were very active in their workplaces. The turn of the twentieth century brought increases in labor activism across the board, and Mexican American workers were very much involved. In Oxnard in 1903, about 800 Mexican and Japanese sugar beet workers joined together to demand better wages and to end what they saw as an unfair contracting system. They created the Japanese–Mexican Labor Association (JMLA), the first multi-racial labor union in the United States. This was no easy task. At their meetings, all discussions were carried out in Spanish, Japanese, and English. Despite these difficulties, the JMLA was able to recruit 1,200 workers to join, which constituted over 90 percent of the sugar beet work force. The sugar beet farmers hired strikebreakers, which led to community tensions and, in March of that year, to violence. Shots broke out over an altercation; 3 workers (1 Mexican and 2 Japanese) were wounded and a Mexican worker was killed. The resulting scandal brought the local farmers to the negotiating table, and ultimately won the JMLA a victory. Shortly afterwards the JMLA petitioned to join the American Federation of Labor (AFL). The AFL refused to allow the Japanese workers to join its union, but was willing to include the Mexican workers. The Mexican JMLA members refused to create a union without their Japanese colleagues and declined the opportunity to join the AFL. Without the AFL's organizational and financial support, the JMLA disbanded after a few years.

Wheatland in California was another site of labor organizing which turned violent. In August 1913, a group of about 2,000 hop pickers working at the Durst Ranch, many of whom were of Mexican origin, gathered around a platform to hear speeches by representatives of the International Workers of the World (IWW). They were considering striking to protest against their abominable working conditions. The pickers earned $1.90 for a 12-hour day of work, and 10 cents of each dollar was held back by the owners as a "bonus" to be paid to them if they remained until the end of the harvest season. They had to sleep outside, many of them without blankets; had to share nine shallow and doorless privies; and their drinking water was contaminated. During the rally, local law enforcement authorities attempted to rush the platform to arrest one of the speakers, IWW organizer Richard Ford. Part of the platform collapsed and a fight broke out. The sheriffs began firing into the crowd, leaving four dead, including a young boy who had been walking by. Hundreds of IWW members were arrested; Ford, along with another

IWW organizer not present at the event, was also arrested and eventually convicted of second-degree murder. Even though the strike never happened, the riot, subsequent trial, and ensuing publicity brought the plight of farm workers to the public's attention. This led to the passage of more than three dozen California state laws designed to improve the conditions of working people. These included an Act creating a commission to investigate farms statewide, and, as the commission found conditions generally not much better than those on the Durst Ranch, the state began enforcing regulations which set standards for farm-worker sanitation and living accommodations.[24]

Mexican Americans in Texas also organized themselves to protest against their second-class status. In 1915, a group of Texas Mexicans called on Blacks, Asians and Indians in Texas to rise up against their "Yankee oppressor" and to establish a new country. When 60 of the rebels raided King Ranch's Norias Division, a group of Texas Rangers was called in and they killed between 100 and 300 Texas Mexicans. Many Texas Mexicans, however, opposed the revolt and turned to more traditional forms of organization. A group of such reformers, many of whom were veterans from the First World War, gathered together in Corpus Christi in 1929 to found the League of United Latin American Citizens (LULAC). Their goal was to fight segregation and discrimination. Given the hostility toward Mexicans in Texas at the time, LULAC chose to emphasize their American roots. They adopted the American flag as their official flag, "America the Beautiful" as their official song, and the "George Washington Prayer" as their official prayer. They also used Robert's Rules of Order[25] as the governing rules during meetings and conventions and conducted all their business in English.

Although LULAC is often described as a Texan organization, it had chapters in New Mexico, Arizona, Colorado, and California. Even though there was contact and coordination among the LULAC chapters, each state organization emphasized different issues and focused on different kinds of social problems. In Texas, because segregation was such a major issue, LULAC focused its energies on fighting discrimination through lawsuits and other kinds of political organizing. In New Mexico, since segregation was present but not as blatant, social issues were more important. The role of women also varied across the organizations. Even though officially women were allowed, after 1934, to organize separate women's chapters, most chose instead to form women's auxiliaries to the men's organizations. In Texas, these auxiliaries were most often relegated to "women's work" – for instance providing food and the like – and were kept separate from the men. In New Mexico, women and men were involved in more joint endeavors, and women attained organizational positions at the state and national levels sooner than the Texas women.[26] In 1939 the Albuquerque LULAC worked to establish a Hispano/Latin American Studies Program at the University of New Mexico, marking the first efforts for this kind of program within a higher education setting. Thus the LULAC example is highly reflective of the diversity of experience among Mexican Americans along the lines of geography, gender, and class. Because the central issues facing the individuals who made up the organization varied in important ways, so did their organizational focus and collective efforts. Across the southwest, the LULAC chapters organized voter registration drives and campaigns to pay Mexican American voters' poll taxes, but much of this work was done quietly; officially, they were not a political organization. The organization was explicitly apolitical; their main goal was to fight the effects of racism, discrimination, and segregation in the Mexican American community.

Another group working to advance Latino civil rights was *El Congreso de Pueblos de Habla Española* (the Congress of Spanish-Speaking Peoples). This was the first national Latino civil rights group organized in the United States. The driving force behind this effort was Luisa Moreno, a Guatemalan immigrant labor activist who was Vice-President of the United Cannery, Agricultural, Packing, and Allied Workers of America (UCAPAWA–CIO).[27] In her work with the UCAPAWA, Moreno successfully organized Mexican American and Jewish female cannery workers, who were able to win important wage increases from their employers and, during the Second World War, child care for their children.

To organize the first *El Congreso* meeting, Moreno worked together with Los Angeles activists Josefina Fierro, Eduardo Quevedo, and Bert Corona, all of whom would take on leadership roles within *El Congreso*. The meeting was held on April 28–30, 1939; between 1,000 and 1,500 delegates attended who represented over 120 organizations. Delegates drafted a comprehensive platform, calling for an end to segregation in public facilities, housing, education, and employment. They also endorsed the rights of immigrants to live and work in the United States without fear of deportation, and they advocated the preservation of Latino culture and the creation of Latino Studies departments in US universities. This organization was very different from LULAC. It was explicitly political and focused on economic, social, and political rights – for citizens and non-citizens alike. Even though it was meant to become a national organization, in the end the delegates were able to organize only a few chapters in southern California. It is important to remember that the 1930s were a period of strong anti-communism and of organized deportation campaigns, particularly in California and the southwest. *El Congreso*'s advocacy of immigrant rights was politically very courageous within this time period. The larger context probably also goes a long way toward explaining why *El Congreso* was not able to expand as widely as the original organizers had hoped. Many feared being seen as communists and deported, a fear which was well justified, given that some of the organization's founders were in fact deported for being radicals. *El Congreso*'s platform is important because many of the basic tenets laid out in 1939 would strongly influence the goals set out by activists in the Chicano Movement during the 1960s.

Thus, up until the Second World War, Mexican Americans had been engaging in labor organizing and in forming organizations to combat the segregation and discrimination which the community faced. But few of these organizations saw themselves as being explicitly "political." This situation changed with the creation of the American GI Forum (AGIF) after the Second World War. It is estimated that 750,000 Mexican Americans served in the Second World War, where, in proportion to their numbers, they earned the highest number of medals of honor among all minority groups. Yet, when these soldiers came home, they encountered difficulty in receiving the veterans' benefits they were eligible for, such as medical services from the Veterans' Administration or access to educational benefits under the GI Bill. To address these concerns, Dr. Hector García founded the AGIF in Corpus Christi, Texas, in 1948. Although the members of the AGIF initially were concerned with veterans' issues, their work soon spread into non-veterans' issues such as voting rights, jury selection, and educational desegregation, and they advocated for the civil rights of all Mexican Americans. Eventually, the AGIF would become one of the most influential Mexican American political organizations in the United States.

The AGIF's first campaign was on behalf of Felix Longoria, a Mexican American private who had been killed in the Philippines in the line of duty. Longoria lived in a small town called Three Rivers. That town had only one funeral home, which was restricted to whites. When Private Longoria's body was returned home, the funeral home refused to allow his family to use the chapel for the wake. The case received national attention. Dr. García sent telegrams to 15 government officials denouncing the funeral home's actions. Then-US-Senator Lyndon Johnson was the only official to respond. He arranged to have Longoria buried in

Arlington National Cemetery with full military honors. This success brought the AGIF to national attention, and chapters were opened throughout the country; the groups also formed a women's and youth auxiliary.

The AGIF, along with LULAC, was a plaintiff in the case of Pete Hernández, a farm worker accused of murder; this was a case brought to the Supreme Court of the United States. In its decision, *Hernández v. Texas* (1954), the Court ruled that Mexican Americans and all other racial groups in the United States had equal protection under the Fourteenth Amendment of the US Constitution. The court held that Hernández was denied equal protection because he was convicted by an all-white jury and that all-white juries existed because of the *de facto*, systematic exclusion of Mexican Americans from jury service in Jackson County, Texas, where Hernández was tried.[28] Until this decision, because Mexican Americans were legally defined as "white" (at least on the federal level), they were seen as not experiencing discrimination in jury selection, since an all-white jury was made up of individuals of the same "race." The *Hernández* decision was the first one in which the Supreme Court held that "nationality" merited protection under the Fourteenth Amendment as well.

The American GI Forum was different from LULAC in a number of ways. It was made up of Second World War veterans, which made it unnecessary for them to "prove" their "Americanness" (as LULAC had to) and provided them with instant moral credibility. The Longoria experience is an excellent case in point. Funeral homes in Texas had long been segregated and had long denied Mexican Americans and African Americans the use of their services. This practice only became controversial because Longoria was a veteran who had died in service to his country. In the face of that sacrifice, it became difficult to justify such blatant discrimination against him.

In California, the post-Second World War period also brought new kinds of political organization among Mexican Americans. In 1947, Antonio Ríos, Edward Roybal, and Fred Ross, Sr. founded the Community Service Organization (CSO). The CSO initially concentrated on organizing citizenship drives, voter registration, and voter turnout drives in Mexican American communities, all across California. Within two years, more than 5,000 people had joined the CSO and the latter had established chapters in 35 cities throughout California. The organization achieved its first major success in 1949, when it was instrumental in electing Edward Roybal to the Los Angeles City Council. Roybal was the first Mexican American to serve on the council during the twentieth century. The CSO was successful at getting Mexican Americans elected to local political office across the state, and would remain a major force in California politics through the 1960s. The organization was significant not only because of its many political successes, but also because it served as the training ground for subsequent Mexican American political activists such as César Chávez and Dolores Huerta, two of the key organizers of the United Farm Workers movement.

César Chávez became a CSO organizer in 1952 and quickly rose to the head of the organization. In that position he worked closely with Dolores Huerta, a veteran political and labor organizer.[29] After working with the CSO for a decade, Chávez urged Huerta to leave the CSO and to join him in order for the two to form the (predominantly Mexican American) National Farm Workers Association (NFWA). Despite improvements in work standards which had been implemented in California after the Wheatland Riot, farm workers were not entitled to collective bargaining rights because they were not included under the 1935 National Labor Relations Act. In April 1965 the Agricultural Workers Organizing Committee (AWOC), a group consisting mostly of Filipino grape-farm workers, went on strike in Delano, demanding the federal minimum wage. One week later, the National Farm Workers Association voted to join their fight. The two groups united to form the United Farm Workers Organizing Committee (UFWOC). In 1966, in addition to the strike, the UFWOC decided to organize a boycott of Schenley Liquor, one of the largest grape producers in California. To raise awareness of their cause, the UFWOC organized a 300-mile march to Sacramento, which garnered national attention. Many Mexican American college students participated in the 1966 march and began supporting the boycott activities. The success of the initial boycott led the UFWOC to call for a national boycott of table grapes. In 1969 the grape growers conceded and signed a contract with the UFWOC. They agreed to provide higher wages, a medical plan, fresh water and toilets in the fields, and to decrease the farm workers' exposure to dangerous pesticides. In 1972 the UFWOC was accepted into the AFL–CIO and changed its name to the United Farm Workers Union (UFW).

The UFWOC grape boycott is important because it taught an entire generation of Mexican American youths about the effectiveness of collective action. This generation of Mexican Americans, because of the educational opportunities afforded by the GI Bill and by the post-Second World War expansion of the US university system, was able to attend college at higher rates than ever before. On campus, students were informed about the work of the UFW and introduced to other kinds of political organizing. Many joined the anti-war movement and began to protest against the unequal educational opportunities available to Mexican American children in public schools. This work, which took place among youths on college campuses and in the general Mexican American community, would serve as the foundation for the Chicano Movement. But the transition to a large-scale social movement only occurred after the many decades of political organizing which Mexican American political and labor organizations across the southwest had engaged in.

Mexican Americans and Electoral Politics

The Second World War was a watershed because of the changes it wrought in Mexican American political organizing, and also in the attitudes of the country at large. Given that the US enemy was fascism, including Hitler's ideology of white racial superiority, it became difficult to justify racial segregation in the United States, because those justifications were often similar to Hitler's arguments about the hierarchy of races. Thus there was a great deal of change in US racial politics after the Second World War. The year 1948 was especially groundbreaking. In that year, President Truman desegregated the US armed forces; the Supreme Court outlawed the use of racially based residential restrictive covenants; and the California Supreme Court struck down the ban on racial intermarriage. These changes did not simply happen; they were the result of decades of political and legal work on the part of organizations like the NAACP and LULAC. The new Mexican American organizations coming out of the Second World War, for instance the American GI Forum and the CSO, moved to expand these gains and to increase Mexican American political influence at the local, state, and national levels. Throughout the 1950s, both organizations worked toward putting an end to segregation and getting Mexican Americans elected to political office.

They were joined by a new, explicitly political Mexican American organization which was formed in 1959: the Mexican American Political Association (MAPA). Bolstered by the CSO's electoral success, MAPA was formed by 150 political activists in California in response to their perception that the California Democratic Party was not supporting Mexican American candidates. Two Mexican Americans had been nominated for statewide office in California during the 1950s: Edward Roybal for Lieutenant Governor in 1954, and Henry López for Secretary of State in 1958. The Democratic Party strongly discouraged both candidates from running and subsequently did not provide support to either campaign. During the López campaign, some Democratic Party officials even refused to join López on the campaign platform. López ended up being the only statewide candidate from the Democratic Party to lose during that year.[30] MAPA's goal was to address this problem, to increase Mexican American political power in California, and to fight for Mexican American civil rights. Edward Roybal, co-founder of the CSO, served as MAPA's first President. To accomplish its goals, MAPA expanded on the work of the CSO, continuing the registration and get-out-the-vote drives, but also lobbying elected officials and working with other civil rights organizations to end segregation.

With John F. Kennedy's candidacy for President in 1960, MAPA and the American GI Forum decided to extend this electoral activity to the national level. Mexican Americans supported Kennedy because the 1960 Democratic National Convention endorsed civil rights, school desegregation, equal opportunity, fair housing, and voting rights. The platform included comprehensive legislation for migrant workers – the first such commitment made by the Democratic Party. Kennedy also promised to appoint a Mexican American to an ambassadorship in Latin America. Kennedy began courting the Hispanic vote in June 1959, when he sent a message of congratulations to the national convention of the American GI Forum in Los Angeles; he joined the Forum in June 1960. Together with Dr. García, Carlos McCormick, one of Kennedy's senatorial staff members who was also a Forum member, came up with the idea of the "Viva Kennedy" movement. The movement would be made up of a network of "Viva Kennedy" clubs which would conduct voter registration and get-out-the-vote drives for the Kennedy campaign. McCormick served as the clubs' national coordinator. In California, MAPA leaders Henry López and Edward Roybal were the state co-chairpersons for "Viva Kennedy."

The "Viva Kennedy" clubs were highly successful in achieving their goals. In Texas, Kennedy won 91 percent of the Mexican American vote. Many believe that the clubs gave Kennedy the margin of victory; Kennedy carried the state by just 30,000 votes. In New Mexico, a state where he won by only 2,000 votes, Kennedy received 70 percent of the Mexican American vote. Kennedy lost to Nixon in California, Arizona, and Colorado, but he won 75 percent of the Mexican American vote in these states. Nationally, Kennedy is estimated to have garnered 85 percent of the Mexican American vote.[31]

Building on this success, Mexican American leaders used these organizational networks on behalf of Mexican American candidates and they were successful. In 1962, the "Viva Kennedy" network helped to elect Henry B. González of Texas and Edward Roybal of California to the US Congress. Seeing the importance of national coordination, leaders from LULAC, MAPA, the American GI Forum, and the CSO met in order to try to develop greater unity among Mexican American political organizations. The result was the creation of the Political Association of Spanish-Speaking Organizations (PASSO or PASO). Although designed to be a national organization, PASSO was especially strong in Texas, where it comprised the first overtly political statewide Mexican American organization. Unlike LULAC and the American GI Forum, PASSO openly endorsed candidates and engaged in electoral campaigning. It also formed coalitions with African American groups to push for the inclusion of minorities in US politics.

One of PASSO's greatest successes was the role it played in the 1963 Mexican American takeover of the city government in Crystal City, Texas. The majority of the city's population consisted of rural migrants or workers at the Del Monte plant, the area's largest employer. The Teamsters organized the Del Monte workers and worked with PASSO to build a coalition so as to influence the city's politics. They encouraged Mexican American voters to pay their poll tax and to support Mexican American candidates. As a result, despite intimidation by the Texas Rangers, five Mexican Americans were elected to the city council, a situation which gave them the council majority. This voter "revolt" was covered in the press nationwide, including in the *New York Times* and in the *Wall Street Journal*. Although the coalition was short-lived (it lost control of Crystal City in 1965), its success was seen as an important, historic victory.

Mexican American Concerns and the White House

Thus the "Viva Kennedy" work led to important, growing electoral success for Mexican Americans in the southwest. Those organizers also hoped that it would lead to political influence on Capitol Hill. Keeping his promise to Mexican American voters, Kennedy appointed Raymond Telles as Ambassador to Costa Rica: he was the first Mexican American appointed to a US ambassadorship. Many of the Mexican American leaders who had campaigned for the new President through the "Viva Kennedy" clubs were, however, disappointed when they did not receive any cabinet-level appointments in the new Administration. In addition, as the civil rights movement began to heat up in the south, there was a perception among the Mexican American leaders that President Kennedy and his successor Lyndon Johnson focused solely on African American racial issues and were ignoring those of the Mexican American community. For example, for its 1964 White House Civil Rights Conference, the Johnson Administration only invited African American leaders; Mexican Americans, Asian Americans, Puerto Ricans, and Native Americans were excluded.

Mexican Americans benefited economically from Johnson's "War on Poverty" programs, yet Mexican American leaders wanted more overt support from the President. In particular, they began lobbying Johnson for a White House conference on Mexican American issues. The Johnson Administration had held two conferences on the problems facing African Americans. In 1966, a group of American GI Forum members marched in front of the White House on Easter Sunday to express increasing frustration with the White House's unresponsiveness and to protest against the Equal Employment and Opportunity Commission's (EEOC) exclusion of Mexican Americans from a conference in Albuquerque. They called their demonstration a *huelga* ("strike"), to underscore their solidarity with the Californian UFWOC farm workers, who were on strike. In an effort to ease tensions, Johnson met with leaders from the American GI Forum, LULAC, and MAPA in the White House in May 1966. They reiterated their desire for a White House conference on Mexican affairs and requested the appointment of a Mexican American White House aide. President Johnson rejected the provision of an aide (he is quoted as saying that otherwise every group would want one) but promised to begin planning a conference to be held in spring 1967.[32]

Yet the planning moved slowly. Johnson felt he needed the support of southwestern state governors, particularly of Texas Governor John Connally, before he could move forward with the conference. Connally refused to respond to White House requests, making Johnson less and less inclined to support a meeting. In response, on February 12, 1967, the major Californian organizations, "expressing unanimous frustration, disappointment, and impatience," announced "their own White House conference on their community problems."[33] In an attempt to address the growing strain, Johnson's domestic policy adviser Henry McPherson had breakfast with Mexican American leaders on February 17 to discuss the conference planning. In a memo to the President reporting on the meeting, McPherson assessed the leaders as "pretty level-headed activists [who] told me that the Mexican community wants a conference, expects a conference, will be bitterly disappointed without a conference, and that their bitterness would have serious political consequences."[34] McPherson concluded by telling the President that "the Mexicans are a major political factor in five states and we should not risk losing them; that risk is greater if we deny them the conference . . . than if some hell is raised." President Johnson responded to the memo with a terse "Keep this trash out of the White House," effectively vetoing the possibility of any conference on Mexican American issues being held there.[35]

Instead, the White House decided to organize a Mexican American conference to be held in El Paso, Texas, in October 1967, and timed to coincide with President Johnson's signing of the Chamizal Treaty with Mexico – a treaty which resolved the last border dispute between the two nations, returning about 300 acres of land to Mexico. The meeting was to be organized as a cabinet hearing, with the 1,000 invited leaders being given the opportunity to meet and discuss their issues with a number of cabinet secretaries. The Director of the "War on Poverty" would attend, as would the first Mexican American EEOC Commissioner, American GI Forum member Vicente Ximenes, the conference organizer. Having waited for years for a conference at the White House, many Mexican American leaders saw this meeting as insufficient. MAPA boycotted the meeting as an organization, but allowed individual members to attend if they so chose. César Chávez declined the invitation to attend on account of Johnson's refusal to support the farm workers' cause. Other prominent leaders also refused to attend, citing the exclusion from the meeting of a number of important political figures such as Corky Gonzáles and Reies López Tijerina (who are discussed below, pp. 83–8). In the end, however, most invitees attended, and the conference included 50 panels on Mexican American issues (5 of which addressed women's issues).

Those in opposition to the meeting organized protests outside the hearings. The protesters called their gathering "La Raza Unida," which means "our people united." The speakers argued for a new political movement, one which was more militant and radical than what had gone before. They expressed their disillusionment with the fruits of two cycles of political activism within partisan presidential campaigns and argued that Mexican Americans needed their own political party – La Raza Unida Party – to achieve their goals. This event reflected the radicalization of many organizers who, up to that point, had believed that their political goals could be reached through traditional electoral politics. The lack of attention to Mexican American issues within the

Kennedy and Johnson Administrations made them change their minds and join those members of the community who advocated a less traditional approach to political activity. This meeting marked a move toward more radical politics among some Mexican Americans and the coming together of three separate political movements which, collectively, are now commonly referred to as "the Chicano Movement."

The Chicano Movement

Even though the political organizing by Mexican American communities in the late 1960s and early 1970s is commonly referred to as "the Chicano Movement," there was not one unified movement, but rather a number of distinct groups organizing activities in different geographic areas. There was contact among the groups and some attempts at coordination (which we saw above in El Paso in 1967 and will see more of below), but the consolidation was never fully successful. The "heyday" of Chicano organizing is considered to go from 1963 (beginning with La Alianza) to 1972. Originally the word *Chicano* was a pejorative for "Mexican American," but it was purposefully adopted by Mexican American activists in the 1960s as a way to transform a negative stereotype into something positive. The name was meant to denote not only a particular national origin but also a leftist political consciousness. For some Mexican Americans, the use of the name remains controversial to the present day.

Reies López Tijerina and La Alianza

Reies López Tijerina arrived in New Mexico in 1956, "with the checkered past of a fugitive from the law and the fire of a Bible Belt fundamentalist turned political insurgent."[36] A former evangelist, he soon became fascinated by the history of land grants in the area. Over the next five years he investigated land grant law extensively and traveled to Mexico and Spain in order to conduct his research. He was convinced that the people of New Mexico had had their land grants stolen, or in any case taken away from them illegally. In order to ensure their rightful return, Tijerina drafted the first plan for *La Alianza Federal de Pueblos Libres* (the Federal Alliance of Free Peoples) in 1962; it called for an alliance of towns and settlers to join together to have their rightful lands returned to them. The group was incorporated officially on February 2, 1963, the 115th anniversary of the signing of the Treaty of Guadalupe Hidalgo, with Tijerina elected President. La Alianza had one goal: the return of historical lands to the "Hispano" settlers of New Mexico.[37]

La Alianza published a weekly newspaper called *The News Chieftain*, and sent letters to the governments of the United States and Mexico reminding them of their responsibilities under the Treaty of Guadalupe Hidalgo. By 1964 La Alianza had 6,000 members, and that number increased to 14,000 within the following year. La Alianza's 1966 convention included 20,000 people of varied class backgrounds. In 1965 Tijerina began broadcasting a daily radio program, which he turned into a television program in 1966.

The group staged protests and set fires to the homes and barns of Anglo ranchers whom they believed not to have a right to their land. They organized a three-day march from Albuquerque to Santa Fe, at the end of which they met with the State Governor and asked him to investigate the theft of communal landholdings. When the Governor failed to act, La Alianza began to take more radical action. In 1966 it occupied a section of the Carson National Forest which had been part of the San Joaquín del Río de Chuma land grant. La Alianza proclaimed that area to be the "Republic of San Joaquín del Río de Chuma." When 2 US forest rangers tried to remove La Alianza, they were arrested by it at gunpoint. The rangers were tried, convicted of trespassing, given suspended sentences, and released along with their trucks. After five days of occupation, the members of La Alianza turned themselves in to the authorities. Of the 300 people involved, only 5, including Tijerina, were arrested. They were charged with assault on the rangers and with the conversion of government property for personal use; their bail was set at $5,000.

Tijerina's legal difficulties increased with an event that La Alianza is most famous for: the Río Arriba Courthouse raid. It is important to keep in mind that in New Mexico individuals of Mexican descent constituted a large proportion of the population and never lost political power completely. Thus the Tierra Amarilla District Attorney was a Mexican American, Alonso Sánchez. He, like many Mexican Americans in New Mexico, was strongly opposed to La Alianza's tactics, particularly their use of violence. On June 3, 1967, Sánchez ordered the police to raid an Alianza meeting and to arrest all those attending. The police complied and took 11 members into custody; Tijerina managed to avoid arrest. On June 5, Tijerina led an armed raid on the Río Arriba County Courthouse in Tierra Amarilla, New Mexico. His goal was to free the arrested Alianza members and to perform a citizen's arrest on District Attorney Sánchez for violating La Alianza's constitutional right of assembly. When the raid occurred, however, Sánchez was not in the courthouse and two of the sheriff's deputies were shot during the confrontation. Tijerina escaped, but New Mexican authorities organized the largest manhunt in the state's history to capture him. Tijerina ended up surrendering to authorities in Albuquerque a few days later and was charged with 54 criminal offenses, including kidnapping and armed assault. Tijerina was incarcerated for 35 days before trial. His case garnered national attention and he was visited in jail by Corky Gonzáles (discussed below, pp. 85–8). At his trial, Tijerina defended himself with the help of two court-appointed lawyers. He was acquitted of all charges stemming from the courthouse raid and was released. Legally, he did not fare as well with regard to the national park occupation. In that trial, he was convicted of destruction of federal property and assault on a federal officer, for which he was sentenced to two years in prison. In early 1970 he was brought to trial again, on charges related to the courthouse raid. The presiding judge rejected the defense's claims of double jeopardy (being tried twice for the same crime, which is barred under the constitution). He was sentenced to another two years in federal prison.

When Tijerina went to prison in 1969, the La Alianza movement lost much of its momentum. One of the terms of his release in 1971 was that he could no longer engage in activities for La Alianza. Even though the movement achieved a great deal in terms of raising awareness of land grant issues and some grants were returned, little substantive change resulted from this campaign. Tijerina is still alive and lives in Mexico, where he continues to speak out on issues of justice. With translation help from José Angel Gutiérrez (discussed below, pp. 88–92), he published his memoir, *They Called me "King Tiger": My Struggle for the Land and Our Rights*, in English in 2001 (the Spanish-language version had been published in 1978).[38]

Corky Gonzáles and the Crusade for Justice

Rodolfo "Corky" Gonzáles started his career as a very successful boxer. He retired from boxing in 1953, but his success in the ring gave him celebrity and a name recognition that would help him with his political work. In the late 1950s he began his political career by engaging in traditional politics. An American GI Forum member, he joined the Democratic Party and was one of the key organizers of "Viva Kennedy" in Colorado. He was later made the head of Denver's National Youth Corps, a "War on Poverty" program. Dissatisfied with the degree of attention Colorado's Democratic Party paid to Mexican American issues and their unwillingness to support Mexican American candidates, he resigned from his post and from the Party in 1965 and began looking for alternatives to address the issues facing Colorado's Mexican American community. In a 1966 speech in front of Denver City Hall, Gonzáles stated: "We are on a crusade for justice." The name stuck. The Crusade worked for better education for Mexican Americans, greater economic opportunities, better housing, an end to segregation in public facilities (including parks and swimming pools), and the return of all land grants stolen after the US–Mexico War.[39] The group ran its own school in Denver, *Escuela Tlatelolco*, and provided college scholarships to *barrio* youths.

The Crusade organized and supported high-school walkouts, demonstrations against police brutality, and legal cases seeking Mexican American civil rights. It also organized mass demonstrations against the Vietnam War. Gonzáles began to speak out against the war in 1966, saying: "Would it not be more noble to portray our great country as a humanitarian nation with the honest intentions of aiding and advising the weak rather than to be recognized as a military power and hostile enforcer of our political aims?" "If we, who are privileged to live in the United States, enjoy a prosperity built on the backs of poor nations," he asked, "are we not living the good life at the expense of the blood and bones of our fellow human beings?"[40]

As a leader, Gonzáles is credited with capturing the attention of the urban Mexican American youth, a feat which he accomplished through the issues he focused on and through a poem he wrote, called "I am Joaquín," which galvanized the nascent Chicano student movement. In this text he lays out what many see as the defining parameters of the new Chicano identity, emphasizing his indigenous roots and connecting their current struggles to Mexico's long history. The poem was an instant success, and was published in Mexican American newspapers across the country. Its success was attributed to the degree to which it addressed the identity issues facing many of these youths. As the scholar and movement participant Carlos Muñoz writes, "this search for identity and the dilemmas that it posed are the key to understanding the Chicano Movement of the 1960s . . . the movement was a quest for identity, an effort to recapture what had been lost through the socialization process imposed by US schools, churches, and other institutions."[41]

In May 1968, Gonzáles and Tijerina were elected to lead the Chicano contingent to the Washington DC march of Martin Luther King's "Poor People's Campaign." Despite significant setbacks, such as the assassination of Dr. King and the bombing of Tijerina's Albuquerque home, both

Selection from Poem "I Am Joaquín" by Rodolfo "Corky" Gonzáles

Yo soy Joaquín,

perdido en un mundo de confusión:

I am Joaquín, lost in a world of confusion,

caught up in the whirl of a gringo society,

confused by the rules, scorned by attitudes,

suppressed by manipulation, and destroyed by modern society.

My fathers have lost the economic battle

and won the struggle of cultural survival.

And now! I must choose between the paradox of

victory of the spirit, despite physical hunger,

or to exist in the grasp of American social neurosis,

sterilization of the soul and a full stomach.

Yes, I have come a long way to nowhere,

unwillingly dragged by that monstrous, technical,

industrial giant called Progress and Anglo success. . . .

I am Cuauhtémoc, proud and noble,

leader of men, king of an empire civilized

beyond the dreams of the gachupín Cortés,

who also is the blood, the image of myself.

Source: www.latinamericanstudies.org/latinos/joaquin.htm (last accessed July 22, 2013).

of which occurred in April of that year, the march went ahead. Gonzáles and Tijerina, with busloads of their followers, joined Mexican Americans from Los Angeles and Texas and a group of Puerto Ricans from New York, in order to take part in the campaign. While there, Gonzáles issued his "Plan of the Barrio," which called for better housing, education, *barrio*-owned businesses, and restitution of *pueblo* lands. This plan would serve as the blueprint for the *Plan de Aztlán* (see below). The Poor People's Campaign was supposed to bring attention to poverty and inequality in the United States and to create a broad-based multi-racial movement for economic justice. Without King's leadership, however, the campaign failed to have a significant impact on economic policies within the United States.

In March 1969, the Crusade for Justice hosted the Annual Chicano Youth Liberation Conference in Denver, which brought together 2,000 Chicano youths from across the United States. The 1969 meeting resulted in the production of a document entitled *El Plan Espiritual de Aztlán* (The Spiritual Plan of Aztlán), which laid out a nationalist call for Mexican American self-determination and included a set of political, social, and economic demands for Chicanos in the United States. The second Chicano Youth Conference, in 1970, moved this call for self-determination further by leading to the formation of the Colorado Raza Unida Party. The Crusade remained active until 1978, and Gonzáles remained active in Denver politics until his death in 2005, at the age of 76.

Student Groups: UMAS, MAYO, and Others

In the mid-1960s, Mexican American student groups began organizing in California, Texas, Arizona, New Mexico, and the midwest. The students organized groups such as the United Mexican American Students (UMAS), the Mexican American Student Confederation, the Mexican American Student Organization, the Mexican American Youth Organization (MAYO), and others.[42] The first MAYO was co-founded by José Angel Gutiérrez in 1965 at St. Mary's College in San Antonio, Texas. Echoing the 1939 platform laid out by *El Congreso de Pueblos de Habla Española*, the student organizations called for increased Mexican American educational opportunities and for programs dedicated to the study of the Mexican American experience. By 1967 there were a number of MAYO groups in existence in Texas and California. In California, student activists were involved in the UFW movement, participating in the 1966 march to Sacramento, delivering food to the strikers, and picketing grocery stores to support the grape boycott.

Their activism reached another level in 1968, when UMAS, in cooperation with other Chicano groups, organized the "blow-outs" in Los Angeles. One morning, 1,000 Mexican American students walked out of Lincoln High School in East Los Angeles to protest against the low quality of education they were receiving there. They called for freedom of speech in school, for the hiring of Mexican American teachers and administrators, and for the addition of classes on Mexican American history and culture. By afternoon, several thousands of other students had walked out of five *barrio* schools. When the "blow-outs" ended one week later, over 10,000 students had walked out of school. The protest made the national news, and the *Los Angeles Times* called it "the birth of Brown Power."[43] The mastermind of the strike was not a student but rather a teacher, Sal Castro.[44] He, like many of the activists we have seen, attended college as a result of the GI Bill and had been active in the "Viva Kennedy" campaign and Democratic Party politics. Disillusioned with the slow pace of change, he believed that Mexican Americans needed their own civil rights movement.[45] He was suspended from his teaching post when the school board learned of his role in the strike.

Three months after the strike, 13 Mexican American activists were indicted by a Los Angeles County grand jury for their roles in organizing it. Called the "Los Angeles Thirteen," they were accused of "willfully destroying the peace and quiet of Los Angeles."[46] Interestingly, all of the activists targeted by the police were men, despite the fact that Mexican American women played important roles in organizing and coordinating the walk-outs.[47] If convicted, the 13 could have faced up to 66 years in prison. This indictment only increased Chicano student activity across college campuses in California. In Crystal City and Denver, activists organized high-school strikes modeled after the Los Angeles actions. This student and youth activity culminated in the 1969 Youth Conference in Denver, which brought together Mexican American youths from across the country and included Puerto Rican youths from Chicago and New York. The conference called for community control over the schools, for the establishment of Chicano Studies programs, and for bilingual education programs designed to ensure Mexican American cultural maintenance.

In California, in 1969, the Chicano Coordinating Council on Higher Education (CCHE) held a conference at the University of California, Santa Barbara, in order to attempt to implement the *Plan de Aztlán*. At the meeting, the CCHE adopted *El Plan de Santa Bárbara: A Chicano Plan for Higher Education*. The plan outlined a proposed curriculum for Chicano/Latino Studies, including laying out a role for the community in Chicano education. The plan also was the founding document for *El Movimiento Estudiantil Chicano de Aztlán* (the Chicano Student Movement of Aztlán or MEChA). The various Mexican American student organizations agreed to drop their names in favor of being called MEChA. The document laid out two goals for the new organization: (1) to remain tied to the social life of its communities and to continue to work for Chicano social, economic, and political development; and (2) to work on campus to get university attention and resources directed at Chicano students and Chicano communities. The organization saw the university as key to community development, both individually and institutionally, and as a source of political change.

The Chicano Moratorium

In addition to its campus organization, MEChA in California played a key role in organizing the Chicano Moratorium in 1970. The movement's central goal was a moratorium on the Vietnam War draft. Participants also called for an increase in social justice in the United States. They organized a large-scale march, called the Chicano Moratorium, to bring attention to their concerns. Approximately 25,000 people attended the march, coming from Chicano organizations across the southwest. The crowd was non-violent and included many families with children. The Los Angeles police and county sheriff's deputies attacked the crowd with clubs and tear gas, sparking a riot, with Chicano youth burning cars and businesses along Los Angeles' Whittier Boulevard. In the end, 3 Mexican Americans were dead, hundreds injured, and over 200 protesters were arrested, including Corky Gonzáles. Among the dead was *Los Angeles Times* columnist Rubén Salazar, who was "accidentally" shot in the head with a tear gas canister by a Los Angeles police officer while he was sitting in a local bar.

La Raza Unida Party

The preceding discussion contains a unifying thread: a general dissatisfaction among Mexican American political activists with the responsiveness of the Democratic Party and its leaders to the needs of their communities. In 1967 this frustration coalesced in El Paso into the formation of La Raza Unida Party. Not a great deal happened beyond this initial statement until 1970, when Corky Gonzáles in Colorado and José Angel Gutiérrez in Texas organized La Raza Unida committees for their respective states. In 1971 the party spread to California, and in 1972 to Arizona and New Mexico. But by far the most successful organizing committee was Gutiérrez' party apparatus in Texas.

Gutiérrez was instrumental in organizing MAYO in south Texas in 1965. This group organized a program called the Winter Garden Project, which was funded by the Ford Foundation, Volunteers in Service to America (VISTA), and the Office of Economic Opportunity (OEO) (the latter two being federal "War on Poverty" programs). The goal of the Winter Garden Project was to direct social, political, and economic resources to a ten-county area of south Texas which had extremely high levels of poverty. The program was expanded through the creation of a Texas Raza Unida Party committee in 1970. Shortly after calling their first organizational meeting, the Texas La Raza committee filed preliminary papers to establish themselves as a party in all the counties of the Winter Garden region.[48] The new party was thrown off the ballot in all the partisan races, but its candidates were able to remain on the ballot for the non-partisan city council and school board contests. La Raza Unida filed candidates for all available offices in the three cities in the area. Of a total of 16 races for which they fielded candidates, they won 15. In Crystal City they were able again to take control of the city council, Gutiérrez himself being one of the candidates elected. Between 1970 and 1972, the party grew in power and won additional city-level positions in Crystal City, Cotulla, and Carrizo Springs. In the 1971 party convention, La Raza Unida decided to field statewide candidates; they held their first statewide nominating convention in San Antonio in June 1972. The meeting was attended by 500 delegates from 25 counties.[49] The movement to statewide elections, however, was not successful. La Raza Unida did best in south Texas, because that was the region where Mexican Americans constituted a majority. Beyond that area, it was difficult for them to surpass the 50 percent threshold necessary to win election. That being said, they were quite successful at the local level in terms of winning elections, and they mobilized large numbers of Mexican Americans into electoral politics.

The national La Raza Unida Party never really got off the ground because of internal factionalism and the lack of a clear program. In 1972, Corky Gonzáles called for a national convention of La Raza Unida. In September that year, 300 delegates from 18 states and from the district of Columbia attended the convention held in El Paso. There were two main factions at the meeting: supporters of González and of the Crusade for Justice, and supporters of Gutiérrez and of La Raza Unida in Texas. The delegates from other states were caught in the middle. The convention also took place during an ideologically heated presidential campaign between George McGovern and Richard Nixon. Gonzáles went to the convention expecting to be elected as party President in time for the presidential campaign, in which he hoped that La Raza Unida might play a role. This was not to be. Instead, the convention refused to endorse any candidate for president; Gutiérrez was elected Party Chairman over Gonzáles; and the fundamental split in the party between the two factions made it impossible for it to move forward as a coherent political organization.[50]

What is true is that La Raza Unida managed to mobilize large numbers of people and to get them to question the two-party system for the first time. La Raza's threat of organizing Latinos outside the two traditional parties helped those Mexican American political leaders working within the Democratic Party, like Henry B. González of Texas, to convince the party to take Mexican American issues seriously. Henry González and José Angel Gutiérrez had a notoriously conflictual relationship. González, like many centrist Mexican American leaders, strongly disagreed with La Raza Unida, its nationalism, and its tactics. Yet its more radical approach helped to make the demands of more mainstream Mexican American leaders more palatable. As we will also see in the case of Puerto Rican political activity, Mexican American political organizing in the 1960s followed two tracks: one was more radical, sometimes violent, and more demanding of a fundamental change in the system; the other was more traditional and middle-of-the-road, asking for substantive, if not fundamental, change in the opportunity structures available to Mexican Americans. The work of the more traditional groups, such as LULAC and the American GI Forum, laid the groundwork for the activism of the late 1960s. That activism changed the rhetoric and the strategies exercised by the more traditional organizations and helped to move the Democratic Party and its elected officials to be more responsive to Mexican American social, economic, and political concerns in general.

Women and the Chicano Movement

One of the main tenets that brought together these disparate groups of Chicano activists was the idea of *Chicanismo*: a cultural nationalist view which argued in favor of a uniform experience of discrimination and exclusion that united all Chicanos toward a common purpose. Even though this nationalist ideology worked well in bringing very disparate groups of activists together, many Chicana women within the movement became critical of the movement's inability to address the gender inequality that existed among Chicanos and the effects of homophobia.[51] Although most of the movement leaders were male, Chicana women were highly involved in all of this political activity. They helped to coordinate and organize events and worked to develop community social networks. Some of these activist women, for instance Anna Nieto Gomez, María Varela, and Elizabeth Martínez, complained that the assumption of a uniform "Chicano" experience across region, class, sexuality, and gender made it impossible for the inequalities which did exist in the community to be eradicated. This created conflict and tension within the movement; many Chicanas and Chicanos called the feminists disloyal and *vendidas* – "sellouts" to white feminism and not true supporters of the movement. Not surprisingly, no real attempts were made to address or incorporate the feminists' concerns, as is reflected in the official movement documents. Neither *El Plan de Santa Bárbara* nor *El Plan Espiritual de Aztlán* mentions women, or gays and lesbians. In both plans, women are only present as part of the Chicano *familia*, which is defined as heterosexual and is seen as the basis for Chicano organizing. This silence is especially telling with regard to the *Plan de Santa Bárbara*, which was meant to lay out the blueprint for research on the Chicano community. Its lack of any discussion of women or sexuality makes it clear that the activists drafting the plans did not see issues of gender or sexuality as necessary areas of focus for that research.[52]

These gender issues were never resolved within the movement and continued to play themselves out in Chicano Studies programs and organizations in academic settings. The conflict undermined the cohesion and effectiveness of movement organizations and often led to feminist Chicanas forming their own, separate organizations. It also led to the development of a new feminism of the Chicana – one which criticizes Chicano cultural nationalism, white middle-class feminism, and heterosexism. This movement has expressed itself through art, poetry, theatre, literature, and academic writings focused on the experience of the Chicana woman.[53]

The End of the Movement and its Consequences

Gender conflict was only one of the sources of factionalism that led to the end of the movement. Personality conflicts were also present, and they were exacerbated by the organizational infiltration of FBI agents as part of the COINTELPRO (Counter Intelligence Program). These agents were tasked to become part of the organization not only in order to keep watch over what members were doing, but also to foment conflict and mistrust within the groups as much as was possible. In the heated political environment of the late 1960s and early 1970s, the FBI agents were quite successful. As a result, many of the groups splintered into factions and most of the intensive mobilization within the movement had ended by 1973.

Nonetheless, the Chicano Movement has a significant long-term legacy. Most importantly, for the first time in US history, the movement

Plate 3.2 *Rosie Castro Working for the Committee for Barrio Betterment.*
Source: Reproduced with the permission of the University of Texas at San Antonio Libraries Special Collections.

Rosie Castro: the Birth of a Texas Political Legacy

Born in San Antonio and raised by a single mother, Maria del Rosario Castro, or Rosie, was an unlikely political activist.[54] Raised on the segregated West Side of San Antonio, she was President and Valedictorian of Little Flower Catholic High School where she organized the Catholic Youth Club. While attending Our Lady of the Lake College, she organized the Young Democrats on campus. She served as President of the Bexar County Young Democrats, and as Vice-President of the women's division of the Young Democrats at the state level. After college in 1969, she worked to increase Chicano representation on San Antonio's city council, supporting a slate backed by the "Committee for Barrio Betterment." Rosie and other organizers knocked on doors, registered people to vote, and turned them out to vote on Election Day. In 1970 she was arrested during the boycott of the San Antonio Savings Association, which was organized after owner and San Antonio's Mayor, Walter McAllister, made derogatory remarks about Chicanos in a news documentary. In 1971, she and other Chicana organizers demanded that they be put on the ballot as well. They were the first Chicanas to run for city council in San Antonio. After defeats in the 1969 and 1971 races, Rosie turned to organizing for La Raza Unida Party and worked to move San Antonio elections to single-member districts in order to make it easier for Chicanos to achieve representation. She was the party's Director in Bexar County, which includes San Antonio. During her professional career, she has worked in higher education and local government while remaining involved in political and social issues. She helped to organize the Coalition for Hispanic Woman Leaders, a group that addressed issues of domestic violence, and San Antonio's Hispanic Municipal Women's Association. In 1974, Rosie gave birth to twin boys –Joaquín and Julián Castro. They have become involved in politics as well. Joaquín was a Texas state representative and was recently elected to the US House of Representatives. Julián was elected Mayor of San Antonio in 2009 and re-elected in 2011. In his 2012 keynote address to the Democratic National Convention, Julián said, "My grandmother never owned a house. She cleaned other people's houses so she could afford to rent her own. But she saw her daughter become the first in her family to graduate from college. And my mother fought hard for civil rights so that instead of a mop, I could hold this microphone."

caused Mexican American issues to be recognized and addressed at the state and national levels. It was only after the movement mobilization that Mexican Americans were included under the Voting Rights Act and under other civil rights legislation such as laws on equal employment and housing, and affirmative action programs. Those pieces of legislation opened up the US political process to Mexican Americans for the first time and gave thousands of them access to higher education, fair employment, and housing.

Another important part of the legacy of the movement is the institutionalization of a new Mexican American political identity, one that values Mexican history, culture, and language. As a result, older organizations like LULAC changed their platforms, allowing for greater support for the maintenance of Mexican culture. In addition, there was a movement among Mexican American organizations to include all members of the community – immigrants and US-born alike. LULAC, for example, rescinded their requirement that all members must be US citizens. Thus the movement caused changes in the way older Mexican American organizations approached issues of cultural maintenance and membership. It also led to the creation of a new set of Mexican American organizations, for instance the Mexican American Legal Defense and Education Fund (MALDEF) and the National Council of La Raza (NCLR). Both are highly successful national organizations which work to ensure that Latino civil rights are protected, and to promote the social, political, and economic well-being of Latinos living in the United States. Similarly, the Southwest Voter Registration Education Project (SVREP) was created in 1974 to register Mexican Americans to vote and to educate them in the political process. With offices in California and Texas, SVREP continues to register and conduct get-out-the-vote drives targeting hundreds of thousands of Latinos during every electoral cycle. They, like MALDEF,

NCLR, LULAC, MAPA, and the National Association of Latino Elected and Appointed Officials (NALEO), now focus on issues facing Latinos generally, and not simply Mexican Americans. Yet it is important to remember that these national groups began from a Mexican American focus and that, because Mexican Americans make up the majority of immigrants of Latin American origin in the United States, they remain a key part of each group's constituency.

In addition to these national organizations, movement activists went on to work within thousands of smaller, locally based social service organizations within their respective communities. Many became labor organizers, social workers, or teachers, and allowed their experience in the movement to inform their professional careers. This legacy has contributed to the economic development and social well-being of Mexican American and Latino communities throughout the United States.

On university campuses, the movement led to the establishment of Chicano Studies programs, which housed scholars engaging in the systematic study of the Mexican American experience in the United States. These programs not only greatly expanded the amount of information available on the Mexican American experience, but also added to the university curriculum by offering courses on community history, literature, culture, and politics. On high school and university campuses across the country, MEChA chapters continue to exist, to engage in efforts toward improving the educational opportunities available to Mexican American and Latino students, and to ensure the academic success of the latter. Many chapters also engage in cultural programming in order to educate their members and their campus communities about Mexican American culture and experiences in the United States.

Mexican American Politics Today

The period from the end of the Chicano Movement until today can be seen as the institutionalization of Mexican American politics in the post-civil rights era. Legislation passed in response to Chicano Movement activity opened up the political process, educational and economic opportunities, and improved the social well-being of all ethnoracial groups in the United States. In order to promote these gains, politically minded Mexican Americans have engaged in a wide range of activities, including political officeholding, community activism, labor organization, philanthropy, and social work. The result has been a growth in collective organizational structures within Mexican American communities and the development of coalitions with other, similarly situated, groups in American politics.

From a political standpoint, this development has led to a greater representation of Mexican Americans at all levels of government, as elected and appointed officials. On the federal level, in 2004 Colorado voters elected Ken Salazar as the first Mexican American US Senator from that state; he served until 2009, when he became Secretary of the Interior under President Obama, an office he held from 2009 to 2013. A number of Mexican Americans served in the 113th Congress (2013–15), including: Xavier Becerra (D-CA), Tony Cárdenas (D-CA), Joaquín Castro (D-TX), Henry Cuellar (D-TX), Bill Flores (R-TX), Pete Gallego (D-TX), Raúl Grijalva (D-AZ), Jaime Herrera Beutler (R-WA), Rubén Hinojosa (D-TX), Ben R. Luján (D-NM), Michelle Luján Grisham (D-NM), Gloria Negrete McLeod (D-CA), Grace Napolitano (D-CA), Ed Pastor (D-AZ), Raúl Ruiz (D-CA), Lucille Roybal-Allard (D-CA), Linda Sánchez (D-CA), Loretta Sánchez (D-CA), Juan Vargas (D-CA), and Filemon Vela (D-TX). Congresswoman Roybal-Allard was the first Mexican American woman elected to the US Congress.

At the state level, there have been a number of Mexican Americans elected governor, including José Antonio Romualdo Pacheco, Jr., in California, and Ezequiel Cabeza De Baca and Octavio Ambrosio Larrazolo in New Mexico during the nineteenth century. Larrazolo was also elected to the US Senate, making him the first Mexican American US Senator. In the twentieth century, Toney Anaya, Jerry Apodaca, Bill Richardson, and Susana Martínez all served as Governors of New Mexico. Raúl Castro was Governor of Arizona and Brian Sandoval is currently serving as Governor of Nevada. Cruz Bustamente served as California's Lieutenant Governor and in the state legislature. Los Angeles Mayor Antonio Villaraigosa also served as Speaker of the California State Assembly, as did Mexican Americans Fabián Nuñez and John Pérez. Mexican Americans have been elected as mayors of a number of major cities and serve on city councils and local school boards across the United States. They also serve in many state legislatures.

On the non-elected side, Hila Solís, who is half-Mexican and a former US congresswoman, served as Labor Secretary during the first Obama Administration. Cecilia Muñoz, who was Senior Vice-President at NCLR, is Director of the White House Domestic Policy Council under President Obama. Previously, she served as Obama's Director of Intergovernmental Affairs. Alberto Gonzales, who served under George W. Bush, was the first Mexican American to serve as US Attorney General. Rosario Marín was the 41st US treasurer, the first Mexican American woman to hold this position – which made her at the time the highest-ranking Mexican American woman in George W. Bush's administration. She was succeeded in that position by another Mexican American woman, Anna Escobedo Cabral. Under Bill Clinton, Henry Cisneros served as Secretary of Housing and Urban Development, and Federico Peña, former Denver Mayor, served as Secretary of Transportation and Energy. Bill Richardson also served in the Clinton Administration as Energy Secretary and US Ambassador to the United Nations. María Echaveste served as Clinton's Deputy Chief of Staff, making her the highest-ranking Latina in his Administration. Janet Murguía, currently President and CEO of NCLR, was Clinton's Deputy Director of Legislative Affairs. Mexican Americans have served as judges at the state and federal levels, including on state supreme courts.

Thus, Mexican American politics today is characterized by growing political representation and a well-developed network of locally and nationally based political organizations. This institutional and organizational development has its roots in the political organizing which has been going on within the community since the nineteenth century. It was pushed forward by the civil rights movements of the 1960s and by the legal changes which came out of that era, all of which resulted in greater political, economic, and social opportunities for Mexican Americans in the United States. Although Mexican Americans remain descriptively underrepresented in relation to their population numbers and still experience high levels of poverty, labor market discrimination, poor access to good-quality public education, a lack of health-care coverage, and other forms of inequality, their presence and voice in American politics has grown dramatically since the mid twentieth century.

Mexican Migration and the Future of Mexican American Politics

Mexicans make up the largest proportion of Latino immigrants to the United States, a fact largely due to the country's geographic proximity, the unique relationship the two countries have had, and the economic dislocations caused by the economic policies implemented by the Mexican government: all these factors have led to significant increases in Mexican migration to the United States after 1970. As the Mexican government began to embrace trade liberalization in the 1980s – a trend which culminated in the passage of the North American Free Trade Agreement (NAFTA) – these flows only accelerated. Those hardest hit by the economic changes wrought by NAFTA were Mexico's rural poor, particularly in the southern part of the country. In 1980, 36 percent of Mexicans worked in agriculture. By 2002, that number had decreased to 17.5 percent. In 2001, 81.5 percent of rural Mexicans lived in poverty and 80 percent of rural families had at least one family member working outside the community. Many of these Mexicans are working in Mexico City, in the border area, or living abroad, so that they can send money home.[55] Northward migration has been Mexicans' response to economic difficulties since the early twentieth century. That process was facilitated by interests and networks in Mexico and the United States which encouraged migration. For example, migration requires resources and support for the journey, which often is beyond the economic reach of the migrant. The migrant often turns to moneylenders and other social network members, who facilitate migration for a profit. Similarly, US agricultural interests continue to recruit workers from Mexico, encouraging their migration and inclusion in these networks. Mexican government actors were often complicit in these activities, as they benefited economically and politically from the migration flows.[56]

As a result of the United States' Great Recession starting in 2008 and improved economic growth in Mexico, these historic flows may be changing. According to a 2012 study by the Pew Hispanic Center, for the first time since the early twentieth century, Mexican migration to the United States has been reduced to zero, or perhaps less.[57] They attribute this change to weakened US job and housing markets, increased border enforcement, the rise in deportations, the growing dangers involved in crossing the border, birth-rate decreases in Mexico, and the strength of the Mexican economy relative to the US economy. According to their analysis, the downward trend in Mexican migration began around 2007 and has also resulted in a decrease in unauthorized migration from Mexico. The change can be explained by a decline in the number of Mexican immigrants entering the United States and by the growing number of Mexican-born immigrants who leave the United States to return to Mexico each year. The Pew analysis estimates that as of 2010, those returning migrants may be outnumbering the Mexican immigrants entering the United States. Whether these trends will continue as the US economy improves remains to be seen. But their findings suggest that we may, over the next few decades, see significant changes in this long-term migratory relationship between the two countries.

The migration flows and the long-term economic connections between the two countries have also led to the growth of transnational political organizing within Mexican immigrant communities. The last two decades have seen the growth of Mexican hometown associations. These organizations developed from social networks made up of Mexican migrants from the same hometowns or villages. They host social and cultural events in the United States, and also work to raise money to fund public works in their hometowns in Mexico. Mexican immigrants had long sent remittances to support their families at home. The Congressional Budget Office estimated that Mexicans sent about $20 billion in remittances to Mexico in 2009, which makes remittances one of Mexico's top three sources of foreign exchange. That number, however, has been decreasing during the Great Recession in the United States. The hometown associations take an activity which used to be individual or family-focused and make it community-focused by pooling immigrants' remittance money in order to address the economic development needs of their hometowns. Although these kinds of organizations have existed in Mexican communities since the 1950s, the numbers have expanded dramatically over the past two decades; there are now well over 600 Mexican hometown clubs and associations registered in 30 different cities in the United States.[58] This transnational political engagement has grown because of decreases in transportation and communication costs, which make the clubs' work much more feasible. The clubs and associations often coordinate their work with the Mexican government.

These hometown associations form another, important part of the growing organizational resources available within Mexican-origin communities in the United States. Because of the organizational and political infrastructure which had developed within US Mexican American communities by the early 1970s, Mexican American organizations were better able to respond to increases in Mexican migration, and the new migrants had access to resources and services which had not been available to previous generations of migrants. Thus, the structural environment which Mexican Americans faced after 1970 was very different, as were the opportunities available to them. Through their hometown associations, these migrants are also creating a new structural environment across borders. The economic development programs they are funding are likely to have important effects on the economic situation in Mexico, and may have already begun to affect migration patterns between the two countries.

By and large, Mexican immigrants historically have settled in the US southwest, including in states like Arizona, California, New Mexico, Colorado, and Texas. There has always been a significant Mexican

Table 3.1 The States with Greatest Growth in Mexican-Origin Population, 1990–2010

State	Mexican-origin population, 1990	Mexican-origin population, 2000	Mexican-origin population, 2010	Percentage increase, 1990–2010
Alabama	9,509	44,522	119,013	1,152
Arkansas	12,496	61,204	137,443	1,000
Georgia	49,182	275,288	511,939	941
Kentucky	8,692	31,385	77,713	794
Minnesota	34,691	95,613	174,789	404
Nebraska	29,665	71,030	127,868	331
Nevada	85,287	285,764	548,914	544
North Carolina	32,670	246,545	472,282	1,346
South Carolina	11,028	95,076	132,856	1,105
Tennessee	13,879	77,372	180,662	1,202

Source: US Department of the Census, 1990 and 2000; for 2010 data, US Department of the Census, American Community Survey 2007–11 5-year estimates; compiled by the author.

population in Illinois too, particularly in the Chicago area. Those areas, in turn, were the location of the bulk of twentieth-century Mexican American political activism and mobilization. In recent times, because of increases in the cost of living in traditional immigrant-receiving states, coupled with growing economic opportunities in other parts of the United States, Mexican immigrants have begun to settle in non-traditional locations, outside of the southwest. Table 3.1 lists the states with the greatest growth in Mexican migration since 1990.

In addition, there are states outside of the southwest which have a growing and significant population of Mexican origin: Iowa, Kansas, Michigan, Missouri, Oregon, and Wisconsin. Such states are struggling to address the needs of this fast-growing population. Similarly, US-born Mexicans and Mexican immigrants settling in the new states are adjusting to life in places which – in terms of services and community organizations – lack the kind of community infrastructure which exists in the more traditional immigrant-receiving areas. These differences will probably affect the opportunity structures immigrants face in the new communities, as well as their ability to engage effectively with the political system and make it address their concerns. The history of migration and settlement among Mexicans suggests that this change in geographic location and settlement patterns will continue into the future.

Conclusion

Upon arriving in the United States, each subsequent generation of Mexican Americans has faced different challenges and has been assisted by the ongoing social, economic, and political mobilization which took place within the community. Those arriving during the period when segregation was legal in the United States faced particular hardships, especially those living in Texas. Across Mexican American communities during this period, individuals experienced limitations in terms of their access to education, well-paid employment, and good-quality housing. Through labor organizing, political activism, and legal challenges, the community was able to respond to these structural constraints and to improve the opportunity structure, which in turn has benefited subsequent generations of Mexican immigrants. Yet Mexican Americans in the United States still face many social, economic, and political challenges. As more Mexican Americans settle in non-traditional locations such as Georgia, North Carolina, and Iowa, they will face a different set of obstacles and a less-developed organizational infrastructure. Only time will tell in what ways the settlement experiences of these new arrivals are similar to or different from those of the immigrants who chose to locate in areas with more established Mexican American communities. At any rate, the Mexican American experience in the United States will continue to vary according to area of settlement, generation, gender, and class status. All these factors will have an impact on the quality and depth of Mexican Americans' incorporation into the US political system.

QUESTIONS FOR DISCUSSION

1 How has the United States' unique relationship with Mexico affected the migration and political incorporation of the United States' Mexican-origin population?
2 How has geography affected the political opportunities and levels of discrimination faced by Mexican Americans in the United States?

3 What are some examples of Mexican American efforts to challenge their second-class status in the United States?
4 Why did Mexican Americans move toward more radical politics at the end of the 1960s?
5 What are the Chicano Movement's most important legacies? Do they remain relevant today?

GUIDE TO FURTHER READINGS

García, Mario. 2011. *Blowout! Sal Castro and the Chicano Struggle for Educational Justice*. Raleigh: University of North Carolina Press.

González, Gilbert G. and Raúl A. Fernández. 2003. *A Century of Chicano History: Empire, Nations, and Migration*. New York: Routledge.

Menchaca, Martha. 2001. *Recovering History, Constructing Race: The Indian, Black, and White Roots of Mexican Americans*. Austin: University of Texas Press.

Montejano, David. 2010. *Quixote's Soldiers: A Local History of the Chicano Movement, 1966–1981*. Austin: University of Texas Press.

Ruiz, Vicki. 1998. *From Out of the Shadows: Mexican Women in Twentieth Century America*. New York: Oxford University Press.

Zavella, Pat. 2011. *I'm Neither Here Nor There: Mexicans' Quotidian Struggles with Migration and Poverty*. Raleigh, NC: Duke University Press.

CHAPTER FOUR

Puerto Ricans:
From Colonized People to
Political Activists

Objectives
- Understand why the US entered into the Spanish–American War and the effects this had on Puerto Rico, including what it means for Puerto Rico to be a US commonwealth
- Understand the role US economic policy has played in Puerto Rican development and migration patterns
- Understand the obstacles faced by Puerto Rican migrants in the United States
- Understand in what ways the Puerto Rican movement reflected a shift in Puerto Rican identity within the United States

Introduction

Puerto Rico was one of Spain's last colonies in the new world. Its proximity to the United States meant that Puerto Rico had significant economic ties with the United States prior to the Spanish–American War. These ties, and the United States' subsequent occupation of Puerto Rico after the war, have had important effects on the presence of Puerto Ricans in the United States, as well as on their politics.

The indigenous population of Puerto Rico was that of the Taínos. The Taínos are thought to have lived across much of the Caribbean. After the Spanish conquest, many of the Taínos died of disease and mistreatment, but their legacy remains an important part of Puerto Rican history and national identity. The Taínos in Puerto Rico called the island "Boriquen"; hence, Puerto Ricans on the island and in the United States often refer to themselves as "Boricua." The demise of the Taínos also changed the demographic make-up of Puerto Rico, creating a need for the Spanish to import large numbers of African slaves to provide labor for the Puerto Rican economy. Thus, Puerto Ricans are of European, indigenous, and African descent. Puerto Rican geneticist Juan Martínez Cruzado recently conducted an islandwide DNA survey and found that a majority of

Puerto Ricans have Indian blood: 61 percent have Amerindian mitochondrial DNA, 27 percent African, and 12 percent Caucasian.[1] Thus it is not by accident that the island's Taíno heritage and indigenous practices remain important parts of Puerto Rican culture.

Until the mid nineteenth century, the Puerto Rican economy was based on sugar production, which was centered in the coastal areas. From then on, Puerto Rico also began to develop its coffee production, which was located inland. The largest market for these goods was the United States. Because of Spanish colonial restrictions, Puerto Rican producers were able to trade with the United States only on a limited basis until 1819, when Spain and the United States signed the Adams–Onis Treaty, formally renewing commercial ties between the two countries. From that point forward, US trade with Puerto Rico grew rapidly. As a result of this interaction, small numbers of Puerto Ricans began settling in the United States, mainly in the New York City area.

The Puerto Rican independence movement began in 1868, with the *"Grito de Lares"* (the Revolt of Lares). As other Spanish colonies gained their independence in the nineteenth century, Puerto Ricans began to demand greater autonomy from the Spanish government. There was also economically rooted animosity building up against Spain in Puerto Rico. In 1868 sugar prices fell dramatically and Spain, in order to raise revenue and quell a rebellion in the Dominican Republic, increased the tariffs on Puerto Rican goods. Faced with mounting economic pressure, Puerto Ricans began to feel even more strongly that they needed to have control over their economy and government. The autonomy movement culminated in 1868 with an uprising in the town of Lares. The rebel group, the *Comité Revolucionario de Puerto Rico* (the Puerto Rican Revolutionary Committee), took over the town church and city hall, demanding Puerto Rican independence. The Spanish militia quickly stopped the rebellion, imprisoning about 475 rebels. These were initially sentenced to death, but the new Spanish Governor released them in 1869 in an attempt to ease tensions on the island. Even though this rebellion failed to achieve Puerto Rican independence, it did move Spain to grant Puerto Rico more autonomy. Puerto Rican representatives had long been urging Spain to abolish slavery on the island, which Spain did in 1873. In 1897, after much negotiation, Spain passed the *Carta Autonómica* (the Autonomy Charter), which, for the first time since the conquest, granted Puerto Rico political and administrative autonomy. The Autonomy Charter established an independent government for Puerto Rico, gave the island representation in the Spanish parliament, and allowed it to

Plate 4.1 *Political Cartoon from the Popular Press.*
Source: Wisconsin Historical Society, PH 2714.

negotiate trade agreements directly with the United States and other countries. The new Puerto Rican government was also granted the right to accept or reject any trade agreements negotiated for Puerto Rico by Spain. Elections were held and Puerto Rico's new autonomous government began to function in 1898.

The year 1898 was also a time of mounting tensions between the United States and Spain. In the United States there was increasing concern about the situation in Cuba and growing support for Cuban independence. By early 1898, it became clear that the United States was likely to intervene in Cuba. Puerto Rican leaders wrote letters to President McKinley in March 1898, to ensure that Puerto Rico was included in any US invasion plans. They also provided the United States with intelligence about the Spanish military presence on the island. After the war began, little of the fighting occurred on Puerto Rican territory, and Spain ceded the island, along with its other holdings, to the United States under the Treaty of Paris, which was signed in December 1898. General John R. Brooke subsequently became the first US military Governor of Puerto Rico.

The Status of Puerto Rico

The US occupation of Puerto Rico began the ongoing, and still unresolved, debate over the status of the island. The fact that Puerto Rico remains in a political "limbo" – neither being a sovereign nation nor having the rights of a US state – has been a central issue in Puerto Rican politics, both among Puerto Ricans living in the United States and among those living on the island. All the political parties on the island are organized according to their position on the status question, and the status question has been a key part of all the forms of political organization which Puerto Ricans have undertaken in the United States.

Puerto Rico was under US military rule until 1900, when the US Congress passed the Foraker Act. This Act established a civil government and free commerce between Puerto Rico and the United States. The Puerto Rican government would include a governor appointed by the US President, an appointed executive council (the equivalent of a senate), and an elected legislature with 35 members. The legislature could override a governor's veto with a two-thirds vote. President McKinley appointed the first Executive Council in June 1900; it included 5 Puerto Rican members and 6 US members. The first legislative elections took place in November. The Act also allowed Puerto Rico to have a non-voting representative in the US Congress (this representative was called a Resident Commissioner). The Act established a Puerto Rican Department of Education, which was headed by an American. Teaching in the new public school system was conducted entirely in English, with Spanish being treated as a special subject. However, both Spanish and English were considered official languages on the island.

In addition to establishing the parameters of the Puerto Rican government, the Foraker Act also made Puerto Rico, officially, an unincorporated territory of the United States. In 1902 Puerto Rico became a US territory. With the passage of the Jones Act in 1917, Puerto Ricans officially became US citizens. The Act was passed despite opposition from the Puerto Rican legislature. But this is a "statutory" citizenship – a citizenship status granted by law rather than by right of birth, as in the case of citizens born in the mainland United States. Thus Congress may revoke the citizenship of Puerto Ricans if it can be shown that the revocation serves a legitimate federal purpose. Congress could also decide that Puerto Ricans born in the future will no longer be considered US citizens. This means that Puerto Ricans born on the US mainland have a citizenship status which is different from that of Puerto Ricans born on the island insofar as birth-right citizenship may be lost only as a result of a person's own actions (for instance through their renouncing it), rather than by an act of Congress.[2]

The Jones Act also altered the Puerto Rican governmental structure, establishing two legislative houses (a 19-member Senate and 39-member House of Representatives), which would be popularly elected. The Governor of Puerto Rico was still to be appointed by the US President, and he (along with the President and the US Congress) retained the right to veto any act of the Puerto Rican legislature. The Governor's cabinet appointments had to be approved by the US Senate. The Jones Act also made English the official language of Puerto Rico.

Despite the fact that the Jones Act gave Puerto Ricans more direct control over their government, it did not satisfy many Puerto Ricans' desire for self-determination. The Puerto Rican independence movement had continued after the US occupation and gained strength in the 1930s and 1940s. The movement was led by the Puerto Rican Nationalist Party, which was founded in 1922. In 1930, the Party elected Pedro Albizu Campos as its leader. Albizu Campos had attended Harvard University and had served in the US army (in a segregated African American unit) during the First World War. Shortly after Campos' election as Party President, the US-appointed Governor of Puerto Rico, Blanton Winship, began cracking down on the Party and its activities. Leaders were jailed and supporters were subjected to harassment. For example, police and nationalist supporters clashed in 1934 on the campus of the University of Puerto Rico in Ríos Piedras. Four nationalists were left dead, and one police officer was wounded. The officers involved were never prosecuted. In 1936 Albizu Campos was arrested for sedition, along with other members of his party. In the initial trial, with a jury of seven Puerto Ricans and five Americans, Albizu Campos was found not guilty. The judge ordered a retrial and the new jury, made up of ten Americans and

two Puerto Ricans, found Albizu Campos guilty. In 1937, a group of supporters appealed against the verdict, but the Boston Court of Appeals
(which had jurisdiction over federal matters in Puerto Rico) upheld
the ruling. Albizu Campos and the other nationalist leaders were sent
to federal prison in Georgia. Shortly afterwards a group of nationalist
supporters held a peaceful march in the city of Ponce to protest against
their imprisonment. The police opened fire on the marchers, killing 19
people, including a seven-year-old girl who was passing by. Police used
guns and clubs, wounding over 100 marchers. This event is called the
"Ponce Massacre."

In response to the uprisings and violence, some Puerto Rican leaders,
such as Luis Muñoz Marín, moved away from advocating independence.
They pushed instead for commonwealth status for Puerto Rico, which
would entail more autonomy and a greater amount of self-determination
in island affairs. Those favoring commonwealth status began negotiations with President Roosevelt; they were successful under the Truman
Administration. In 1946, President Truman appointed the first Puerto
Rican-born Governor of the island, Jesus Piñero. The following year, the
United States granted Puerto Rico the right to elect their Governor. In
the 1948 elections, Luis Muñoz Marín became the first democratically
elected Governor of Puerto Rico. He would serve in that capacity for 16
years, until 1964.

Yet many nationalists did not consider these moves sufficient. They
began to plan the Jayuya uprising, which took place in October 1950.
Nationalist leaders took up arms in seven Puerto Rican cities, including
San Juan, Ponce, and Jayuya. In Jayuya, the nationalists raised the Puerto
Rican flag in the town square (between 1898 and 1952 it was illegal to
carry the Puerto Rican flag on the island) and held the town for three
days. The US government declared martial law on the island and called
in the Puerto Rican National Guard. Jayuya was attacked by US bomber
planes from the air and by US artillery on the ground; the city was
destroyed. The top leaders of the nationalist party, including Albizu
Campos, were arrested and sentenced to long prison terms. Two nationalists, Griselio Torresola and Oscar Collazo, were living in the United
States at the time and devised a plan to assassinate President Truman.
They attempted it unsuccessfully at Blair House in November 1950.
Torresola was killed and Collazo was arrested and sentenced to death.
President Truman commuted his death sentence into life imprisonment.

In response to this violence, President Truman allowed for a democratic referendum to be held in Puerto Rico, to determine whether

Puerto Ricans wanted to draft their own constitution.[3] The referendum passed, and the new constitution was adopted in July 1952. That constitution established Puerto Rico as a US Commonwealth (on the island, the status is called *Estado Libre Asociado*), which is the status the island holds today. Puerto Rico is considered by the US government to be an unincorporated organized territory of the United States, subject to the powers of the US Congress and with the right to establish a constitution for the internal administration of government and on matters of purely local concern. In other words, Puerto Ricans on the island may directly elect their Governor and their legislature, and those bodies may pass laws relating to local issues on the island. But this is subject to the discretion of the US Congress, which can rescind these rights at any time. Should the US Congress disagree with any of the island government's actions, it may reverse them. The head of state for Puerto Rico is the US President, not the island's Governor. Yet Puerto Ricans do not have the right to vote in US presidential elections.[4] Puerto Rico has an elected, non-voting representative in the US Congress. From a financial standpoint, Puerto Ricans on the island pay federal payroll taxes (Social Security, Medicare) but do not receive the level of Medicare benefits they would be entitled to if they were a state. They also pay taxes to support the Puerto Rican government.

The establishment of the Puerto Rican Commonwealth did not end the independence movement; the nationalists wanted nothing short of independence for the island. In 1954, in order to bring attention to the Puerto Rican status issue, a group of nationalists led by Lolita Lebrón attacked the US House of Representatives. Lebrón was a poor single mother who had migrated to New York City during the 1940s in order to be able to support her daughter. There she experienced racial discrimination and became a follower of Albizu Campos. The nationalists chose March 1 as the day of the attack, in order to mark the anniversary of the passage of the Jones Act. Four nationalists, Lebrón, Rafael Cancel Miranda, Irving Flores, and Andrés Figueroa Cordero, unfurled a Puerto Rican flag from the balcony of one of the visitors' galleries and opened fire in the House of Representatives chamber. Lebrón is quoted as yelling: "I did not come to kill anyone; I came to die for Puerto Rico! ¡Viva Puerto Rico Libre!" According to Miranda, Lebrón shot her pistol toward the ceiling (so that she would not hurt anyone) and Figueroa's pistol jammed. Miranda is credited with causing most of the injuries. Despite the fact that an estimated 240 House members were on the floor that day, none was killed; 5 members were wounded. A bullet from the attack may still be found in the podium used by Republicans to speak on the floor of the House. The nationalists were arrested immediately and sentenced to death. President Eisenhower commuted their death sentences, and they were sentenced instead to imprisonment for life. After this attack, Albizu Campos was sent back to prison too. In an attempt at national reconciliation, Governor Muñoz Marín had pardoned Albizu Campos in 1953, but he revoked that pardon after the events of 1954. Albizu Campos remained in prison until 1964, when Muñoz Marín pardoned him for the last time.

None of these events served to resolve the issue of status. Since 1952, three referenda have been held to determine what the island's status should be: in 1967,[5] 1993, and 1998.[6] Each time the result has favored maintaining the status quo rather than independence or statehood. Interestingly, in the 1998 referendum, less than 47 percent of Puerto Ricans supported statehood and over 50 percent chose "none of the above," which suggests a general frustration with the choices offered. Independence has not had strong support in these referenda – which is not surprising, given the political repression and violence which have surrounded the independence movement and the economic uncertainty which accompanies the prospect of independence for the island. We will see below that Puerto Ricans in the United States have always been more supportive of independence than Puerto Ricans on the island, and that working to free political prisoners fighting for Puerto Rican independence has been an important part of Puerto Rican politics within the United States.

The Puerto Rican Economy: Operation Bootstrap and the Great Migration

For the first four decades of the twentieth century, Puerto Rico was an agrarian economy, with sugar as its primary export. The crash of sugar prices during the Great Depression decimated the Puerto Rican economy, leading to widespread misery and malnutrition. During the New Deal, the US government had begun developing plans to diversify and industrialize the Puerto Rican economy, so that it would no longer be so dependent on the sugar revenue. That plan accelerated during the Second World War. The US government built factories in Puerto Rico to provide goods for US domestic consumers and for the US military in the event of a possible German naval blockade of the Atlantic. After the war, the United States moved from state-driven industrialization to a system using tax and economic incentives to encourage private industry to invest on the island. In 1947 the Puerto Rican legislature approved the Industrial Incentives Act, which provided tax breaks, low-cost labor, and land to US businesses to encourage them to move manufacturing to the island. US government officials referred to this act as "Operation Bootstrap." The idea behind the plan was that Puerto Rico would help itself, pulling itself up by its metaphorical bootstraps in order to become industrialized. But they still received assistance from the United States in order to accomplish this. Until the 1970s, the US government sent nearly $600 million annually to Puerto Rico in order to support the program.[7] The industrialization process was also helped by Puerto Rican access to US markets: these became the destination of choice for Puerto Rican exports. As a result, from 1958 to 1977, Puerto Rico experienced dramatic economic growth, averaging over 9 percent a year. Factory employment doubled during the same period and the number of factories grew by about 20 percent.[8] The industrialization also coincided with a dramatic decline in the agrarian sector. In 1950, 40 percent of the labor force worked on farms; by the late 1980s, that number had fallen to 3 percent.[9] Thus, in a very short period of time, the Puerto Rican economy was transformed from an agrarian-based system to an industrialized one.

This transformation led to significant social dislocations within Puerto Rican society, in particular to the mass migration of Puerto Ricans to the United States. Puerto Rico's dramatic rates of economic growth did little to affect employment levels on the island. In fact, total employment in Puerto Rico actually decreased, from 603,000 jobs in 1951 to 543,000 in 1960; employment did not return to the level it had in 1951 until 1963. The growth in industrial jobs was not able to keep up with the population growth, or to compensate for job losses in the agricultural sector or in the home needlework industry.[10] Some scholars argue that what made the Puerto Rican economic model sustainable was the provision of US federal transfer money, particularly in the form of food assistance, to the island. This assistance made it possible for the Puerto Rican population to survive despite the lack of available employment. In 1950, transfer payments from the US federal and Puerto Rican governments constituted about 12 percent of personal income; by 1980, that proportion had risen to 30 percent.[11] This injection of funds served to increase Puerto Rican per capita income and helped to maintain consumer demand on the island.

Another important factor in the maintenance of this industrialization program in the face of high unemployment was the free movement of Puerto Ricans to the United States. Since the United States takeover of Puerto Rico, the US government has often used the Puerto Rican population as a source of low-cost labor. Starting in 1898, Puerto Rican workers began to be sent by the US government to different locations to be used as contract laborers. The first group was sent to Hawaii. Later groups of Puerto Rican workers were sent to the Dominican Republic and to Cuba. The most common destination, however, was the US mainland. In 1917, the United States' Bureau on Insular Affairs issued a memorandum outlining plans for addressing the "overpopulation" of Puerto Rico. One proposal was "to bring to the US from 50,000 to 100,000 laboring men to be used on farms as agricultural laborers, for which they are best fitted, or as right-of-way laborers on the railroads or similar work requiring manual labor."[12] Various US government agencies followed through with these plans, using Puerto Ricans, as they used Mexicans, as contract laborers in US agriculture, particularly in places like Arizona, New Mexico, and Ohio.

Because Puerto Ricans are US citizens, they require no immigration documentation or visas in order to migrate to the United States. In response to the economic dislocation which took place in the 1950s, large numbers of Puerto Ricans began leaving the island and settling in the United States. This large movement of people is known as the "Great Migration." Even though Puerto Ricans had been settling in the United States since the turn of the twentieth century, this process accelerated rapidly in the post-war period. An estimated 470,000 Puerto Ricans left Puerto Rico during the decade of the 1950s – a number which represented 21 percent of the island population. Most of these migrants settled in New York City. By 1964, Puerto Ricans made up over 9 percent of the city's population. As is clear from figure 4.1, the bulk of this migration flow occurred from the 1940s to the 1960s. Since then, Puerto Rican migration has continued, but at much lower rates.

There were a number of factors that drove this increased migration. First, the industrialization program being carried out on the island had significantly increased unemployment, making it necessary for Puerto Ricans to seek their livelihoods elsewhere. Second, improved medical care during the twentieth century had lowered the Puerto Rican mortality rate and had increased population growth, creating more economic pressures. Third, air travel became much less expensive after the Second World War, putting the cost of a ticket to the United States within the

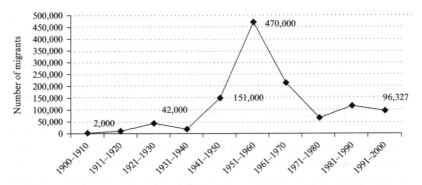

Figure 4.1 *Puerto Rican Migration to the United States, 1900–2000*

Source: *E. Acosta-Belén and C. E. Santiago, Puerto Ricans in the United States: A Contemporary Portrait (Boulder, CO: Lynne Rienner, 2006), p.81.*

reach of ordinary families. Some scholars argue that the Puerto Rican government facilitated this air travel by asking the Federal Aviation Administration (FAA) to approve low rates for transportation between Puerto Rico and the United States.[13] After centuries of immigration by boat, the Puerto Rican Great Migration became the first large-scale air-borne migration in US history. Fourth, many Puerto Ricans had served in the US armed forces during the Second World War and therefore had earned college tuition benefits under the GI Bill. Many of them traveled to the United States in order to attend college. Finally, US companies began to see Puerto Rico as a source of cheap labor and recruited heavily on the island. US government officials participated in this recruitment as well. For example, New York Mayor Robert F. Wagner, Jr., began a campaign to recruit laborers to the city to work in its factories. In 1953 he stated publicly that he and all New Yorkers would welcome any Puerto Rican who was willing to work.

Puerto Rican migration to the United States is somewhat unique because of its circular pattern. Many Puerto Ricans participate in life both on the mainland and on the island. When economic conditions are good on the mainland, they move there. When there is an economic downturn, many return to the island. This type of migration is facilitated by the island's geographic proximity to the mainland. Other factors include the availability of inexpensive transportation and the Puerto Ricans' status as US citizens, both of which lower the barriers for re-entry on the mainland.

Puerto Rican Political Life in the United States

Puerto Ricans began settling in the United States during the independence movement of the nineteenth century, and in 1895 they created a Puerto Rican Section of the Cuban Revolutionary Committee. Puerto Rican and Cuban activists formed other organizations, published newsletters, and raised money to support the cause of independence on the islands. They were joined by small numbers of tobacco workers, skilled laborers, and their families, who joined these groups and settled in Manhattan and Brooklyn.[14] Economically, Puerto Ricans were initially concentrated in the cigar trade – a very skilled type of work which brought high pay and good working conditions. In 1919 the cigar-makers engaged in a strike which, although successful, marked the end of their craft, because shortly afterwards the producers began mechanizing their industry. In the 1920s, Puerto Ricans in the United States were concentrated in cigar-making, factory work, and laundry. It is estimated that 25 percent of Puerto Rican women worked outside the home during this period as cigar-makers, domestics, typists, and operators in the needle trades.[15]

After 1898, new Puerto Rican organizations arose in these communities: organizations which, much like the *mutualistas* in Mexican American communities, helped community members to deal with the problems of daily life by assisting with housing and employment, by providing food for needy families, and by organizing recreational activities such as baseball. Often these organizations were formed in response to the fact that Puerto Rican migrants were not welcomed with open arms. They arrived in the United States at the height of racial segregation, at a time when Puerto Ricans on the island were depicted in newspaper cartoons as "aboriginals" or "negroes" incapable of governing themselves. Puerto Ricans found their legal residency questioned by many, and there were reports of Puerto Ricans being refused the right to vote and the right of access to public services.[16] Many reported seeing signs in restaurants which read "No dogs or Puerto Ricans allowed." There were also numerous incidents of violence against Puerto Ricans. In the summer of 1926, 50 people were injured during a week of violence directed at Puerto Ricans in Harlem. The altercations were initiated by Jewish gangs hired by merchants who were concerned about the expansion of Puerto Rican-owned *bodegas* (markets) in the area. In response, the Puerto Rican Brotherhood, one of the first Puerto Rican organizations in New York City, called for a mass meeting which resulted in the formation of two new organizations designed to provide protection for the community.

Luisa Capetillo: Transnational Labor Organizer and Political Activist[17]

Luisa Capetillo was a fiery Puerto Rican labor organizer and feminist activist during the early twentieth century. She was born in Puerto Rico on October 28, 1879. She started her career as a labor activist as a *lectora* (reader) in a cigar factory in Arecibo, where she joined *La Federación Libre de Trabajadores de Puerto Rico* (FLT; the Free Federation of Workers of Puerto Rico), one of Puerto Rico's strongest and most radical labor unions. As a reader, her job was to entertain and inspire the workers as they produced cigars. She quickly became a leader in the male-dominated FLT and traveled throughout the island rallying workers to the cause. A prolific writer throughout her life, she published her first book, *Ensayos libertarios* (Liberating Essays), in 1907, which she "dedicated to the workers of both sexes." Capetillo had a strongly feminist vision in her writings, arguing in favor of broadening women's education and job opportunities, and speaking out against conventional marriage. She is credited with pushing the FLT to take women's issues more seriously. She was one of the first women to wear trousers publicly, an act for which she was jailed in Cuba and Puerto Rico. She visited New York City in 1912, meeting with labor activists, giving lectures, and organizing workers in New York's cigar industry. After New York City, Capetillo visited Ybor City in south Florida, working again as a cigar factory reader, speaker, and journalist. Capetillo engaged in organizing in Cuba and then returned to Puerto Rico where in 1916 she helped to organize one of the largest sugar-cane workers' strikes in the island's history. She returned to New York City in 1919–20, continuing her transnational organizing efforts. While in New York, she ran a boarding house, providing vegetarian meals to her boarders, engaging in political debates, and devoting herself to radical causes. After returning to Puerto Rico, she died of tuberculosis on April 10, 1922; she was 42. Despite her short life, through her writings and activism Capetillo inspired workers and feminist organizers in the United States and across the Caribbean, and is seen as one of the founders of Puerto Rico's women's rights movement.

Many Puerto Rican organizations, like the *Liga Puertorriqueña* founded in 1922, were explicitly apolitical. Between 1922 and 1930, 30 "civic" organizations were created in the Puerto Rican community.[18] What made this rich organizational life possible was funding from key sectors of the community. In Manhattan, the cigar-makers, because of their economic resources, were able to support these institutional structures. In Brooklyn, the *boliteros* (or "numbers runners") became quite successful during the 1920s and were able to contribute significant amounts of money to Puerto Rican associations. In 1913, the Spanish-language newspaper *La Prensa* was founded as a weekly; it became a daily in 1918. By 1927 there were a number of periodicals serving the community, including *El Gráfico, Metropolis*, and *El Machete Criolla*.[19]

Also in 1918, the Puerto Rican community in Brooklyn began establishing political clubs. They soon had clubs active in a number of assembly districts. These clubs provided social services and functioned as brokers between the Puerto Rican community and the local Democratic Party. Such clubs did not flourish in the Manhattan *barrios* because the Manhattan Democratic Party was controlled by Tammany Hall, which frowned upon non-white participation in city politics. Politics in Brooklyn, on the other hand, was a little more open and allowed Puerto Ricans to exercise some influence in party politics. But that influence was mediated by two non-Puerto Rican party bosses: Jimmy Kelly and George McCure. They did not allow Puerto Ricans themselves to assume leadership positions and ensured that any contact with the Party went through them, a fact which kept Puerto Ricans distant from party politics. The main political issues of concern to the community during this period were the political status of Puerto Rico; the United States' policies toward Latin America; the Spanish civil war; and New York City politics.

In terms of formal political participation, prior to the Second World War, Puerto Rican engagement in New York City's electoral arena was limited. Sánchez-Korrol argues that having to subject themselves to registration and an English literacy test discouraged many Puerto Ricans from engaging in electoral politics. In addition, many felt they had little to gain from their participation, as one Puerto Rican activist from the period remarked:

> Many Puerto Ricans did not exercise their right to vote. In addition, it was not an easy matter to vote at that time. The officials submitted the aspirant to an interrogation with the purpose of frightening them and making them abandon their original political persuasions. This only served to keep Puerto Ricans away from the polls. But they [Puerto Ricans] also believed that they had nothing to look for in American politics. [20]

Yet some Puerto Ricans did exercise the right to vote. It is estimated that over 7,000 Puerto Rican voters participated in the 1918 New York gubernatorial election, and in 1926 there were over 5,000 Puerto Ricans reported to be registered to vote in the city of New York.[21] In 1937, the first Puerto Rican elected official in the United States, Oscar García Rivera, was elected to the New York State Assembly with the support of the Republican Party and the American Labor Party. He would serve one term.[22] Starting in the 1930s, Italian party boss Vito Marcantonio began reaching out to Puerto Rican voters. He expressed his support for Puerto Rican independence, criticized the United States' treatment of the island, and pushed for aid to the poor in Harlem. In 1936 Marcantonio traveled to Puerto Rico to defend nationalist leader Albizu Campos and helped to organize a march in August of that year, in support of Puerto Rican independence, that attracted about 10,000 protesters.[23] These efforts resulted in strong electoral support from Puerto Rican voters in his runs for Congress. Marcantonio was elected as the US representative for East Harlem in 1934. He lost the seat in the 1936 election, but won it back in 1938 and held that office until 1951. In the 1940 election, over 30,000 voters were registered in Latino (mostly Puerto Rican) districts in New York, and over 80 percent supported Franklin D. Roosevelt for the presidency and Marcantonio for Congress.[24]

Marcantonio was a member of the American Labor Party, the only political party credited with a large-scale mobilization of the Puerto Rican vote. Even though, as we saw above, there was an ongoing, informal relationship between the Puerto Rican community and the Democratic Party, that party did not embrace the community until the 1960s. In fact, neither of the two major political parties focused much energy on organizing the Puerto Rican vote during the first half of the twentieth century.

The 1930s and 1940s marked the height of Puerto Rican engagement in New York electoral politics prior to the 1960s. That engagement was driven largely by the outreach to the community which had been undertaken by politicians such as Marcantonio and New York City Mayor Fiorello La Guardia. During this period there was a strong relationship between New York City politics and politics on the island, with island politicians visiting and speaking before the mainland community and New York organizers spending time on the island in support of candidates and causes. As the post-war period began, a number of factors combined to decrease Puerto Rican engagement in the electoral sphere. In 1948, Puerto Rico's Department of Labor set up its first Migration Office in New York City. The head of that office was appointed by the Governor of Puerto Rico, and the funds came from the island government. The office was meant to help Puerto Rican migrants to adjust to life in the United States and, in particular, to help them to secure jobs and access to social services. In order to ease tensions in the New York area, the office also tried to settle Puerto Rican migrants in other parts of the United States. As such, the Migration Office took on roles which community politicians and political leaders often assume. The office often spoke for the community, and city leaders would contact the Migration Office to discuss problems facing the Puerto Rican community in New York City.

This delayed the development of a New York-based Puerto Rican leadership structure; the implication was that the community could look to island officials in the Migration Office rather than to politicians in local or state government to solve their problems.

Other factors combined to decrease the Puerto Rican presence in New York City politics during the 1950s. Organizational life diminished as funding for the organizations dried up. The large-scale mechanization of the cigar industry decreased the number of cigar-makers left in the community and limited their ability to provide financial assistance to Puerto Rican community groups. Similarly, starting in the 1930s, the income generated by the *boliteros* began to decrease, which rendered them, too, unable to provide the financial backing they had offered in the past. In addition, starting in the 1930s, the Puerto Rican Democratic Clubs began distancing themselves from what was considered an illicit activity, and so started to depend solely on membership dues and other sorts of fund-raising rather than on funding from the *boliteros*.[25] On the political side, in light of growing civil rights struggles in the south, the Democratic Party was becoming more clearly a party of whites only, which in the northeast meant that it was a party of ethnic whites. Puerto Ricans, being seen as non-white, were defined as "a threat to the city's white population."[26] Besides, the Democratic Party may have seen the community's politics as being too far to the left. The Puerto Ricans' strong support of Marcantonio, an outspoken leftist, and of Puerto Rican independence, became less acceptable after the Truman assassination attempt and after the 1954 nationalist attack on Congress. Thus "the backdrop of Cold War tensions and McCarthyism may have added to the Democrats' reticence to embrace the city's Puerto Rican electorate."[27] This happened despite the fact that most Puerto Ricans in the early twentieth century identified with the Democratic Party.[28]

The 1950s saw another shift in Puerto Rican politics in New York: a move toward more of a focus on the US Puerto Rican experience. In 1958, what had been the "Hispanic Day" parade in New York City became the Puerto Rican Day parade, an event designed to showcase Puerto Rican life and culture in the United States. This new sense of group identity, which was rooted in Puerto Rican experiences on the US mainland, continued to grow during the 1960s. The establishment of a new set of Puerto Rican organizations helped the development of this new identity. Lyndon B. Johnson's "War on Poverty" programs provided funding to these new groups, which slowly began to challenge the role the Migration Office played in the lives of Puerto Ricans in New York. These organizations

Plate 4.2 *Puerto Rican Day Parade.*
Source: © *Bo Zaunders/Corbis*

included the Puerto Rican Day Parade Committee; the Congress of
Puerto Rican Hometowns; and an educational advocacy organization
called Aspira. They organized in order to address the problems of poverty, inadequate housing, nutrition, education, and health care faced
by New York's Puerto Rican community. They were quite successful. For
example, in the mid-1960s Aspira protested against a proposed change
to the college admission standards for the City University of New York
(CUNY). Aspira activists picketed in front of New York Governor Nelson
Rockefeller's home; they were dressed as "mothers," "fathers," and
"children" and they carried caskets and signs asserting that Rockefeller
had "killed the future of high school Puerto Rican youth."[29] Rockefeller
reacted, meeting with Aspira and other Puerto Rican groups. The outcome was that all the students affected were granted admission to CUNY
the following academic year.

By the end of the 1960s, the war in Vietnam and the end of the Johnson
Administration also signaled the end of the "War on Poverty." Many of
the Puerto Rican organizations which had flourished at the beginning
of the decade found themselves struggling to find funding from state or
local government. Some of their leaders turned to the electoral arena
in order to influence the budgetary priorities at city and state levels.
One such leader was Herman Badillo, a political moderate who entered

politics through the reforming arm of the Democratic Party. He became Bronx President in 1965 and went on to be, in 1970, the first Puerto Rican elected to the US Congress. One of his first acts upon being elected was to fly to Puerto Rico to consult with key island officials. In an interview during his trip, Badillo stressed that he considered the island to be a part of his constituency.[30] Similarly, Ramón Velez was very active in anti-poverty programs in the Bronx. Once the funds dried up, he ran for a number of political offices and served as a New York City councilman. Other Puerto Rican political leaders during this period included Carlos Rios, a district leader in East Harlem, and Gilberto Gerena Valentín, an avowed socialist who became head of the Puerto Rican Council of Hometowns in 1963.[31] In 1965 Valentín was the head of the newly formed National Association of Puerto Rican Civil Rights and went on to serve in the New York City municipal government until 1971.

Other Puerto Rican activists, who were becoming increasingly frustrated with the slow pace of change in their communities and were influenced by the Black power movement,[32] turned to more violent tactics in order to achieve their political goals. By the 1960s, the Puerto Rican community in the United States had changed. There was now a larger proportion of individuals born in the United States who had never lived on the island. For example, in 1950 only a quarter of the community was born in the US; by 1970 the US-born comprised almost half of the Puerto Ricans in the United States. This demographic situation led to a shift toward US-based issues in the community's political organizing. It also meant that the community was quite young. Although Puerto Ricans made up only 7.9 percent of New York City's population in 1960, they accounted for "11 percent of all youth aged 15 through 19, 11 percent of those 10–14 years old, 12 percent of those 5–9, and 14 percent of all children under 5."[33] Given these demographic changes, it is not surprising that the youth born in the US formed the backbone of the community's political movement and were highly focused on issues concerning children and the young.

The Puerto Rican Movement

As we saw in the Chicano Movement, there was no one group that constituted "the Puerto Rican Movement," but rather a collection of different organizations. The most successful of these organizations was called the Young Lords, which originated as a youth gang in Chicago's Lincoln Park neighborhood. While in prison, one of the gang's founding members, José "Cha Cha" Jiménez, met Fred Hampton and other Black Panther Party members. They discussed the exploitation and oppression of Latinos, African Americans, and poor people in the United States. When he was released from prison in 1968, "Cha Cha" took back to the gang what he had learned and transformed the Young Lords into an organization committed to human rights and the liberation of Puerto Rico.

Soon afterwards, the Young Lords were restructured into ministries, in an attempt to build better organization and a Puerto Rican equivalent of the Black Panthers. The group became known as the Young Lords Organization (YLO). They did not have an official uniform, but all wore purple berets. In July 1969, the New York regional chapter was founded. It soon became independent from the national headquarters in Chicago, changing its name to the Young Lords Party. Branches were also organized in Philadelphia, PA; Bridgeport, CT; Newark, NJ; Boston, MA; and Puerto Rico. The Young Lords set up community programs: free breakfast for children, community testing for tuberculosis and lead poisoning, free clothing drives, cultural events, and Puerto Rican history classes. In Chicago they also set up a free dental clinic and a free community day-care center. The Young Lords worked to improve conditions for incarcerated Puerto Ricans and for the rights of Vietnam War veterans. They coordinated a great deal with the Black Panther Party, and their membership was not made up exclusively of Puerto Ricans; chapters often included African American members and Latinos of other national-origin backgrounds. The group's overarching goal was Puerto Rican self-determination in the United States and on the island.

Unlike in the Chicano Movement organizations, women's rights were a key concern for the Young Lords from the beginning, largely because the founding members often included women. In Chicago, a sub-group of the Young Lords led a group of women called "Mothers and Others." The group centered around women's rights and worked to educate the male members and the community at large about the issues facing Puerto Rican women. In New York, one of the first steps undertaken by the new organization was establishing a 13-point program delineating what the Young Lords stood for. Point 10 included a sentence stating that "Machismo must be revolutionary and not oppressive." The female members protested that machismo can never be revolutionary because it is always oppressive. The men agreed, and the platform was revised; point 10 was deleted and a new point 5 was added which said: "We want equality for women. Down with machismo and male chauvinism." This was the only change made to the original document. The female members demanded the organization provide child care, so that women could attend the meetings; and they made the point that every issue of the newspaper should contain articles about women's issues as well as articles written by women.[34]

The Young Lords quickly became famous for taking dramatic actions. Like the Black Panthers, the Young Lords based their strategy on using social service provision as a means of offering political education. For example, many of the chapters would play the Puerto Rican national anthem while serving children breakfast, as a way of encouraging cultural maintenance. In Chicago, the Young Lords, along with some members of Students for a Democratic Society (SDS), occupied the McCormick Theological Seminary. They demanded that the seminary provide funds for low-income housing in the community, a children's center, a cultural center for Latin Americans, and legal assistance. They occupied the seminary for seven days. As a result, the Lincoln Park neighborhood received $600,000 for low-income housing. The seminary also agreed to open its facilities for community use. The Chicago Lords also established a free breakfast program for children and proposed starting a day-care center. They approached the head of the Methodist Church, asking him to provide space for housing the center. He was receptive, but the congregation was not; so the Young Lords occupied the church. In the end, they were able to establish their day-care center. Their final major project was the creation of a free health clinic for the community, which provided preventive care, prenatal care, eye exams, and other important health services for the individuals living in the area.

The New York chapter of the Young Lords engaged in similar activities as the groups in Chicago and elsewhere, but this one was able to garner the highest media attention and national recognition. Part of the reason was that this group of organizers was very adept at using the media; it published its own newspaper (*Palante*, meaning "*Forward*") and produced a local weekly radio show, also called "Palante." In order to decide what their first major action should be, the group canvassed the residents of Spanish Harlem. Much to their surprise, the issue that was mostly on people's minds was that of trash, specifically the fact that the city sanitation department picked up the *barrio* trash only sporadically. In the summer of 1969, the Young Lords spent a number of days sweeping up the trash into piles, so that the sanitation department could collect it more easily. When the city still did not pick up the trash, the activists moved the piles into the middle of one of Manhattan's major avenues

and set the piles on fire, making their point quite dramatically and gar-
nering a great deal of media attention in the process.

The New York Young Lords then turned to establishing children's
breakfast and free clothing programs. As the programs grew, the organization needed more space. Just as in Chicago, one of the neighborhood
churches happened not to be used during the week, and this made
it an ideal location to house these programs. When the Young Lords
approached the pastor, a Cuban refugee, to see whether they could use
the church basement for their programs, he refused. The Young Lords
then attended the church one Sunday to address the congregation
directly. When they began to speak, a signal was given to the police,
who were stationed throughout the church. Chaos quickly ensued, with
the police beating and arresting Young Lord members. The next day's
headlines read: "Young Puerto Ricans ask Church for Food Programs
for Children. Thirteen arrested."[35] Three weeks later, the Young Lords
occupied the church, renamed it the "People's Church" and set up "serve
the people" programs, which included free breakfast and clothing programs, a liberation school, free health services, and community dinners.
After 11 days the police moved in, arresting 106 Young Lords and their
supporters. The People's Church drew national media attention and led
to a national focus on Puerto Rican issues for the first time.

Health issues were also a priority for the Young Lords in New York.
They went door-to-door collecting urine samples from *barrio* children,
and from these samples they documented high levels of lead poisoning
in the community. Similarly, they went door-to-door to conduct tuberculosis testing, finding very high levels here too. They tried to convince the
city health department to bring their X-ray truck into the neighborhood
for tuberculosis testing; the city refused. So the Young Lords "liberated"
the truck and brought it to the *barrio*. The driver and the technician
agreed to stay and test people, hundreds of whom were tested as a
result.[36] Finally, the South Bronx was home to Lincoln Hospital, a facility
which had been condemned (or found unfit for human habitation) by
the city of New York 25 years earlier, but had yet to be replaced. This was
the only medical facility serving this largely Puerto Rican community.
To protest against the conditions there, in July 1970 the Young Lords
occupied the hospital for one day; they staged a similar takeover a year
later. They demanded that a new hospital be built and that preventive
health care programs be established for the community. In 1976 the city
responded by building a new Lincoln Hospital. The Young Lords of New
York were also active in prison issues. During the 1971 riot at Attica State

Prison, its leaders were asked to mediate the conflict. The mediation and the subsequent negotiations resulted in improved conditions for prisoners throughout the New York State prison system.

Over time, however, it proved difficult to maintain this level of activity and activism. The Young Lords' heyday was from 1969 to 1972. Like other radical organizations of the time, the Lords were subject to surveillance and infiltration by the FBI's COINTELPRO, which increased infighting and paranoia within the group. The group also experienced difficulty when it tried to expand to the island of Puerto Rico itself. Puerto Ricans on the island did not embrace the organization and many in the US leadership thought it more important for the Young Lords to focus on issues on the mainland. This tension between focus on the island or focus on the US was one of the key factors which undid the Young Lords' organization. Many of the group's activists went on to careers in the media, or continued community-level activism. In the early 1970s, some of the New York Young Lords formed a new organization, the Puerto Rican Revolutionary Workers Organization (PRRWO).

Like the Chicano Movement, the Puerto Rican Movement also included a number of student groups. The Puerto Rican Student Union (PRSU), or *La Unión*, as it was often called, was the most important Puerto Rican student group at the time. Most powerful in New York City, *La Unión* established chapters on campuses throughout the northeast. It also established a community office in the South Bronx (later the office moved to East Harlem), to emphasize the fact that Puerto Rican college students needed to maintain their ties to the community (a sentiment quite similar to that of MEChA). In 1970, the PRSU, in cooperation with the Young Lords, organized the first national conference of Puerto Rican students. Within higher education, the group advocated the establishment of Puerto Rican Studies programs, the use of culturally sensitive curricula, and admissions and retention services for Puerto Rican and Latino students.[37] The PRSU was critical in the founding of the Center for Puerto Rican Studies in CUNY, the first program of its kind in the nation. It also helped to organize the "Free Puerto Rico!" movement together with the Young Lords. In 1971, the two groups mobilized 1,000 students to attend a conference at Columbia University. The purpose was to set up "Free Puerto Rico Now!" committees in high schools and colleges across the country. After the conference, organizers put together a mass demonstration in which 10,000 people marched from *El Barrio* to the United Nations to demand Puerto Rican independence, freedom for Puerto Rican political prisoners, and an end to police brutality. Even though the

PRSU worked closely with the Lords, they were a separate organization. In the early 1970s, however, they chose to merge completely with the Lords' successor organization, the PRRWO.[38]

At the same time as this more radical political activity was occurring within the community, other Puerto Rican leaders were using more mainstream methods to achieve the community's goals. Politicians like Herman Badillo ran for local office and were successful. One of the factors explaining their success was the existence of this more radical arm within community politics. The existence of groups like the Young Lords drew public attention to Puerto Rican issues; it also made it more politically expedient for the city and state leadership to satisfy the demands of the more mainstream politicians. In this way, Puerto Rican politics in the 1960s and early 1970s contained two prongs – one moderate and one radical – and each helped the other. For example, leaders like Badillo were able to negotiate with city police so as to ensure that the Young Lords would not have to serve time in jail for occupying the People's Church. On the other hand, the Young Lords increased media scrutiny on city leaders and brought attention to the many problems that needed to be solved. This helped the mainstream political leadership to make their case and to prompt the city government to address these problems. It is unlikely that either group would have been as successful on its own, without the other.

There were a number of other leftist Puerto Rican organizations active during this period, including the MPI–PSP (Movement for Independence, Puerto Rican Socialist Party), *El Comité* (which became the MINP), and the MLN (Movement for National Liberation). Like the Young Lords, these groups proposed broad-based programs designed to improve the status of the community. Although there was some coordination among these different groups, there was also a great deal of infighting. The one issue that managed to unite all of them was working to free the Puerto Rican nationalists imprisoned after the attack on the US Capitol. In the end they were successful; President Jimmy Carter granted them all a pardon in 1979. These leftist organizations also included one paramilitary group, the *Fuerzas Armadas de Liberación Nacional* (FALN; Armed Forces of National Liberation). Made up of activists and former Chicago Young Lords, from 1974 to about 1980 this group engaged in armed actions against the US government and military, actions which included an estimated 120 bombings in Chicago and New York. Its members were eventually captured in a series of arrests in the 1980s: 16 were sentenced to terms in jail ranging from 35 to 105 years, despite the fact that none was connected directly to any bombing or to any injury to a person. Once the nationalist prisoners were released in 1979, Puerto Rican activists focused their attention on securing the release of the FALN prisoners. They were successful in 1999, when President Bill Clinton granted all 16 a presidential pardon; they had served more than 19 years in prison at the time of their pardons.

This activism on the part of Puerto Ricans had a number of effects. Most broadly, it made Americans more aware of the issues facing Puerto Ricans in the United States, and it forced elected officials to take those concerns into consideration. The Democratic Party, which was the dominant political actor in most of the cities with large Puerto Rican populations, finally included Puerto Ricans in its leadership structure; this led to many Puerto Ricans being elected to public office at the local level and being appointed to government positions as well. The use of both insider and outsider tactics on the part of political activists thus produced very tangible results. At the national level, Puerto Ricans were included under civil rights legislation, including the Voting Rights Act, and were recognized as a group which had experienced historical discrimination in the United States. In 1972, Puerto Rican activists formed the Puerto Rican Legal Defense and Education Fund (PRLDEF), now called Latino Justice, which continues to use the legal system in order to ensure full political and social rights for Puerto Ricans and other Latinos in the United States. In New York City, the movement led to a new expression of Puerto Rican cultural identity – one that had its roots in the community's experiences in the United States as well as in Puerto Rico. The new identity, for which the term "Nuyorican" was coined, was meant to reflect this bicultural experience and is celebrated through community arts and cultural events, for instance the Puerto Rican Day parade.

In addition to these broad changes, the Puerto Rican Movement also had very tangible successes. It led to the establishment of Puerto Rican Studies programs across the northeastern United States. These programs have become centers for rigorous academic research focusing on the Puerto Rican experience. At the local level, many movement organizations continue to exist, albeit with different names. These organizations continue to work to improve access to services and the quality of life for Puerto Rican communities in the United States. At the international level, movement organizations were successful in keeping the status of Puerto Rico, and the question of colonialism more generally, on the agenda of the United Nations. Although the island was not made independent, it was not annexed to the United States either – which many thought likely to happen.

Puerto Rican Politics Today

Although the Puerto Rican middle class has grown substantially in the United States since the 1980s, poverty and a lack of socioeconomic mobility are still important concerns facing Puerto Rican communities there. In addition to becoming more class-differentiated, the mainland Puerto Rican community has changed with regard to its geographic dispersion. Until the 1970s, the majority of Puerto Ricans in the United States lived in New York City. This situation has changed dramatically, and there are now 14 states which contain a Puerto Rican population greater than 45,000. Table 4.1 summarizes the Puerto Rican population in the 10 states with the highest concentrations, with Puerto Rican populations greater than 75,000. Consistent with the decrease in the Puerto Rican percentage of the overall Latino population in the United States (from 9.6 percent in 2000 to 9.3 percent in 2010), we see the Puerto Rican proportion of the Latino population in each of these states has remained flat or decreased in every state but Florida. In each of these states, Puerto Ricans make up a very different percentage of the total Latino population. In states like California and Texas they are likely to have political

Table 4.1 The Puerto Rican Population by Selected States, 2000 and 2010

State	2000		2010	
	Puerto Rican population	Percentage of whole Latino population	Puerto Rican population	Percentage of whole Latino population
California	140,570	1.3	189,945	1.4
Connecticut	194,443	61.0	252,972	52.8
Florida	482,027	18.0	847,550	20.1
Illinois	157,851	10.3	182,989	9.0
Massachusetts	199,207	46.5	266,125	42.4
New Jersey	366,788	33.0	434,092	27.9
New York	1,050,293	37.0	1,070,558	31.3
Ohio	66,269	31.0	94,965	26.8
Pennsylvania	228,557	58.0	366,082	51.0
Texas	69,504	1.0	130,576	1.4
Total US	3,406,178	9.6	4,623,716	9.3

Source: US Department of the Census, 2000 and 2010 summary files; compiled by the author.

influence only in coalition with Mexican Americans. In Massachusetts and Pennsylvania, in contrast, Puerto Rican concerns will likely play a prominent role in policymaking relevant to Latinos in these states. Thus, dispersion involves differences in settlement experiences and also in political power and coalition building within particular localities.

The final change which has occurred in Puerto Rican politics since the 1950s is the expansion of traditional officeholding. As was mentioned above, the Puerto Rican Movement paved the way for Puerto Ricans to run for political office on a major party ticket. Puerto Rican Maurice Ferré served in the Florida State House in the 1960s and was Mayor of Miami from 1973 to 1985. Fernando Ferrer was a Bronx Borough President for 14 years and ran failed bids for Mayor of New York in 1997 and 2001. In 1994, Carmen Arroyo became the first Puerto Rican woman to hold a New York State Assembly seat. Bonnie García was a Republican member of the California State Assembly from 2002 to 2008. Four Puerto Rican representatives served in the 113th US Congress: Luis Gutiérrez (D-IL), Raúl Labrador (R-ID), José Serrano (D-NY), and Nydia Velázquez (D-NY). Puerto Rican representatives also currently serve in the Connecticut, Massachusetts, and Florida state legislatures.

Conclusion

Puerto Rican migration to the United States has been strongly affected by the status of Puerto Ricans as US citizens and by the United States' designation of Puerto Rico as a US territory after the Spanish–American War. The status of the island has always been a key concern in Puerto Rican politics, and, given that it remains unresolved, this concern will continue. The largest wave of Puerto Rican migrants arrived in the United States at the height of racial segregation. Because of its mixed-race background, the Puerto Rican community had difficulty fitting into the United States' Black/white racial binary. The racialization of its members limited their integration into the major political parties and restricted their economic opportunities in the United States. Yet, through their organizing and activism, Puerto Ricans were able to define a new identity for themselves – one that included the community's experiences in the United States. Through this organizing, they were also able to improve the quality of life in Puerto Rican communities and to get Puerto Rican issues included in US political discourse. By so doing, they increased their opportunities to hold political office and their political influence. They were also able to alter some of the structural constraints surrounding Puerto Rican socioeconomic mobility and adaptation in the United States. The one main constraint that remains, however, is the unresolved status of the island of Puerto Rico.

QUESTIONS FOR DISCUSSION

1 Why did the United States remain in Puerto Rico after the Spanish–American War? How has that affected the island's development and Puerto Rican migration patterns?
2 How has the status of Puerto Rico affected Puerto Rican political engagement in the United States?
3 When and why did Boricua politics begin focusing more on the Puerto Rican experience in the United States?
4 What are the similarities and differences between the Puerto Rican and Chicano movements? Which factors best explain what is the same and what is different?
5 What are the legacies of the Puerto Rican Movement? Do they remain relevant today?

GUIDE TO FURTHER READINGS

Briggs, Laura. 2002. *Reproducing Empire: Race, Sex, Science, and US Imperialism in Puerto Rico*. Berkeley: University of California Press.
Jennings, James and Monte Rivera, eds. 1984. *Puerto Rican Politics in Urban America*. Westport, CT: Greenwood Press.
Sánchez, José Ramón. 2007. *Boricua Power: A Political History of Puerto Ricans in the United States*. New York: New York University Press.
Sánchez-Korrol, Virginia. 1994. *From Colonia to Community: The History of Puerto Ricans in New York City*. Berkeley: University of California Press.
Torres, Andrés and José E. Velázquez, eds. 1998. *The Puerto Rican Movement: Voices from the Diaspora*. Philadelphia: Temple University Press.

CHAPTER FIVE

Cuban Americans: Occupation, Revolution, and Exile Politics

Objectives

- Understand the political and economic relationship Cuba has had with the United States
- Understand the effect of the Cuban revolution on that relationship
- Understand how the United States' geopolitical concerns affected the treatment and benefits received by Cuban exiles in the United States
- Understand how the exile experience and US government support facilitated Cuban political incorporation

Introduction

Cuba is located 90 miles off Key West, Florida. This proximity has resulted in an intimate relationship between Cuba and the United States since the nineteenth century. That relationship was the foundation of the United States' response to the Cuban revolution in 1959 and of its approach to Cuban migration since that time. No country in Latin America, and no Latin American immigrants, experience the same treatment as Cuba and the Cubans. The unique legal standing that Cuban-origin migrants have when they arrive in the United States, and the island's relationship to US concerns during the Cold War, have had a profound impact on the social, economic, and political status of Cubans and Cuban Americans in the United States.

In the mid nineteenth century, Cuba and Puerto Rico constituted the last of Spain's holdings in Latin America. In the 1860s, a strong movement for independence began in Cuba, starting with the *Grito de Yara* in 1868. That event began what is called the Ten Years' War, in which Cuban *independencistas* fought the Spanish. Neither side was successful in defeating the other, so the Spanish Crown offered Cuba a limited autonomy in order to put a stop to the violence. The independence movement did not end, however. Many of the pro-independence forces left the country in order to gather financial support from abroad. The vast majority, including journalist and poet José Martí, one of the principal leaders of the movement, settled in the United States. Martí published writings, gave speeches, and worked toward increasing American awareness of the situation in Cuba. In New York City, in 1892, he formed *El Partido Revolucionario Cubano* (the Cuban Revolutionary Party). Initially, the Party had chapters only in New York and Philadelphia, but it quickly spread to Tampa, Florida, and Key West. Fighting between the insurgents and the Spanish began anew in 1895. On February 24, 1895, Martí returned to Cuba to participate in the armed struggle; he was killed on May 19.

Plate 5.1 *Paulina Pedroso.*

Source: Reproduced courtesy of the Florida Memory Archive.

Paulina Pedroso: An Advocate for Racial Justice and Cuban Independence

Paulina Pedroso, born in 1845 in Cuba's Pinar del Río, would become one of the most prominent women advocating for Cuba's independence in the late nineteenth century.[1] Her parents had been slaves, but Paulina was born free. When she was 15, she moved to Havana with her husband, then continued on to Key West, Florida. She and her husband owned a boarding house in Ybor City which catered to cigar-makers and, later, political activists. Her home became the headquarters for José Martí when he visited Ybor City. Martí would host events with the Pedrosos, and Paulina and Ruperto pushed Martí to ensure that the Cuban revolution would result in racial as well as political equality. As an expression of their desire to ensure interracial equality in the United States as well, Paulina and Martí were said to have often strolled the streets of Ybor City hand in hand, a controversial act in what was a southern city under Jim Crow, even if the ethnic parts of the city historically had been integrated. Paulina and her husband hosted events and worked tirelessly to raise money for the Partido Revolucionario Cubano. After the turn of the twentieth century, their interracial vision took a blow when Anglo residents of Ybor City decided to enforce Jim Crow laws within the Cuban mutual aid societies. Up until that point, *El Club Nacional Cubano* (the Cuban National Club) had been integrated. After complaints from Anglos that the queen in the 1899 Labor Day parade was too "dusky," the club split. Those Cubans claiming to be white stayed in *El Club Nacional*, which they renamed *El Círculo Cubano*. Those who identified as Afro-Cubans, including Paulina Pedroso, formed *Los Libres Pensadores de Martí y Maceo* (the Free Thinkers of Martí and Maceo) and *La Unión* (the Union), which combined to form *La Unión Martí–Maceo* (the Martí–Maceo Union) in 1904. Founded in the Pedrosos' home, the new organization purposely spoke to Cubans' biracial roots: the white José Martí and the Afro-Cuban revolutionary general Antonio Maceo. The Pedrosos moved back to Cuba in 1910. Their house in Ybor City was donated to the Cuban government in 1956, in honor of José Martí. The house was demolished and the Batista regime donated money to establish a park with a statue of José Martí on the site. After the Cuban revolution, this created an ownership dilemma since the land officially belongs to the Cuban government. The park is now run by a Cuban American organization and is kept locked except for during specific hours. Paulina Pedroso died in Cuba in 1925 and was inducted into Florida's women's hall of fame in 1993.

Martí was successful in his efforts and attracted the attention of William Randolph Hearst, publisher of, among other newspapers, the *New York Journal*. Hearst began publishing stories about the plight of the Cuban people under Spanish rule. These stories became all the more powerful when, in response to a growing insurgency on the island, Spanish General Valeriano Weyler y Nicolau instituted a policy of *reconcentración* (reconcentration) to control Cuban insurgents. Seeking to starve out the rebels operating in the countryside, he herded the rural population into garrisoned towns and placed the entire island under martial law in February 1896. The result was widespread misery and starvation, much of which was photographed and documented for the American audience by Hearst's newspapers. It is estimated that at least 30 percent of those housed in the camps perished from lack of proper food, poor sanitary conditions, and lack of access to medicine.

Yet the United States had had interests in Cuba long before Hearst began publishing his stories. During the Ten Years' War, American sugar interests bought up large tracts of land in Cuba. Noting the growing American economic interests on the island, in 1869 the US government offered to buy Cuba from Spain for $100 million; Spain refused. Despite this, Cuba's economy continued to become more closely linked with that of the United States. On the one hand, the Cuban cigar industry was partially transplanted to Florida. Trying to flee unrest in Cuba, Spanish-born cigar-maker Vicente Martinez Ybor moved his cigar manufacturing from Cuba to Florida's Key West in 1869. Needing room to expand in the 1880s, Ybor decided to establish a company town just north of Tampa, Florida, which he named Ybor City. Ybor recruited Cuban and Spanish cigar-makers to come to Ybor City, which comprised the first major Cuban settlement in the United States and became a major center of US cigar production.

On the other hand, due to a sharp drop in sugar prices that took place from early 1884, the old Cuban "sugar nobility," unable to mechanize the trade and to cut costs, began to disintegrate and lose its dominant role in the island's economy and society. This facilitated US penetration of the Cuban economy. Sugar estates and mining interests passed from Spanish and Cuban to US hands, and it was US capital, machinery, and technicians that helped to save the sugar mills by making them competitive with European beet sugar. In 1894, nearly 90 percent of Cuba's exports went to the United States, which in turn provided Cuba with 38 percent of its imports. That same year, Spain took only 6 percent of Cuba's exports, providing it with 35 percent of its imports. By 1895, the United States had more than $50 million invested in Cuba, and US annual trade with Cuba was worth nearly $100 million. These economic interests were an important factor in moving the United States toward military intervention in Cuba.

There were also political and strategic reasons for the United States to maintain an interest in Cuba. In 1896, both the US Senate and the House of Representatives overwhelmingly passed resolutions calling for the recognition of the Cuban insurgency and of Cuban independence. Also, in the 1890s US military strategists were recommending the development of US naval power, combining the establishment of naval bases in the Caribbean with the construction of a fleet of armor-plated, steam-driven battleships. This strategy was endorsed by Theodore Roosevelt when he was Secretary of the Navy. The first major test of this new naval strategy would be in the Spanish–American War.

Thus, by 1897, there was a variety of American interests, economic and political, favoring US intervention in Cuba. Newly inaugurated President William McKinley was anxious to become involved; that interest only grew when the *New York Journal* published a copy of a letter from Spanish Foreign Minister Enrique Dupuy de Lôme criticizing the American

President. Events moved swiftly after the explosion aboard the *USS Maine* in Havana harbor in February 1898. On March 9, Congress passed a law allocating $50 million to build up American military strength. On March 17, Vermont Senator Redfield Proctor, who had traveled to Cuba at his own expense in February, told his Senate colleagues and the US business community that the situation in Cuba was so dire that US military intervention was the only answer. On March 28, the US Naval Court of Inquiry (incorrectly) found that a Spanish mine had blown up the *Maine*.[2] On April 4, the *New York Journal* printed an issue dedicated to the independence fight in Cuba, in which the publishers called for the immediate entry of the United States into war with Spain; they printed 1 million copies. On April 19, the US Congress, by a vote of 311 to 6 in the House and of 42 to 35 in the Senate, adopted the Joint Resolution for war with Spain. The resolution included the Teller Amendment, named after Senator Henry Moore Teller (R-CO), which stated that the United States had no intention of exercising jurisdiction or control over Cuba and would leave the island as soon as the war was over. President McKinley signed the resolution on April 20 and both countries formally recognized their being at war on April 25, 1898.

American forces immediately were in contact with Cuban rebels, who supplied the United States with military maps, intelligence, and a core of rebel officers to coordinate US efforts on the island. The rebels also fought alongside the US in a number of skirmishes with the Spanish. Despite having almost 200,000 troops on the island, the Spanish were quickly defeated. Representatives of Spain and of the United States signed a peace treaty in Paris on December 10, 1898. The treaty established the independence of Cuba; ceded Puerto Rico and Guam to the United States; and allowed the United States to purchase the Philippine Islands from Spain for $20 million. No Cuban or Puerto Rican representatives were present during the treaty negotiations. The war had cost the United States $250 million and 3,000 lives; 90 percent of these victims had perished from infectious diseases such as yellow fever.

In January 1899, the United States installed a provisional military government in Cuba and began a debate as to what should happen to the country. Although many Americans still supported Cuban independence, there was growing sentiment that the United States should annex Cuba. By September 1899, Cubans on the island were taking seriously the threat of annexation. In an interview with the *Chicago Chronicle*, Cuban General Carlos García warned that Cubans would not surrender their independence and that, if the United States attempted to annex the island, it would

The Platt Amendment, 1901

The United States occupied Cuba for five years after 1898. In 1901, Secretary of War Elihu Root drafted a set of articles (later known as the Platt Amendment) as guidelines for future United States–Cuba relations. Despite considerable Cuban resistance, they became a part of the 1902 Cuban Constitution. In subsequent years the United States used the amendment several times to send troops to maintain or place friendly governments in power and to protect US investments. The amendment was abrogated in 1934.

Whereas the Congress of the United States of America, by an Act approved March 2, 1901, provided as follows:

Provided further, That in fulfillment of the declaration contained in the joint resolution approved April twentieth, eighteen hundred and ninety-eight, entitled "For the recognition of the independence of the people of Cuba, demanding that the Government of Spain relinquish its authority and government in the island of Cuba, and withdraw its land and naval forces from Cuba and Cuban waters, and directing the President of the United States to use the land and naval forces of the United States to carry these resolutions into effect," the President is hereby authorized to "leave the government and control of the island of Cuba to its people" so soon as a government shall have been established in said island under a constitution which, either as a part thereof or in an ordinance appended thereto, shall define the future relations of the United States with Cuba, substantially as follows:

I.   That the government of Cuba shall never enter into any treaty or other compact with any foreign power or powers which will impair or tend to impair the independence of Cuba, nor in any manner authorize or permit any foreign power or powers to obtain by colonization or for military or naval purposes or otherwise, lodgement in or control over any portion of said island.

II.   That said government shall not assume or contract any public debt, to pay the interest upon which, and to make reasonable sinking fund provision for the ultimate discharge of which, the ordinary revenues of the island, after defraying the current expenses of government shall be inadequate.

III. That the government of Cuba consents that the United States may exercise the right to intervene for the preservation of Cuban independence, the maintenance of a government adequate for the protection of life, property, and individual liberty, and for discharging the obligations with respect to Cuba imposed by the treaty of Paris on the United States, now to be assumed and undertaken by the government of Cuba.

IV.   That all Acts of the United States in Cuba during its military occupancy thereof are ratified and validated, and all lawful rights acquired thereunder shall be maintained and protected.

V.   That the government of Cuba will execute, and as far as necessary extend, the plans already devised or other plans to be mutually agreed upon, for the sanitation of the cities of the island, to the end that a recurrence of epidemic and infectious diseases may be prevented, thereby assuring protection to the people and commerce of Cuba, as well as to the commerce of the southern ports of the United States and the people residing therein.

VI. That the Isle of Pines shall be omitted from the proposed constitutional boundaries of Cuba, the title thereto being left to future adjustment by treaty.

VII. That to enable the United States to maintain the independence of Cuba, and to protect the people thereof, as well as for its own defense, the government of Cuba will sell or lease to the United States lands necessary for coaling or naval stations at certain specified points to be agreed upon with the President of the United States.

VIII. That by way of further assurance the government of Cuba will embody the foregoing provisions in a permanent treaty with the United States.

Source: "The Platt Amendment," in C. I. Bevans, ed., *Treaties and Other International Agreements of the United States of America, 1776–1949*, Vol. VIII (Washington, DC: US Government Printing Office, 1971), 1116–17.

be met with armed resistance. In November, General Máximo Gómez was quoted in the *New York Times* as saying: "The honorable Cuban should place before himself the ideal of the republic, remembering that every day on which the sun sets until the establishment of the republic is an injury to the Cubans."[3] In November and December of that year, Cubans staged a series of protests and rallies calling for a speedy end to the US occupation.

The first municipal elections held in Cuba after the war, which took place in June 1900, also demonstrated Cuban opposition to annexation. The Cuban National Party and the Republican Party, both strongly against annexation, won almost all of the races. The Democratic Union Party, which openly favored annexation, did not win control of any city. These electoral defeats led the American military governor, General Leonard Wood, to call for an election to choose delegates to a Cuban Constitutional Convention. The draft of the Constitution of the Republic of Cuba was published in January 1901. The new constitution was modeled after the US Constitution. Shortly afterwards, the US House and Senate passed the Platt Amendment, which stipulated that Cuba had only a limited right to conduct its own foreign and debt policy. It also gave the US an open door to intervene in Cuban affairs. Under the amendment, Cuba also agreed to sell or lease to the US "lands necessary for coaling or naval stations at certain specified points to be agreed upon."

The passage of the amendment provoked massive protests and denouncements of it in Cuba. On February 27, the Cuban Constitutional Convention passed five declarations which clearly expressed their opposition to the terms laid out for Cuban governance by the Platt Amendment. These were:

1 The Government of Cuba will not make a treaty or agreement with any foreign power which may compromise or limit the independence of Cuba, or which may permit or authorize any power to obtain by means of colonization or for military or naval purposes, or in any other manner, any foothold or authority, or right over any portion of Cuba.

2 The Government will not permit its territory to be used as a base of operations for war against the United States or against any foreign nation.

3 The Government of Cuba accepts in its entirety the Treaty of Paris, in which are affirmed the rights of Cuba to the extent of the obligations which are explicitly indicated, and especially those which the international law imposes for the protection of life and property, substituting itself for the United States in the pledge, which they assumed in that sense according to Articles 12 and 102 of the Treaty of Paris.

4 Cuba recognizes as legally valid all acts of the Military Government during the period of occupation, also the rights arising out of them, in conformity with the joint resolution and the Foraker amendment and the existing laws of the country.

5 The Governments of the United States and Cuba ought to regulate their commercial relations by means of a treaty based on reciprocity, and with tendencies toward free trade in natural and manufactured products, mutually assuring ample special advantages in their respective markets.[4]

In the face of increasing Cuban opposition, General Wood wrote to the US Secretary of War, Elihu Root. He asked: "Can you indicate our [the US] action in case the Cuban Convention should refuse to accept the Platt Amendment?" Root responded: "The Platt Amendment is, of course, final and the members of the Convention who may be responsible for refusing to establish relations on that basis will injure only themselves and their country. If the Convention takes such a course it will have failed to perform the duty for which it was elected and the duty must be performed by others."[5] Despite this threat, in April 1901 the Cuban Constitutional Convention rejected the motion to accept the Platt Amendment by a vote of 24 to 2. A second vote, held six days later, rejected the amendment again, 18 to 10. In May, after long discussions with President McKinley and Secretary Root, the Cubans accepted the amendment by a vote of 15 to 14. The document approved by the convention included not only the exact words of the Platt Amendment, but Article I of the Treaty of Paris, as well as long extracts from Root's various explanations of the purposes of the amendment, including the assurance that "the Platt law has for its object the guaranteeing of the independence of Cuba, and does not mean interference with its government or the exercise of a protectorate or of sovereignty."

Secretary Root immediately rejected the actions of the Cuban Constitutional Convention and insisted that Cubans could not expect the American army to withdraw until the Platt Amendment was adopted verbatim, with no changes or additions. The convention delegates acceded to this request in June, accepting the amendment verbatim by a vote of 16 to 11. After the passage of the amendment, Orville H. Platt, one of the amendment's authors, argued in the *Independent* that the amendment was necessary because "Cubans are incapable of stable self-government" and "in many respects . . . they are like children."

Thus began Cuba's existence as an independent nation. The United States was intimately entwined in the country's economics and politics and routinely exercised its power to influence both. On the economic side, in 1903 the two countries signed a reciprocity treaty which gave preference to Cuban sugar in the US market, reduced duties on American imports, and encouraged US investment in the island, thus tying the Cuban economy even more tightly to the US market. This agreement was renegotiated in 1934. The Cuban *peso* was also pegged to the US dollar, which meant that Cubans had no say about their monetary policy; the latter was set by the US Federal Reserve. By 1913, US investments in Cuba were estimated at $220 million, which constituted 17.7 percent of the total US investment in Latin America. By 1928, the United States controlled about three-quarters of the Cuban sugar crop and was responsible for the move to large-scale plantations for sugar production.

On the political side, by 1906 the new Cuban government was in crisis: an armed rebellion attempting to take down the regime of President Estrada Palma was just beginning. President Theodore Roosevelt was quoted as saying, in response to this crisis:

> I am so angry with that infernal little Cuban republic that I would like to wipe its people off the face of the earth. All we have wanted from them is that they would behave themselves and be prosperous and happy so that we would not have to interfere. And now, lo and behold, they have started an utterly unjustifiable and pointless revolution and may get things into such a snarl that we have no alternative save to intervene."[6]

Despite the President's frustration, the US government intervened, taking control of the island until new elections were held and a new government installed in 1909. This intervention laid the groundwork for US–Cuba relations throughout the first half of the twentieth century. The US military repeatedly intervened in Cuban governmental affairs. In 1912, the United States entered Cuba to quell an armed Afro-Cuban revolt in the eastern province of Oriente. In 1917, it forced Cuba to hold a special election. The US military remained in Cuba until 1922, to "advise" the new president. In 1933, the US government played an integral part in compelling dictator Gerardo Machado to leave office. Then the US appointed his successor. As part of Franklin Delano Roosevelt's "good neighbor" policy, the Platt Amendment was rescinded in 1934, but the United States continued playing an important role in Cuban politics behind the scenes.

After Machado left office, a group of army soldiers led by Sergeant Fulgencio Batista took over the government. The 1930s saw a succession of puppet presidents who ran Cuba, with Batista remaining the controlling figure behind the scenes. In 1940 he took over the presidency directly, in an election widely considered fraudulent. Under his presidency, Cuba passed a new constitution in 1940. Considered one of the most progressive constitutions of the time, it provided for land reform, public education, and a minimum wage. Unfortunately, most of its provisions were never implemented. After a series of corrupt governments during the 1940s, Batista returned to power in a *coup* in 1952. One of his first acts was to suspend the 1940 constitution and to halt all elections.

The United States strongly supported Batista's dictatorship. In 1958, the United States provided Batista's government with $1,000,000 in military aid. All of Batista's arms, planes, tanks, ships, and military supplies came from the United States, and his army was trained by a joint mission of the three branches of the US armed forces. Batista's government largely supported US economic interests, which, by the late 1950s, were substantial. American companies controlled 90 percent of Cuban mines, 80 percent of public utilities, 50 percent of railways, 40 percent of the sugar production, and 25 percent of bank deposits. Yet this high level of investment did not generate significant employment. In 1957, American firms employed only about 1 percent of the Cuban population.

Cubans were increasingly opposed to the Batista government, which was highly repressive. The opposition included a growing guerrilla movement led by Fidel Castro, Che Guevara, and Camilo Cienfuegos which attacked Cuban government outposts in the Sierra Maestra. The guerrilla movement obtained positive news coverage in the United States, including a May 1957 interview with Castro which was aired by CBS. By 1958 Batista was beginning to lose US support. In December,

Plate 5.2 *Fidel Castro with Vice-President Richard Nixon, April 1959.*
Source: Bettmann/Corbis.

millionaire William Pawley offered Batista the use of his home in Florida if he agreed to go into exile; Batista refused. But after additional pressure from the CIA, Batista decided to flee the country after all on January 1 1959. Guevara and Cienfuegos led the rebels into Havana; Castro did not arrive in Havana until January 7, the very day when the US government officially recognized the new Cuban government.

At this point the United States was not terribly concerned about what would happen in Cuba. As historian Terence Cannon writes: "The US did not send in the marines for one basic reason: it did not fear the revolution. It was inconceivable to the US policy makers that a revolution in Cuba could turn out badly for them. After all, US companies owned the country."[7] Their concern began to increase, however, as the new Cuban government started to round up former police and army officers from the Batista regime and to execute them after publicly held trials. By March, almost 500 individuals had been executed in this fashion.

The new Cuban government also nationalized the telephone system and passed an agrarian reform bill, both of which raised US government concerns. In April 1959, Castro made an "unofficial" visit to the United

States (he was invited by a group of journalists) in order to talk about the revolution in Cuba. President Eisenhower, who was feeling increasingly uneasy about the regime, snubbed Castro by saying that he was busy playing golf. Instead, the Cuban leader met with US Vice-President Richard Nixon on April 19, 1959.

The meeting lasted three hours and occurred right after Castro made an appearance on NBC's *Meet the Press* program. In a confidential memo which he wrote in order to brief Eisenhower and other cabinet officials on the meeting, Nixon said he felt that Castro's goal was "to win support for his policies from American public opinion." He went on to say that Castro's "primary concern seemed to be to convince me that he was sincere, that he was not a communist and that his policies had the support of the great majority of the Cuban people." Nixon's evaluation of Castro was prophetic. He told Eisenhower that Castro

> has the indefinable qualities which make him a leader of men. Whatever we may think of him he is going to be a great factor in the development of Cuba and very possibly in Latin American affairs generally. He seems to be sincere, he is either incredibly naïve about Communism or under Communist discipline – my guess is the former . . . But because he has the power to lead to which I have referred we have no choice but at least to try to orient him in the right direction.[8]

Given the tone of this memo, it is not surprising that, on May 2, the United States signed a four-point agreement with Cuba, consenting to provide technical cooperation so as to help Cuba in carrying out its agrarian reform. On May 17, Cuba enacted its Agrarian Reform Law, distributing all farmlands of over 1,000 acres in size to Cuban peasants and workers. The law prohibited foreign ownership of Cuban land. This was a major change: at that point in time, 75 percent of Cuban land was in foreign hands. The government agreed to purchase foreign-owned land using 20-year government bonds set at a 4.5 percent interest rate. The price the Cuban government would pay was to be based on the land's valuation as given in the Cuban tax rolls. Many of these value assessments had not been updated in 30 or 40 years – which had been a boon to foreign owners: they paid much lower taxes than a current valuation would have required. But when it was announced that these same valuations were to be used to provide compensation, the landowners cried foul.

Since many of those landowners were US-based companies, the Agrarian Reform Law quickly led to increased opposition to the Cuban regime in the United States. In mid-June, the US government officially protested against the compensation levels which the Cuban government planned to provide for US-owned land. Landowners from other countries were also unhappy with the plan. Over the course of the year, the Cuban government successfully negotiated compensation agreements with landowners from Britain, Canada, France, Italy, Mexico, Spain, and Sweden. US landowners were the only group to refuse negotiation. In January 1960, Cuba expropriated 70,000 acres of land held by US sugar companies which had refused to sell the land at any price. This expropriation included 35,000 acres held by the United Fruit Company (now Chiquita Banana), which at that time owned 235,000 acres of land in Cuba.

This expropriation soured US–Cuba relations significantly. The United Fruit Company had many high-level supporters in the Eisenhower Administration and began to push for US intervention in Cuba. The calls for intervention only increased in June 1960 when, after US oil companies refused to refine some crude oil which Cuba had purchased from the Soviet Union, Cuba expropriated its oil refineries, all of which were US-owned. In August, the Cuban government took the final step of expropriating all the remaining US-owned companies and land in Cuba.

Thus there was only a brief window, in early 1959, when US–Cuba relations may have moved in a more positive direction. In his memo to Eisenhower, Nixon states on multiple occasions that he doubted whether his arguments made any impression on Castro. It seems that, with the four-point plan, the United States was attempting to "orient" the Castro government. But the terms of the Agrarian Reform Law caused the US government to doubt its own ability to influence Castro himself. At that point, we see the US government moving toward taking more drastic action to remove Castro from power. The subsequent expropriations most probably only solidified the Eisenhower Administration's sense that they could not control what was happening within the Castro regime.

In September 1960, Fidel Castro prepared to give a speech at the United Nations (UN). The US government required that his movements be restricted to the island of Manhattan; he was to remain as close as possible to the UN headquarters. The same limitations were placed on the Soviet leader Nikita Khrushchev, on the Hungarian leader Janos Kadar, and on the Albanian leader Mehmet Shehu. This was the first time that such restrictions were imposed on persons of rank visiting the General Assembly. In retaliation, Cuba announced that US Ambassador Philip Bonsal would be restricted to the Vedado district of Havana during the period when Castro was restricted to Manhattan.

In the course of that visit to the United States, the Castro delegation received less than favorable treatment from New York's Shelburne Hotel. The hotel refused to allow all the members of Castro's multi-racial delegation to stay there. In response, the Castro group moved to the Hotel Theresa in Harlem. There Castro had a meeting with the Black civil rights leader Malcolm X, with the author Langston Hughes, and, later, with the Soviet Premier Nikita Khrushchev, along with the leaders of Egypt, Syria, and India. Castro's meeting with Krushchev solidified Eisenhower's perception of him as a communist who therefore must be removed from power.

There was another group interested in removing Castro from power: the Cuban exile community. Responding to the political upheaval in Cuba, Cubans had begun fleeing the country as early as 1958. By 1960, the number of exiles had grown significantly. These exiles quickly learned that they had a common and powerful ally: the US government. The Eisenhower Administration's desire to isolate the Castro regime rested heavily on the shoulders of the community in exile. The Cuban exiles served two purposes. On the one hand, their presence in the United States and their desire to flee their homeland provided strong support for the Administration's depiction of the Castro regime as repressive and anti-democratic. On the other hand, the Administration knew that any plan to overthrow the regime would require explicit support of the community in exile, most directly in the form of organizing a "government in exile" which the United States could quickly recognize after any sort of military intervention on the island. This meant that, as early as 1960, the US government was providing material and personnel to support the development of nascent Cuban exile organizations in the United States. After the Administration decided, in March 1960, to invade Cuba, the CIA (which was planning the invasion) established a number of recruiting offices in south Florida, and Cuban exile volunteers were sent to training camps in Nicaragua, Guatemala, and other parts of the Caribbean to prepare for the invasion.

But the community of Cubans in exile included at least 50 disparate political factions of varied ideological stripes, all claiming to speak for the "community." In order to develop a reasonable alternative to the Castro regime, the United States needed these disparate forces to unite into one cohesive group which could form a reasonably legitimate provisional government. That fairly simple goal, however, would prove to be elusive and led the US government to provide significant economic resources to fund the operations of a number of exile organizations before and after the Bay of Pigs invasion.

The CIA's first attempt to organize the exiled community into a coherent political group led to the creation of the *Frente Revolucionario Democrático* (FRD; the Revolutionary Democratic Front). This was the group designed to invade Cuba and establish the new government. But the group was not able to muster much support in the Cuban community at large. So Kennedy decided to use another group of exiles for the invasion, and he developed another provisional government, the *Consejo Revolucionario Cubano* (CRC; the Cuban Revolutionary Council). The Administration was more involved in the organization of this group, to which it even gave final approval of its manifesto.

In April 1961, the United States went forward with the Bay of Pigs invasion. About 1,500 Cuban exiles, armed, trained, and supplied by the US government, using two ships donated by the United Fruit Company for use in the invasion, landed at the Bay of Pigs (*Bahía de Cochinos*) in southwestern Cuba. The plan had been for US fighter planes to take out Castro's air force before the landing, so as to diminish the regime's ability to repel the invasion. These airstrikes were unsuccessful and left most of the Cuban air force intact. The plan had also called for US air cover for the exiles during the invasion itself. President Kennedy, uncomfortable with a plan he did not create (he inherited it from the Eisenhower Administration), decided to scale back the air cover; but this left the invading troops vulnerable. In addition, the spontaneous Cuban uprising against Castro, which the planners had depended upon for the plan to succeed, failed to materialize. Without any support on the island and without air cover, the invading force was stranded near the landing zone and was soon captured by the Castro government. In the end, 68 of the exiles died and the remaining ones were captured. The Castro regime ended up ransoming them back to the United States for $48 million in food, medicines, and tractors. The regime remained firmly in place.

Despite the failure of the Bay of Pigs invasion, the Kennedy Administration continued to fund the CRC; it is estimated that they received between $100,000 and $200,000 monthly in order to continue their activities. The Department of Defense also created a program to enlist Cubans into the US military in order to train them in case they were needed for another military operation. As a follow-up to the Bay of Pigs, the Kennedy Administration organized "Operation Mongoose," a program designed to incite open revolt in Cuba. Cuban exiles were very involved in the execution of this plan, particularly in gathering intelligence, conducting small-scale raids, and engaging in economic sabotage on the island. The Kennedy Administration canceled this program, however, after the Cuban missile crisis. One of the commitments the United States made toward the Soviet Union during that crisis was not to invade Cuba. This made it impossible for the US government to work overtly toward overthrowing the regime. But US plots against the regime continued; they simply became covert. The United States still used Cuban exiles to carry out its plans. Now it simply based these plans in other countries, for instance Costa Rica and Nicaragua. One of the central tenets in many of these plans was the elimination of Fidel Castro. It is estimated that the CIA attempted to kill Castro 638 times. Methods included the use of an exploding cigar, a fungus-infected scuba-diving suit, and a mafia-style shooting. Castro is reported to have said, in regard to the numerous attempts on his life: "If surviving assassination attempts were an Olympic event, I would win the gold medal."

By 1963 the Castro regime had consolidated power, and the basic parameters of the US–Cuba relationship for the next 50 years had been established. Currently, the United States maintains an economic embargo against Cuba, forbidding US companies to trade with it and barring all US exports there except for food, medicines, and humanitarian aid. The embargo was codified in the 1992 Torricelli Bill and strengthened under Helms–Burton in 1996. Helms–Burton expanded the embargo to include foreign companies trading with Cuba, barring them from trading with the United States. The United States also bans travel to Cuba. Cuba remains the only country in the world to which US citizens cannot travel freely.[9] The United States does not have formal diplomatic relations with Cuba; both countries maintain interest sections within the Swiss embassy in the other's country.

Cuban Exiles in the United States

The post-1959 Cuban migrants to Florida were not all that different from the Cubans who had settled in Florida during the nineteenth century. Those earlier community members saw themselves as fighting for Cuban independence while at the same time quite successfully integrating themselves into the US economy and politics. The post-revolutionary exiles continued this tradition, working to change the regime on the island while establishing successful political and economic institutions in the United States. This meant that their politics, while starting with a strong focus on the situation in Cuba, evolved toward encompassing and even privileging issues of importance to the community in the United States. That being said, as María Cristina García points out, the Castro regime still looms large in community politics today: "In a community of largely first-generation immigrants for whom the memory of the revolution is an open wound, Cuba plays a tremendous role in public debate and consciousness."[10] More than 50 years after the revolution, a pro-Castro Cuban or Cuban American candidate, even if they are running for school board, has little to no chance of winning public office in Miami.

This anti-Castro bent within the Cuban community in the United States has led many observers to describe Cubans as politically monolithic: all speaking with one opinion and one voice on political issues. Yet it is important to remember that, from the beginning, the Cuban community in exile in the United States was made up of individuals representing a variety of political ideologies and perspectives. In the early 1960s there were three main political leanings in this community regarding the future of Cuba: (1) the right wing (that is, former associates of Batista) wanted a conservative, authoritarian government – like that of Batista; (2) the moderates wanted a return to the democratic process as guaranteed under the 1940 Constitution; and (3) the left wing (former rebels who had fought with Castro) wanted social, economic, and political change, but not necessarily socialism. These ideologically disparate exiles found themselves living side by side in Miami and being united against a common enemy: Fidel Castro. The common enemy gave the political exiles a common ground; and this is something which makes political migrants – as opposed to economic migrants – unique. First, the bulk of Cuban migrants arrived at the same time and had similar experiences. Second, their common story of oppression and loss of homeland, and the common enemy they could blame for that suffering, gave them as a community a strong sense of identity, unity, and shared purpose.

During the first few years after arrival in the US, the community of Cuban exiles was focused on survival and on returning to the homeland. They did, however, experience a mixed reception in the United States. Even though the US government supported the exiles, local residents of Miami were not happy about this large influx of foreigners into their midst. Cubans who arrived in the first wave experienced significant discrimination, and it was common to find signs posted in apartment buildings that read: "No Pets, No Kids, No Cubans."[11] Local politicians pressured the US government to relocate these new arrivals, so the US government created a program that provided Cuban migrants with financial assistance if they immediately relocated away from Miami. The federal government paid for their transportation, helped them to find housing and employment in the new locations, and provided financial support until each migrant secured employment. More than 300,000 individuals were resettled out of Miami under this program.

Yet in spite of the discrimination and of the resettlement programs, the vast majority of Cubans remained in the Miami area. As time went on, they began to place an emphasis on preserving *cubanidad* in exile so that they (and their children) would be ready to return to Cuba when the Castro regime fell. The result was a re-creation of Cuban social institutions in exile. For example, Belén had been a very prestigious Jesuit boys' school in Havana (and one which Fidel Castro attended). The majority of the school's academic board, including the principal, ended up fleeing to Miami, and so they created a new "Belén" school in the United States, with most of the same teachers, curriculum, and materials. In fact, the first bilingual education programs in the United States were begun by Cubans in Florida, since they believed it was very important for their children to know Spanish so as to be able to return to Cuba with their parents when the time came. This strong imperative for cultural maintenance was another unique characteristic of Cuban exiles. At least over the first decade of their residence in the United States, these immigrants were certain that their return home was imminent. Even though they were integrating themselves into the US economy quite successfully, it was also very important to them to maintain their *cubanidad*. As a result, the Miami community, in exile, constructed a new sense of what it meant to be "Cuban." It developed Spanish-language media, particularly talk radio, and Cuban-oriented schools to deliver its message. Historically, it emphasized nineteenth-century Cuban heroes like José Martí, since Cubans of different ideological beliefs could agree on them. The result was a new understanding of what life in Cuba was like, and a very specific understanding of what "good" (read "anti-Castro") Cubans should think politically. This new identity would serve as the foundation for future political organization and activity among Cuban Americans.

Cuban Exiles and Government Support

With the consolidation of the Castro regime in the early 1960s, Cuban exile politics began to move on two tracks. On the one hand, exile political organizations continued to engage in paramilitary activities to overthrow the Castro government and worked to develop the support of the US government for their foreign policy goals. On the other, exile leaders needed to address the serious economic and settlement issues facing their community. Both tracks benefited from Cuba's perceived strategic importance to the United States. Because of this importance, exile organizations were given a great deal of access to the US President to discuss US–Cuba policy. The CRC reportedly met with Kennedy himself at least four times before the Bay of Pigs invasion, and continued to have access to him afterwards. The CRC dissolved in 1964, but other groups took its place and received significant financial and political support from the US government. For example, *the Movimiento de Recuperación Revolucionario* (MRR) is reported to have received between $3 million and $6 million to train and maintain a paramilitary force of about 200 Cuban men in Central America.

This high-level political access is important in terms of the material support it resulted in; but it is also important because it means that Cuban exile leaders could discuss other community-level issues during these high-level meetings. As we saw in chapter 3, Mexican American political organizations worked for years to try to get a White House conference on Mexican American concerns, and without success. Cuban exiles, because of the historical relationship the United States had with Cuba and because of the United States' concerns about the Cold War, were able to have even higher-level access, which included one-on-one meetings with the president, and these enabled them to bring attention to their economic and settlement concerns in a more informal fashion. No other Latino national-origin group has had this level of access to top US government decision-makers across multiple presidential administrations.

This access, and the symbolic importance of Cuba, also resulted in significant material benefits for the Cuban exile community in the United States. It is estimated that this community received at least $4 billion in direct aid from the US government between 1960 and 1996 – apart from the CIA-sourced funding to Cuban paramilitary organizations discussed above. The US government provided this aid because it served its political interests, both at home and abroad. Internationally, the aid encouraged Cuban migration to the United States, which discredited the Castro regime. Domestically, it offset resentment and political opposition from local leaders in Miami Dade by helping them to pay the costs of Cuban settlement. No other immigrant group in the United States has received this level of direct economic assistance from the US government.

Between 1959 and 1962, 215,323 Cubans migrated to the United States.[12] The first program created to provide aid to these Cuban migrants was the Cuban Refugee Program, which was established by the Kennedy Administration in January 1961. The program provided direct relief, resettlement assistance, and employment assistance to all Cuban migrants. Direct relief included cash payments, food distribution, and access to health services. On the educational side, the federal government provided funding to assist local public schools with the cost of educating their new Cuban students. The government also provided adult refugees with training and educational opportunities, including English-language classes and re-training or licensing programs for professionals. During its tenure, the program provided aid to an estimated 700,000 Cubans and it cost the US government about $1 billion.[13]

The support provided to Cuban exiles under the Refugee Program, and to the Cuban migration in general, was especially controversial in the African American community in Miami. The Cuban migration occurred in the midst of the civil rights movement. African Americans in Florida had been working since the 1950s to improve their political and economic opportunities and to end segregation in the state. Although, as is mentioned above, the Cuban immigrants did experience significant discrimination in Miami, they were not segregated, unlike African Americans in the city; Cuban children were allowed to attend white-only public schools. In addition, the job assistance provided by the Refugee Program tended to situate Cuban immigrants in job sectors that had traditionally been staffed by African Americans, limiting the latter group's economic opportunities. Finally, African American leaders complained that US-born Blacks and other immigrants did not have access to the kinds of financial assistance the US government was providing for the Cuban exiles. This animosity between Cubans and African Americans would remain, and it erupted into race riots in Miami in 1980, 1982, and 1989. Thus the members of the Cuban community benefited not only from this direct government assistance, but also from the fact that they arrived in the United States after the start of the civil rights movement, and were therefore not subject to segregation and exclusion in the same ways Mexican Americans or Puerto Ricans had been.

The Cuban Refugee Program was followed by funding provided by the US government for the Camarioca boatlift and airlift, which took place from 1965 to 1973. In September 1965, Castro announced that those Cubans with relatives in the United States could leave Cuba if their relatives asked for them.[14] This announcement created an immediate refugee crisis. Initially, relatives in Miami took boats to pick up their relatives. When this proved dangerous, the United States negotiated with the Castro government to arrange for a safer means of travel. The United States agreed to pay for the costs of flights from Varadero (a city east of Havana) to Miami. The flights would carry 3,000 to 4,000 people per month and began in December 1965. The total cost is estimated to have been $100–120 million per year. Officials in Florida were outraged. To that point, after the initial wave from 1959 to 1962, Cuban migration had averaged about 35,000 people per year. This made their absorption into US society fairly easy. The boatlift/airlift would lead to much larger-scale migration to south Florida. From 1965 to 1973, 260,561 Cubans were brought to the United States through this program; it was the largest airborne refugee operation in US history.

The airlift more than doubled the Cuban population in the United States and led to the codification of Cubans' migratory status as refugees, which meant that they received preferential treatment under US immigration policy. In November 1966, the US government passed the Cuban Refugee Adjustment Act. Under this Act, any individual who was a native Cuban or a citizen of Cuba and had been admitted into the United States after January 1, 1959 was eligible for permanent residence after just one year. Most other immigrants had to reside in the United States for a more extended period in order to receive permanent residence, and they were not guaranteed that their applications would be approved. Under this Act, Cubans received not only an expeditious route to permanent residence, but also a blanket guarantee that their petitions would be granted. People fleeing from other countries, even from communist countries during the Cold War, had to prove that they were being persecuted; Cubans did not. These were benefits unique to Cuban migrants, and they were the result of the historical relationship between the US and Cuba and of the symbolic importance of Cuban migration during the Cold War. Thus, even though on arrival in Miami Cuban migrants faced significant discrimination and the trauma of finding themselves in the United States with little to nothing in terms of material resources, they also received significant financial support from the US government and preferential treatment in terms of US immigration policy. These factors facilitated their economic and political integration into the United States.

Cuban Exile Politics

During the 1960s, the Cuban exile community was concerned mainly with survival in a new country. Whatever politics they did engage in tended to be focused on the home country, and their political organizations often were paramilitary groups working to overthrow the Castro regime. By the 1970s, however, this focus began to change. After spending more than a decade in their new country, many Cubans came to accept that they would be staying indefinitely in the United States. As a result, they started to naturalize at much higher rates. This change in orientation led to changes in the kinds of policies advocated by their community. Some new organizations were created which argued for a more diplomatic approach toward Cuba. Some Cubans showed willingness to visit the island, softening what had been very hard-line positions against such a move. In the face of these changes, the paramilitary sector became increasingly desperate, and this led to growing violence in Miami. For example, from 1973 to 1976, there were 100 bombings and at least 10 assassinations in the Miami area alone.[15] Cuban hardliners would threaten, beat, and sometimes kill any Cuban who spoke out in favor of the normalization of relations with Cuba, or who complained about the violence propagated by their groups. Some of these hardliners were arrested, but many cases remain unsolved to this day. This violence prompted many Cuban Americans to re-evaluate the tactics they had been using and led to a movement toward using incorporation into US politics as the preferred way to effect change in Cuba.

The other aspect of life which changed in the Cuban exile community in the 1970s was the increased success of Cuban-owned businesses. As of 1997, there were almost 90,000 Cuban-owned businesses in Florida. These businesses served two important purposes. On the one hand, their owners were able to employ new Cuban migrants as soon as they arrived, helping to facilitate their settlement in the United States. On the other hand, the public policy needs which arose from their business interests – for example regarding zoning policy, tax policies, or other economic development issues – served as another catalyst for Cuban integration into US politics. These business owners quickly learned that, if they wanted to influence this decision-making at the local, county, or state levels, they needed to get allies elected to political office.

This feeling only increased after the Mariel boatlift. In April 1980, Castro announced that anyone wanting to leave Cuba could do so from the port of Mariel. Cuban exiles used whatever vessels they could find to travel to Cuba and retrieve their relatives. Similarly, Cubans from the island used any available boat to make the trip to Florida. From April to October 1980, 124,776 Cubans arrived in the United States – forming the third wave of Cuban migration. This influx of new immigrants put a tremendous amount of strain on social services in the Miami area. The US government constructed tent cities to house migrants while they were processed. Those with sponsors stayed only for a few days; those without, for more than a year. Initially, Americans were sympathetic to the Cubans' plight. But, as word spread that the Castro government had used the exodus to rid the country of criminals and of the mentally ill, the tide of US public opinion quickly shifted.

The Carter Administration, sensitive to these concerns during an election year, determined that the Mariel Cubans did not satisfy the definition of "refugee" under the 1980 Refugee Act. They were called instead "entrants" and given limited government assistance. The states where the migrants settled were also given 100 percent reimbursement for the cost of all education, social services, and health care they provided to the migrants. But, even so, the Mariel migrants remained deeply unpopular, even within the Cuban exile community. Earlier waves of migrants were concerned that the new arrivals would not be able to adapt to American society and would hurt the community's reputation. Despite this ambivalence among Cubans, the community raised money and provided services to assist with the resettlement of the *marielitos*. It worked toward regularizing their migration status and addressing the status of the many migrants who remained in a legal limbo (and in jail) years after their arrival in the United States. This experience made it even more clear to the Cuban community that they needed to have a greater say in government at all levels in order to influence the policies affecting their communities.

Cubans, the Political Parties, and Bloc Voting

To accomplish this, initially these Cubans turned to the Democratic Party. As late as 1979, 49 percent of Florida's Cubans were registered as Democrats, compared to only 39 percent for the Republican Party.[16] Historically, Cubans in Ybor City and other parts of Florida had been strongly Democratic, and the post-1959 immigrants followed this trend, at least initially. Yet Miami, like many cities in the south, was controlled by the Democratic Party. Party registration in the city was so overwhelmingly Democratic that Republican candidates had little or no chance of winning elections. Therefore, most elections were one-party contests, with competition within one party rather than between them. This meant that whichever candidate the Democratic Party chose to support most often won. Yet, when Cubans competed for the Party nomination, Democratic Party voters did not support Cuban candidates. The Republicans, on the other hand, facing almost certain defeat, were happy to let Cuban candidates onto the ballot.

What happened then was a surprise to many in Miami: the Cuban candidates won. This was due to two key factors: (1) the geographic concentration of the Cuban community; and (2) strong Cuban bloc voting. In terms of geography, even though many Cubans were resettled to other parts of the United States, a significant number of them ended up returning to Miami. According to the 2010 census, 68 percent of all Cubans in the United States live in Florida, and 48 percent of all Cubans in the United States live in just one county – Miami Dade.[17] As we saw in chapter 2, residential segregation plays an important role in ensuring that minority groups can achieve representation within a majoritarian system, because it helps them to surpass the 50 percent threshold. The second factor driving Cuban political representation, which also helped in relation to the majoritarian problem, was their bloc voting. Because of the development of *cubanidad* discussed above, when Cuban candidates ran for office, other Cuban exiles voted for them overwhelmingly. Cubans have the highest voting rates of any Latino national-origin group; in fact they vote at rates higher than those of the US population generally. High turnout combined with bloc voting led to electoral success. A good example is Ileana Ros-Lehtinen's initial run for US Congress in 1989. Her Democratic opponent, when told by Republicans that the seat should go to a Cuban, declared that it should remain "an American seat," a statement which Ros-Lehtinen called "racist." Miami Spanish-language media rallied to her cause, going as far as to say that a vote for the Democrat was a vote for Fidel Castro. In response, an incredible 90 percent of Cuban voters supported Ros-Lehtinen. This overwhelming support, combined with high voter turnout in Little Havana, gave her the margin of victory, despite the fact that 96 percent of Black voters and 88 percent of white voters voted against her.[18]

This combination – geographic concentration, high voter turnout, and bloc voting – has led to significant levels of Cuban political representation at all levels of government. The first Cuban to win statewide office was Ileana Ros-Lehtinen, who was elected to the Florida State House in 1982. She was elected to the Florida State Senate in 1986, and she became the first Cuban American member of Congress in 1989. In 1985, Xavier Suarez became the first Cuban-born mayor of the city of Miami. All three of the current Latino US senators are of Cuban origin: Ted Cruz (R-TX), Robert Menéndez (D-NJ), and Marco Rubio (R-FL). Former US Senators John Sununu (R-NH) and Mel Martínez (R-FL) were also of Cuban origin. In the 113th Congress, there were four Cuban American members of the US House of Representatives: Republicans Ileana Ros-Lehtinen and Mario

Díaz-Balart from Florida, and Democrats Joe García from Florida and Albio Sires from New Jersey. Before being elected to Congress, Joe García served as the Department of Energy's Director of the Office of Minority Economic Impact and Diversity under President Obama. There also were a number of high-ranking Cubans in George W. Bush's Administration, including Secretary of Commerce Carlos Gutiérrez; Emilio González, who was Director of the US Citizenship and Immigration Service (formerly the INS); and Mel Martínez, who served as secretary of Housing and Urban Development (HUD). At the state level, Bob Martínez was governor of Florida and the first Cuban American state governor in the United States. Before joining the US Senate, Marco Rubio served as speaker of the Florida State House. At the local level, Cubans have often served as mayors of Miami and of Miami Dade County, and have held numerous positions in Miami city government, local school boards, and local planning commissions.

The importance of Florida in national presidential campaigns also ensures continued Cuban American political influence. It is estimated that 75 percent of Cuban American voters supported George W. Bush in the 2000 presidential race, in an election which was decided on the basis of a few hundred votes. Yet that strong Republican bloc voting seems to have shifted in recent years. An exit poll of Florida's Latino voters found that 48 percent of Cuban American voters supported President Obama in 2012.[19] The shift seems to be a generational one, with younger, US-born Cubans more likely to vote Democratic than the older, exile generation. That same exit poll found that 60 percent of US-born Cuban Americans supported Obama, compared to only 45 percent of Cuban-born voters. US-born Cubans are seen as being more concerned with social issues important to them in the United States than US policy toward the island. Given that Cubans are the only Latino national-origin group that favors abortion rights and that Cubans strongly support social safety-net programs, it seems likely that the Cuban American vote may continue to move in a Democratic direction.

If it does, Democrats may have access to the significant political organizational infrastructure Cuban Americans have developed in Florida, including a sophisticated ethnic political machine. Cuban American-oriented pollsters, consultants, and media experts work together to help in turning out the vote; this contributes to explaining why Cuban American voter turnout is so high. This increases their ability to achieve electoral results. Cuban Americans in Miami were also seen as instrumental in putting an end to the vote recount in Florida after the 2000 presidential election, by organizing the protests that took place outside of each vote-counting station. Because of this high level of organization, Cuban Americans were especially supportive of Bush's campaign on account of Elián González and of their feeling that the Clinton Administration should have allowed the boy to remain in the United States rather than returning him to his father in Cuba. The fact that presidential elections in Florida are expected to be close for the foreseeable future means that presidential candidates from both parties, as well as presidents considering their chances of re-election, will attempt to court and maintain the support of the Cuban vote.

Other Forms of Political Influence

In addition to electoral power, the Cuban American community has been highly successful in lobbying US Administrations regarding US–Cuba policy. This process began when Cuban exiles were granted unique access to high levels of the Kennedy Administration. They retained some access with the subsequent Administrations, but there was a general feeling among exiles that the US government was not as serious about getting rid of Castro as they would have liked. All this changed with the election of Ronald Reagan in 1980. Reagan's strong anti-communist rhetoric resonated deeply with the Cuban community. In addition, Reagan was the first presidential candidate to court the Cuban vote. He was successful; an estimated 85 percent of Cuban American voters supported him. In order to capitalize on his election, a group of Cuban American business leaders set up a new political organization in 1981 which was designed to help Reagan to craft a more "realistic" Cuba policy. It was called the Cuban American National Foundation (CANF) and was run by a Bay of Pigs veteran named Jorge Más Canosa.[20] Although the group was headquartered in Florida, they purposely established an office in Washington, DC, and started a Political Action Committee (called the Free Cuba PAC), so that they could influence the Administration and fund supportive congressmen. The Free Cuba PAC was active through the 2004 election and made donations to candidates, party committees, and party leadership PACs. CANF is non-partisan and supports any candidate who supports its policies. This was reflected in the Free Cuba PAC's donations to candidates. In the 2004 electoral cycle, 67 percent of the PAC's contributions went to Democratic candidates, 33 percent to Republicans.[21] CANF also has a lobbying arm that, until recently, spent over $100,000 annually on lobbying various elected officials. CANF itself is a membership organization, with a membership estimated at over 50,000.

Over time, CANF grew so as to become the most influential Cuban American political organization in the United States. Its members were successful at convincing the US government to establish and fund Radio Martí, a US radio station which broadcasts news and information to Cuba. They also are credited with ensuring the passage of the Torricelli Bill, which promoted the Cuban embargo to US law (until then it had been based on an executive order), and with the passage of the Helms–Burton Law, which expanded the embargo so as to prevent foreign companies doing business in the US from doing business with Cuba. Under the George W. Bush Administration, CANF and the Cuban American lobby are largely credited with the administration's tightening of the embargo, which included greater restrictions on travel to Cuba and an increase in prosecutions of those who violate the Helms–Burton Law. In 2009, CANF reversed course, lobbying the Obama Administration to lift restrictions on US citizens' ability to travel to the island and family remittances, causing controversy within the community but perhaps also reflecting a shift in Cuban exile opinions about US–Cuba policy.[22] The perception of CANF as an important and electorally influential political constituency and its ability to provide financial support to members of Congress give it significant political access and influence. This kind of formal political lobbying and cultivation of political connections is another way in which the Cuban American community has been able to exercise its political clout.

Cuban Political Ideology and Opinion

But what are the issues of greatest importance to the Cuban American community? Although it is true that anti-Castro feeling remains high, there is growing diversity of opinion among Cubans regarding the best ways to deal with the problem. According to a 2007 poll conducted by the Cuban Research Institute, just over half of Cubans and Cuban Americans say now that they support establishing a national dialog among Cuban exiles, Cuban dissidents, and representatives of the Cuban government – compared to only about 22 percent who supported that position in 1991. About half of the Cuban-origin respondents in that poll also said that they supported medicines and food sales to Cuba and the allowance of unrestricted travel – positions which were supported by fewer than 30 percent of respondents in 1991. As mentioned above, even CANF, the organization that historically represented the most "hard line" on US–Cuba policy, still does not support lifting the embargo but does now advocate for an increase in people-to-people exchanges between the United States and Cuba.[23] Cubans and Cuban Americans clearly care deeply about what happens in Cuba and oppose the regime there, but their attitudes are not as black and white as the media or some Cuban American organizations portray them.

Cubans' historical affiliation with the Republican Party, combined with their strong anti-communism, has led many to define the community as conservative. Yet public opinion polls have consistently shown Cubans to hold many traditionally "liberal" values. Cubans and Cuban Americans are the only Latino national-origin group to report that they are in favor of abortion rights. They also tend to support government services, including the provision of welfare, health care, and social security programs. The Cuban American members of Congress often vote with the Democratic Latino members on these kinds of social issues, and in support of immigrant rights. Cubans are quite conservative in terms of their attitudes toward homosexuality (they are one of the most anti-gay Latino groups) and in their foreign policy attitudes. But Cuban political ideology does not run neatly toward smaller government, fewer social programs, and opposition to abortion, as one would expect from strong Republican partisans. Their party identification can be explained more readily by the unique context they experienced upon arrival, their being shut out of the Democratic Party, and the loyalty the Republican Party fostered in them when it gave them the opportunity to hold political office. This, combined with the perception Reagan cultivated in his 1980 campaign that Republicans are more anti-communist than Democrats, goes a long way toward explaining Cuban and Cuban American partisanship in Florida. Those experiences, however, were only shared by the exile generation. A recent study of Cuban voters in Miami-Dade found that Cuban migrants who arrived after Mariel are two and a half times more likely than pre-Mariel arrivals to identify as "strong Democrats."[24] Second-generation Cubans are also more likely than the first generation to identify as Democrat.[25] In addition, other observers of Florida politics have argued that vote choice among the exile generation is moving toward the Democratic Party.[26] This is not so surprising, given that another area with a large Cuban population – Union City, New Jersey – is also politically represented by Cubans, but those two Cuban American representatives (Congressman Sires and Senator Menéndez) are Democrats. In addition to their support for President Obama, in

2012 Cubans in Florida elected the first Democratic Cuban American congressman from that state, Joe García. This supports the proposition that partisanship among the exile generation was more a product of context and history than of political ideology, and that partisan identification among all cohorts of Cuban Americans is shifting in a Democratic direction.

The Limits of Cuban Political Influence

The popular perception is that Cubans are the most politically powerful Latino national-origin group. Much of the evidence points in that direction. They turn out and vote at very high rates, and often vote in a cohesive bloc, which strongly benefits their candidates of choice. In proportion to their population, they have the highest number of elected representatives of any Latino national-origin group. The presidential candidates from both parties, and sitting presidents, travel to Miami often in order to court them and construct policies meant to address their needs. Yet what are the policies that Cubans really have influence on? It is generally understood that the Cuban and Cuban American lobby has had an impact on US–Cuba relations. But at no point since 1959 has the Cuban lobby fundamentally *disagreed* with what the US government was already interested in doing in Cuba. Cuban exiles often wanted the United States' position to be stronger; but opposition to the Castro regime has been the goal on both sides. So, does the Cuban lobby have power? Or does its support of standing US government policy simply give that policy legitimacy? It is difficult to know. It would be interesting to see the effect the Cuban lobby might have in the face of an American administration interested in normalizing US–Cuba relations. So far, no US president has expressed an interest in taking that step. Until one does, it is difficult to know how much influence the Cuban American lobby actually has.

A good case in point is the *balsero* ("rafter") migration crisis in 1994 and the changes it wrought in US immigration policy. In 1990, Cubans began migrating on rafts, clandestinely, to the United States. That year, 467 *balseros* were picked up by the US Coast Guard. But in each subsequent year, the numbers increased. From January to August 1994, more than 6,200 rafters were picked up. In mid-August, in the face of a number of government demonstrations, Fidel Castro announced that his government was considering allowing another mass exodus. Unlike previous US administrations, the Clinton Administration quickly warned Cuba that it would not allow another boatlift like the Mariel, and that it was prepared to impose a naval blockade if Cuba attempted to launch a similar exodus.[27] This forced the Cuban government to re-evaluate its strategy. Instead, it instructed the Cuban Coast Guard not to forbid Cuban vessels from leaving Cuba of their own accord. By the end of August, 17,000 Cubans had arrived in the United States. This was in spite of the fact that the Clinton Administration, reversing three decades of US policy, announced in August 1994 that Cubans intercepted at sea would no longer be brought to the United States, but rather sent to the Guantánamo naval base in Cuba or other safe havens around the Caribbean. This announcement led (for the first time since the Cuban revolution) to bilateral negotiations with the Cuban government. As a result, an agreement was reached between the two governments. Cuba would stop the *balsero* exodus. In return, the United States would grant 20,000 visas per year to Cubans petitioning to migrate to the United States, not including the immediate relatives of Cubans already in the United States. Ideally, this would deal with the backlog and prevent another mass (and dangerous) exodus in the future.

In response to the *balsero* incident, in 1995 the Clinton Administration made the first major change in US immigration policy toward Cuban migrants since the 1966 Cuban Adjustment Act. The current policy is popularly called "wet foot, dry foot." This designation refers to the fact that, if a Cuban migrant is intercepted at sea (and therefore has a "wet foot"), the US government returns her to Cuba. If that same migrant is able to touch one toe on dry US land (and therefore has a "dry foot"), she is allowed to settle in the United States. The Cuban community was furious about this change in policy, because they believed it constituted a departure from historical precedent and would lead to differential treatment among migrants. They were correct. The Elián González fiasco illuminated the problems with this new policy. He migrated to the United States with his mother and her boyfriend; his father was left in Cuba, with no notice that they were migrating. Elián's mother and boyfriend drowned en route, leaving him stranded in the ocean until the US Coast Guard found him. Had they simply returned him to Cuba immediately, his feet would have been considered "wet," and he would have gone directly to his father. As soon as the Coast Guard admitted him to a Miami hospital for medical treatment, his feet became "dry," and he was eligible for residence in the United States. Once this occurred, releasing him into the custody of his father, his only living parent, became fraught with political meaning and calculation. This problem led to a direct confrontation between the Miami Cuban community and the Clinton Administration, and resulted in the federal government having to remove Elián forcibly from the home of his Miami relatives, so that he could be returned to his father in Cuba.

Although the "wet foot, dry foot" policy still constitutes a form of special treatment for Cuban migrants in relation to all other immigrants to the United States, it does represent the first change to Cuban migration policy in three decades. It also reflects the growing perception among US policy-makers that Cuban migrants are better characterized as economic migrants than as political refugees. This view is not in line with what members of the Cuban American community believe the US position should be; they see the Cuban government as a totalitarian dictatorship and therefore consider all those living in Cuba to be politically persecuted. Their inability to make that perception the dominant view in Washington may reflect a limitation of their political influence at the national level, even with regard to one of their deepest concerns.

Cuban political dominance in Miami may be overstated as well. It is true that the Cuban American community has been highly successful in getting its members elected to political office. Yet the fact of the matter is that the majority of elected officials in Miami are still white, despite the fact that whites make up a minority of the total population. In addition, over the past 20 years Miami has become increasingly cosmopolitan and is the destination of choice for immigrants from all over the world, but particularly from Latin America. As a result, Cubans now only comprise just over half of the population of Latin American origin in Miami. Only time will tell if they are able to build coalitions with these other groups in order to continue to win elections and maintain their current levels of political representation.

Political Changes in Cuba and US–Cuba Policy

On February 28, 2008, Raúl Castro, younger brother of Fidel Castro, was elected President of Cuba by the Cuban National Assembly. Raúl had assumed this position informally when his brother was taken ill in July 2006. His election in 2008 marked the first time since 1959 that a person other than Fidel Castro was officially elected President of Cuba. Around the world there was immediate speculation about what this would mean in terms of Cuban politics and of Cuba's relations with the United States. The Bush Administration quickly issued a statement making it clear that nothing would change with regard to US–Cuba relations until there was a fully fledged democratic transition in Cuba.

Many Cuba watchers assumed that, without the polarizing presence of Fidel Castro, greater dialog between the two countries might develop. On May 7, 2008, the Cuban government allowed for a historical teleconference to occur directly among President Bush and three Cuban dissidents on the island: Martha Beatriz Roque, Berta Soler, and Jorge Luis García Pérez. Roque, considered to be one of the strongest hardliners of the dissident community and one of its members most supportive of US policies toward the island, asked President Bush to make it easier for Cuban Americans in the United States to visit family members on the island and to send money to their relatives there. The dissidents argued that the teleconference itself was a reflection of the political opening Raúl's leadership was making possible on the island, and that the United States should help Cubans to take advantage of this opportunity. President Bush, however, was not moved. After the call, he reiterated his position that nothing will change in US policy toward the Cuban government until Cubans are allowed to pick their own leaders in free and fair elections and the government releases all political prisoners and respects human rights "in word and deed." The Obama Administration has not deviated significantly from that position. In 2009, the Obama Administration lifted all restrictions on family travel (the Bush Administration had limited family visits to once every three years), removed restrictions on family remittances to Cuba, made a number of changes to facilitate US–Cuba telecommunication and satellite connections, and increased the humanitarian goods that can be sent from the United States to Cuba.[28] In 2013, the Obama Administration agreed to open migration talks with Cuba, but administration spokesmen made clear this did not comprise a significant shift in US–Cuba relations.

Yet, change continues in Cuba. In January 2013, for the first time since 1961, the Cuban government allowed Cubans to travel abroad without securing exit visas, the infamous *tarjeta blanca*. Although international travel remains beyond the financial reach of most ordinary Cubans, this move does have important symbolic and psychological implications for Cubans on the island. In February 2013, Cuban President Raúl Castro announced that his current 5-year term as President would be his last, meaning he will step down in 2018. This would make 2018 the first time since 1959 that a member of the Castro family was not leading Cuba. The 52-year-old Miguel Díaz-Canel Bermúdez, an electrical engineer and former minister of higher education whom Raúl just made his first Vice-President, is seen as the front-runner to be his replacement. In a speech before the Cuban Assembly, Raúl called this a moment of "historic transcendence" for Cuba.[29] For the first time, the reins of power would be handed over to the younger generation – those Cubans who did not fight in the revolution. What this means for Cuba's future is unclear. For the Obama Administration, the change was not great enough to justify a significant revaluation of US–Cuba policy. In a February 25, 2013 State Department press briefing, Deputy Spokesperson Patrick Ventrell was asked about the change in Cuba. He responded: "a change in leadership that, absent the fundamental democratic reforms necessary to give people their free will and their ability to pick their own leaders, won't be a fundamental change for Cuba."[30] Thus, there will be no change, for the foreseeable future, in US policy toward Cuba. Two major stumbling blocks to the thawing of relations are the imprisonment, in Cuba, of US government contractor Alan Gross, who was convicted of illegally distributing communications equipment on the island, and the imprisonment in the United States of four of the "Cuban Five," Cubans found guilty in 2001 of spying for the Castro regime in the United States (one of the Cuban Five, René González, was released on probation and allowed to remain in Cuba after renouncing his US citizenship).

The Bush and Obama Administrations' lack of response to political changes in Cuba could be seen as another sign of the limitations of Cuban American power over US policy toward the island. Under George W. Bush, individuals who historically have been very supportive of US policy, Cuban dissidents, asked the President to consider modifying the policy, given changes on the ground. Although it is significant that they had this level of access to the president, in the end their opinions meant little. The Obama Administration did soften George W. Bush's hardline positions on person-to-person contact with the island, but the embargo remains firmly in place, with no signs of change in the near future. This suggests that, even if there were a sea change of opinion in Miami and among Cuban dissidents regarding the direction US–Cuba relations should take, it is not at all clear that the US government would alter course in response. Looking at the full history of US–Cuba relations, the United States has always believed that it knew what was best for Cuba and for the Cuban people. Since 1959, that view has happened to coincide with that of Cuban exiles in the US and Cuban dissidents on the island. If these views were to diverge, there is little reason to believe that the US government would fundamentally change its Cuba policy.

Conclusion: Is there a Cuban "Model?"

Many political analysts, when considering the lack of Latino political engagement broadly in the United States, point to the Cuban case as a "model" for other groups of Latin American origin. But is there a Cuban model? We have seen in this chapter that there are many things about the Cuban case which cannot be replicated. The first is the high level of importance attached by the US government to what was happening in Cuba because of the close relationship which had existed between the two countries since the nineteenth century. The second is the high level of government access and support accorded to Cuban exiles in order to change what was happening politically in Cuba. The third is the very high geographic concentration of the exile community and its common experience of exile, which gave its members a sense of shared identity and political cohesion strong enough to lead to high voter turnout and bloc voting. And bloc voting, combined with geographical concentration, has made it possible for this minority community to win elections consistently within a majoritarian electoral system. Finally, not only have Cuban immigrants enjoyed privileged status with regard to US immigration policy for almost 50 years, but they have also received an unprecedented amount of direct assistance from the US government – an estimated $4 billion. One can only imagine how much more successful other immigrant communities would be if they had that kind of capital investment to assist with their settlement and economic adaptation to the United States.

This being said, the Cuban story remains one of very effective economic and political adaptation in the face of significant adversity. As the community moves beyond the experience of exile and the regime continues to evolve in Cuba, it will be interesting to see how the community's politics may change, what groups it may turn to for coalition-building, and what kind of political influence it may be able to exercise – locally, nationally, and internationally.

QUESTIONS FOR DISCUSSION

1 What was the nature of the United States' political and economic relationship with Cuba before 1959?
2 How did this relationship affect the United States' response after the Cuban revolution?
3 How have Cubans been treated under US immigration policy,

and how does that vary from the treatment of other US Latino groups?

4 What are the factors that best explain Cuban American political success in the United States?

5 Should recent Cuban immigration be seen as a continuation of Cuban exile politics or something else? What might this mean for the future of Cuban American politics in the United States?

GUIDE TO FURTHER READINGS

Franklin, Jane. 1997. *The Cuban Revolution and the United States: A Chronological History*. Melbourne, Australia: Ocean Press.

García, María Cristina. 1996. *Havana USA: Cuban Exiles and Cuban Americans in South Florida, 1959–1994*. Berkeley: University of California Press.

Masud-Piloto, Félix Roberto. 1995. *From Welcomed Exiles to Illegal Immigrants: Cuban Migration to the US, 1959–1995*. Lanham, MD: Rowman & Littlefield.

Pérez, Louis. 2003. *Cuba and the United States: Ties of Singular Intimacy*, 3rd edn. Atlanta, GA: University of Georgia Press.

CHAPTER SIX

Dominicans: Political Upheaval, Imperialism, and Transnational Activism

Objectives

- Understand the Dominican Republic's turbulent political and economic history, and the historical role the United States has played in the country's economics and politics
- Understand the domestic and international factors that drove Dominican migration to the United States
- Understand the context of reception for Dominicans in New York and how that affected their political incorporation
- Understand the transnational nature of Dominicans' political engagement in the United States

Introduction

Even by Latin American standards, the Dominican Republic has experienced a turbulent political history. Plagued by military conflicts with the colonial powers and with Haiti throughout the nineteenth century, as well as internal political strife, the island's economic infrastructure was repeatedly destroyed, and various Dominican governments were forced to borrow heavily from international creditors in order to pay for their military efforts and support the government's operations. The United States' involvement in the Dominican Republic grew dramatically beginning in the late nineteenth century, leading to two US occupations of the island, in 1916 and 1965, and US control of the island's customs revenue for almost half of the twentieth century. This close and ongoing relationship with the United States meant that when migration became possible for Dominicans after the fall of the Trujillo regime, the United States was the destination of choice. The timing of their arrival, their concentration in New York City, and their unique homeland politics combined to create a dynamic and transnational approach to politics among Dominicans in the United States.

The island of *Española*, which would later become the Dominican

Republic and Haiti, was the first Spanish colony in the new world. Christopher Columbus landed there on his first voyage in 1492. As in Cuba and Puerto Rico, the original inhabitants of the island were Taíno Indians, whose population was decimated after the Spanish conquest by disease and forced labor. The Taíno word for the island was *Quisqueya*, which is why Dominicans are sometimes called *Quisqueyanos*. As was true in other Caribbean islands, *Española*'s early history was driven by conflicts among the great European powers. In *Española*'s case, however, the effects were especially great, limiting the island's political and economic development and resulting in its partition into two countries: the Dominican Republic and Haiti.

As in the rest of the Caribbean, the decimation of the Taíno population on *Española* necessitated the importation of African slaves to shore up the colonial work force. Sugar-cane production began shortly after the slaves arrived and the first sugar mill in the new world was founded on *Española* in 1516. By 1527, the island had 25 sugar mills operating at full capacity.[1] The increased development of sugar production led to an increase in the number of imported slaves, who quickly outnumbered the white population. In 1546, the island's white population numbered 5,000, with 12,000 African slaves. The latter number had increased to 20,000 by 1568.[2] The European colonists found it difficult to control the large numbers of Africans. As a result, *Española* had many fugitive slave communities that periodically launched raids against the European colonists. At the end of the sixteenth century, then, *Española* had a bifurcated economic structure with a small group of wealthy sugar elites, larger numbers of landless European colonists, African slaves, and numerous African and indigenous maroon communities in the island's mountain regions.

Politics and economics were tumultuous in the Caribbean region during the sixteenth and seventeenth centuries, and *Española* was often at the center of these conflicts. *Española*'s Spanish colonists were threatened by raids carried out by French, and later British, pirates. To defend their trade routes against these raids, at the end of the sixteenth century the Spanish Crown made two decisions that had significant effects on the development of *Española*. First, due to its strategic location, they decreed that Cuba would be the designated stopping point for the Spanish merchant fleets, which had a monopoly on royal commerce in the Americas. Second, because Spanish settlements on the northern and western coasts of *Española* had been engaging in illegal trade with the French and Dutch, who at the time were at war with Spain, the Spanish forcibly resettled its colonists there closer to the city of Santo Domingo, located on the southern coast. Those who resisted had their houses burned to the ground by Spanish soldiers.[3] The move was disastrous – over half of the colonists died of disease or starvation and only 2,000 of the estimated 110,000 cattle on the island survived.[4] The result was a dramatic increase in poverty on the island and many colonists chose to emigrate to other parts of the Caribbean. The island's economic difficulties only increased as a result of the Thirty Years War (1618–1648), during which the large number of pirates patrolling the Caribbean made travel to *Española* hazardous, and mostly halted trade to the island.

Seeing that the Spanish had moved their colonists to the southern end of the island, France quickly took control of the island of Tortuga, off the northwestern coast of *Española*. The Spanish army periodically raided Tortuga and captured settlers, but most of the inhabitants managed to escape and return to the island once the Spanish left. The French also settled on the northwestern coast of *Española*; in 1677 the French had 11 villages and more than 4,000 colonists living on the island.[5] Politically, the end of the seventeenth century was marked by yet another war between France and Spain, part of which was waged on the island. For four years, both sides attempted to take control of the entire island. Spain and France agreed to end hostilities in 1697 under the Treaty of Ryswick. The treaty allowed the Spanish and French colonists to engage in commerce with one another, but periodic military conflicts between the French and Spanish continued on the island.

The island's economic situation did not improve. By 1630, most of the slaves had died from disease or fled into the mountains. Sugar production was at a standstill. The hostilities with the French and other foreign powers led to the militarization of the island. A Spanish military elite replaced the small sugar elite. But the military could not protect the island from French incursions, nor natural disasters like the 1668 and 1672 hurricanes that destroyed the island's agriculture and much of its infrastructure. Many families moved out of Santo Domingo into the countryside and turned to subsistence farming in order to survive. The result was a decrease in the population on the Spanish side of the island while the French side was expanding rapidly. The French economy was based on tobacco farming, resulting in a colony that, by 1716, was home to 30,000 free persons and 100,000 Blacks and *mulattos*. This compared to the 18,410 Spanish inhabitants.[6] The French continued trying to expand their territory while the Spanish pushed back, making the "border" between them a moving target (and source of continual conflict) until the signing of the Treaty of Aranjuez in 1777, which finally established a definitive border between the two countries. The island was now officially divided.

The French revolution spurred continued conflict on the island. Wealthy free *mulattos* from the French side petitioned the new revolutionary government to grant them full citizenship rights; the French Assembly refused.[7] The result was open conflict between the white and *mulatto* landowners, with whites calling for the colony's independence from France and the *mulattos* fighting for independence and political equality. Neither group was interested in freeing the slaves, but the slave population saw an opportunity to gain their freedom. In 1791, fighting broke out between the slaves and white and *mulatto* landowners. The different camps allied themselves with the French, Spanish, and British, leading to an international war that would last nearly five years.

The conflict was resolved in 1795 with the Treaty of Basel. In it, the King of Spain ceded the colony to France. The treaty stipulated that Spanish troops would evacuate the towns and relocate their settlers; the Spaniards would be given one year to relocate. The Crown told the colonists they could go to Cuba and would be given lands equivalent to those they were abandoning. The first group of émigrés, though, quickly learned that all high-quality Cuban lands were spoken for and that the Cuban cities had little room for new settlers. Hearing this, many of those remaining on *Española* chose to stay. By 1800, they had formed an armed resistance to Toussaint L'Ouverture, the former slave who had gained control of the French side of the island that same year. Toussaint marched into Santo Domingo on January 26, 1801.[8] Many of the Spanish residents who had resisted him fled to Venezuela. The island was now entirely under French rule, with Toussaint as its Governor.

Toussaint abolished slavery and attempted to reform agriculture in the former Spanish colony. He ordered all landowners to cultivate sugar cane, coffee, cotton, or cacao for export. Agricultural workers would receive a quarter of the profits from farms. He invested in infrastructure to ensure export products could get to market. Yet these changes were not able to bear fruit because the island was again the site of fierce fighting, this time between Toussaint and Napoleon. Napoleon wanted to wrest control of the island from the former slaves and re-establish slavery. His fleet arrived in 1802. More than 50,000 French soldiers and 100,000 Blacks died in the bloody conflict.[9] The French captured and imprisoned Toussaint, but yellow fever, along with fierce fighting by the former slaves, led to a French defeat, and the former French side of the island became the independent Haiti on January 1, 1804. The Spanish side of the island, however, remained under Napoleon's control.

In 1808, Napoleon's forces invaded Spain. Many of the inhabitants of Santo Domingo still considered themselves Spanish and saw this act as an affront to their homeland. In collaboration with the Governor of Puerto Rico, the Dominicans confronted the French in November 1808 and won the battle decisively. This was the beginning of what the Dominicans call "the War of Reconquest." The French chose to surrender to the British instead of the Dominicans, so the British forces took control of Santo Domingo in 1809. To get the British to leave, the Dominicans had to grant the same tariffs to imported British products as had been given to Spanish imports.

The constant state of military conflict that characterized the island during the two decades after the French revolution left the population of the Spanish side of the island reduced by half and the economy decimated. Most of the agricultural land, sugar mills, and cities had been destroyed. All the colony's clergy left except for a handful of priests, the university closed, and all the convents were abandoned (and would remain so for over 100 years), destroying the Dominican educational system.

The Spanish colony rebuilt its economy by exporting mahogany and tobacco. Yet international conflict would again affect the eastern part of the island. Spain was facing uprisings in many of her colonies. South American ships, led by Simón de Bolívar, patrolled Caribbean waters and urged the colonies to revolt. The French, never having accepted the loss of Haiti, made plans to invade the island. It seemed the Spanish were quickly losing control of the situation. In May 1821, the Spanish Lieutenant Governor of Santo Domingo, José Nuñez de Cáceres, proclaimed the independence of Santo Domingo from Spain and sought to join Gran Colombia in South America. In November, a number of Dominican frontier towns proclaimed their independence from Spain and pledged allegiance to Haiti. In December, Nuñez de Cáceres announced the creation of the *Estado Independiente del Haití Español* (the Independent Spanish State of Haiti) which would become part of Gran Colombia. Haitian President Jean Pierre sent a message to Nuñez de Cáceres stating that two independent governments could not coexist on the island. In January 1822 Nuñez de Cáceres accepted Haitian control of the Spanish side of the island. He understood that much of the Spanish population supported unification with Haiti because the Haitian government promised them land reform, the abolition of taxes, and the social and juridical equality of whites, *mulattos*, and Blacks.[10]

The Haitian land reform offered land to all who needed it, with the goal of encouraging the new landowners to produce crops for export. The peasants in the western and eastern parts of the island resisted. Many of these new landowners preferred to produce food for their own consumption, rather than excess production of cash crops for export. In response, the government passed the Rural Codes in 1826, which required peasants to work on plantations to produce export crops. Peasants were required to work for the plantation owner for a minimum of three years. Vagrancy was forbidden and soldiers were assigned to each plantation to enforce the laws.[11] Women were required to work until the fourth month of pregnancy and to return four months after giving birth. The codes failed because rural workers simply ignored them, and the soldiers, many of whom were small producers themselves, would not enforce the laws. Since the peasantry owned small parcels of land on which they could subsist, they had no incentive to go to work for a large landholder.

Independence

The failed Haitian land reform was just one of the reasons underlying the Dominicans' desire to be independent from Haiti. In 1838, a group of young men in Santo Domingo formed a secret society called *La Trinitaria* whose purpose was to gain independence from Haiti. Led by Juan Pablo Duarte, the group's popularity grew rapidly. In 1843, the *Trinitarios* joined with disaffected Haitians to overthrow the Haitian government, with the goal of giving the Dominicans their independence. Haitian President Hérard attempted to quell the rebellion by abolishing many of the laws the Dominicans had resented, particularly the one barring them from writing public and legal documents in Spanish. The Dominicans organized a popular insurrection and marched on Santo Domingo on February 26, 1844. Negotiations with the Haitians ensued, with the Haitians peacefully surrendering power to the Dominicans. The two sides agreed that all Haitians would leave the eastern portion of the island, resulting in the birth of an independent Dominican Republic in 1844.

As the Dominican Republic worked to establish itself as an independent republic, fissures between the conservative and liberal ranks of the elite soon became evident. Tomás de Bobadilla, the first President of the Republic, had been a supporter of French military and political protection for the island. The conservative plan was to make the Dominican

Republic a French protectorate in exchange for the secession of the eastern bay and peninsula of Samaná to France. The *Trinitarios* were strongly opposed to the involvement of any European power in the Dominican Republic. They felt it would threaten the new country's sovereignty. Three months later, in June 1844, the *Trinitarios* carried out a military *coup* to remove the conservatives from power. The conservatives fought back, and regained power with Pedro Santana serving as the new junta president. The *Trinitarios*, including Duarte, were detained and jailed. The archbishop of Santo Domingo declared that those who disobeyed the proclamations of "our wise government" would be excommunicated.[12] Shortly thereafter, the *Trinitario* leaders were exiled for life. The junta sent them to separate countries (Germany, England, the United States, and Venezuela) to prevent them from communicating with one another.

The conservative junta called a constitutional convention in September and developed a new constitution, based on the United States and Haitian constitutions. President Santana, however, opposed the new constitution because he felt that it did not give the president sufficient power to protect the Dominican Republic in a state of war, which the new country now faced. He advocated that political power should rest with military rather than civilian forces. As a result, the following article was added to the constitution: "Article 210: . . . during the current war and while peace has not been signed, the President of the Republic can freely organize the army and navy, mobilize the national troops; and consequently be able to give all orders, decision, and decrees which are fitting, without being subject to any responsibility."[13] To ensure passage of this provision, Santana sent a battalion of soldiers to surround the assembly building and to advise the convention delegates that they should abide by his wishes. Santana was elected President of the Republic and served until his resignation in 1848. The Dominican Republic had its first constitutional government.

Santana faced many challenges in consolidating the new government, including insurrections from various *Trinitarios*, the opposition of the church (who were upset when their confiscated lands were not returned under the new government), and another Haitian invasion in 1845. The Haitians invaded again in 1849 after France recognized the Dominican Republic as an independent nation. This invasion was more protracted and bloody, but the Haitians were unsuccessful. This led the Dominican government to push the United States and Britain to recognize the Dominican Republic in order to help diminish the Haitian threat. They were successful in 1850 when the Dominican Republic signed a treaty with Britain. This was followed by a successful recognition treaty with Spain in 1855.

The Spanish were pushed to support Dominican independence by their concerns about the Dominican government's negotiations with the United States. US President Franklin Pierce had sent Texan General William Cazneau to the island to negotiate the establishment of a US naval base on the Samaná peninsula. President Pedro Santana's opponents (he had returned to office in 1853) were against the US negotiations because they believed US political and military support would give Santana too much power. Santana remained in favor of maintaining a very strong executive in the Dominican governmental structure in order to ensure the nation's security against Haiti. He codified the president's absolute power over the country's affairs in the 1854 Constitution. Santana's worry over a Haitian invasion proved justified in 1855 when Haiti again invaded the eastern part of the island.

Thus, the first decade of Dominican independence was marked by repeated Haitian invasions, internal political strife, and economic stagnation. The new country found itself reaching out to the colonial powers in order to protect its independence from Haiti. That ongoing Haitian conflict also created a semi-authoritarian political system with a very powerful office of the president. The ongoing conflict, along with drought, kept the Dominican Republic from addressing the pressing economic problems in the country. In particular, by 1858 the government was bankrupt, having had to finance repeated mobilizations of its armed forces. The government's strategy for financing these expenditures had been to print more money, resulting in a dramatic 90 percent devaluation of the Dominican peso. Frustrated with the ongoing monetary crisis, a group in Cibao, the tobacco-growing province, decided to revolt in 1858. Their goals were to stabilize the economy and to establish a democratic constitution. The fighting lasted almost a year, and resulted in Pedro Santana returning to power and re-establishing an autocratic, president-controlled state apparatus.

Searching for Imperial Protection

The civil war left the Dominican government in an even more disastrous position economically. President Santana worried that, given its financial state, the country was vulnerable to a US invasion, as had occurred with William Walker invading Nicaragua. These worries deepened in

1860 when a group of US adventurers landed on the islet of Alta Vela, located off the Dominican Republic's southwestern coast. Interested in exploiting the island's guano deposits, the Americans planted the US flag and declared the island a US territory. The Dominicans sent a warship and took the Americans prisoner; they were able to secure US recognition of the Dominican Republic's sovereignty over the island. But the incident left the Dominican government more concerned about its ability to defend itself against the US threat.

This intensified ongoing negotiations between the Dominican Republic and Spain. At first, the Dominicans had asked that Spain make the Dominican Republic a Spanish protectorate. As the negotiations progressed, and particularly after the Alta Vela incident, Santana supported the idea of annexing the Dominican Republic to Spain. The Spanish agreed to amortize the Dominican currency, not to re-establish slavery, and to respect all laws created by the government since 1844. The Dominican Republic would be granted all the rights of a Spanish province. The agreement was announced in 1861 and was a surprise to most Dominicans since the negotiations had been carried on in secret. Santana was appointed the new province's Captain General. The Spanish, however, were not interested in keeping Santana in power and removed him in 1862.

The Dominican public was not in favor of changes wrought by the Spanish regime and rebelled in 1863. In an ironic twist, Haiti offered aid to the rebels, largely because of their concerns about having a slave-holding colonial power next door. The fighting lasted almost two years and cost Spain 10,000 soldiers. In 1865, the Spanish Queen signed a decree annulling the annexation. The Spanish soldiers left and the island's economy was, again, left in ruins. No longer united against a common enemy, the various Dominican political factions took up arms against each other. On one side was the Partido Rojo, who wanted to reinstitute the 1854 Constitution. On the other was the Partido Azul, led by the Cibao liberals who wanted to democratize the Dominican Republic. The conflict between the Rojos and Azules lasted 14 years, during which the island experienced 21 changes in government.[14]

During the conflict, the Dominican government again found itself bankrupt and, in 1868, again appealed to an imperial power: the United States. Dominican President Baez began negotiations with the United States to annex the Dominican Republic. US President Ulysses S. Grant supported the deal, intending to build a US naval base on the Samaná peninsula. The final treaty would have allowed the United

States to purchase Samaná bay and peninsula for $2 million, made the Dominican Republic a US territory, and given the Dominican Republic the opportunity to become a state. Grant supported the plan because he believed the Dominican Republic could serve as a safe haven for African Americans from the US south and that the new naval base would provide protection for the proposed Panama Canal. The plan was controversial in the United States, however, given many senators' concerns about bringing a mixed-race population into the United States. There were also concerns about the Dominican Republic's history of political instability. Great Britain and France also strongly opposed annexation, as did the Dominican exile community. In 1870, the US Senate vote on the treaty was a 28 to 28 tie, so the treaty was not ratified.

President Baez, still in desperate need of funds, negotiated an agreement with a private US company, under the control of Joseph Fabens, called the Samaná Bay Company. In their December 1872 agreement, the company was granted permission to rent the Samaná bay and peninsula for 99 years, at an annual cost of $150,000 in gold.[15] The company was empowered, within its territory, to build canals, railways, and roads, establish a judiciary and police force, set up a bank, levy taxes and port dues, and issue bonds. The *New York Times* called it "a republic within a republic."[16] For every 3 miles (or every league) of railway or canal the company built, they were given an additional 3 square miles of land by the Dominican government. According to the *New York Times*, the company quickly received numerous petitions from wealthy landowners hoping to be granted land in Samaná peninsula to establish sugar plantations.[17]

Almost immediately after signing the agreement, the company fell behind in its rent payments to the Dominican government. At the same time, Baez resigned the presidency in January 1874. Since the agreement with the Samaná Bay Company stipulated that the Dominican government could cancel the agreement if the company failed to make payments, the new Dominican administration, under Ignacio María González, did just that. The Samaná Bay Company, in turn, petitioned the US government to intervene on its behalf.[18] The Grant Administration refused to intervene. The United States considered annexing Samaná again in 1897, just before the Spanish–American War, but abandoned the effort when Spain's defeat made it possible for the United States to establish a naval base in Guantánamo Bay, Cuba, instead.

On November 9, 1874, the González government signed a peace treaty with Haiti, ending decades of conflict. The treaty established the border and allowed for free trade between the two countries. But Dominican politics remained unstable. Soon after the treaty was signed, González was removed from power. After his replacement was unable to establish peace, Baez came into power one last time. Upon his ouster, two Dominican governments were formed – one in Santo Domingo and one in Santiago. The factions continued to fight until the final days of 1879, when the liberal *Azules* were finally able to set up a stable government under the leadership of General Gregorio Luperón.

The new government focused its attention on revitalizing the Dominican economy. By the 1870s, it was highly bifurcated. The Cibao region had been dependent on tobacco production which required the intensive use of small parcels of land. The southern region, on the other hand, had produced mahogany and hardwoods, which depended on large landholdings and required a large low-wage work force to harvest the wood. This began to change in the mid-to-late nineteenth century when thousands of Cuban and Puerto Rican exiles, fleeing the unrest in their countries, settled in the Dominican Republic. The exiles established sugar plantations and built steam-powered sugar mills in the southern and eastern parts of the island. Other foreign investors, mainly from Europe, soon followed, establishing 30 plantations and mills within seven years, an investment valued at $6 million.[19]

The United States also was interested in developing economic ties with the Dominican Republic. In 1884, the United States established diplomatic links with the Dominican Republic for the first time.[20] That same year, the Hayes Administration negotiated a reciprocity agreement with the island nation. The agreement allowed US manufactured goods to enter the country duty-free, and gave the same duty-free status to Dominican products and raw materials. The treaty was ratified in 1891 but never put into effect because of opposition from European countries, especially Germany, who said it would stop buying Dominican tobacco if the treaty went into effect.

The Dominican Debt and Growing US Influence

Throughout the nineteenth century, the country's debt remained a significant problem. Until 1892, the bulk of Dominican external debt was owned by Westendorp, a Dutch company headquartered in Amsterdam. When Westendorp was moving toward bankruptcy at the end of the nineteenth century, a group of American investors, including the US Secretary of State and other government officials, organized the

Santo Domingo Improvement Company (SDIC) to buy the Dominican Republic's debt from Westendorp. The American investors believed the Republic would soon become an American protectorate through the lease of the Samaná peninsula, and that they would reap a large profit once the protectorate was established.[21]

The SDIC purchased the Dominican Republic's outstanding debt and lent the government additional funds. From 1893 to 1897, the Dominican debt multiplied sevenfold from just under $5 million to over $35 million.[22] The SDIC's ownership of the Dominican national debt, which gave them control over the collection of the country's customs receipts, the fact that a few New York broker firms controlled the island's sugar industry, and that Clyde Steamships had a monopoly over the transport of passengers and freight between New York and Santo Domingo, gave the United States significant and growing influence over the Dominican economy and politics. This comprised a significant departure for the Dominican Republic. Until this point, European interests had been dominant in the Dominican economy.

As the turn of the twentieth century neared, the Dominican government continued to face serious financial difficulties. Agreements were signed with the SDIC in 1895 and 1896 that created two new companies – the San Domingo Finance Company and San Domingo Railways Company – which retained control over the country's customs receipts and nascent rail system in exchange for payments to support government operations. It was not enough to avoid the downward spiral. By 1898 the nation's creditors were demanding payment, yet the government had no capital available to meet its obligations. Without access to its customs revenues (which were still controlled by the SDIC), the government could not pay its debts. A series of negotiations ensued, with subsequent Dominican leaders attempting to alter the original agreements in order to regain access to the country's customs receipts. After years of negotiations, in 1903 an agreement was reached. The Company agreed to sell its rights for $4.5 million and to sell $4.25 million in Dominican government bonds at 50 percent of their face value. The form of payment was to be set by three arbitrators, one chosen by the United States, another chosen by the Dominican Republic, and a third selected by both countries. The agreement was highly unpopular among Dominicans and led to another *coup*.

The new President, Carlos Morales, was able to remain in power with the support of the US government. In return for its support, the United States asked the Morales regime to respect the agreements with the Improvement Company and to allow the United States to build lighthouses along the Dominican coast to facilitate the navigation of ships traveling to the Panama Canal, which was under construction. The United States was also concerned about European influence in the Dominican Republic and, by extension, within the United States' sphere of influence under the Monroe Doctrine. In 1900 and 1903, the Italian, Belgian and German governments had sent warships to Santo Domingo to force repayment of their debts. US President Theodore Roosevelt was concerned this European military presence threatened US influence in the hemisphere and its control over the Panama Canal. It was in response to the Dominican debt crisis that President Roosevelt developed his corollary to the Monroe Doctrine (see chapter 1). At the same time, in 1904 the arbitration board agreed that the Improvement Company would accept $4.5 million in payment for its properties and interests in the Dominican Republic. The Dominican government was obligated to set aside its non-sugar customs revenues to pay this debt. This angered European creditors since it limited the Dominican government's ability to service its debts.

Dominican President Morales, however, welcomed this agreement with the United States since he saw this alliance as key to his remaining in power. In 1904, he proposed to the US State Department that the Dominican Republic be made a US protectorate for 50 years. The United States did not go that far, but it did propose taking official charge of all the country's customs offices to distribute revenues among foreign and domestic creditors. The Morales Administration agreed. Under the agreement, the Dominican government kept 45 percent of receipts. The remaining 55 percent was to be used by the US government to pay customs employees and pay off the country's foreign and domestic debt. Until that debt was paid off, there could be no changes in the Dominican Republic's customs duties or export taxes, or increases in the public debt, without the consent of the President of the United States. The US Senate refused to ratify the agreement because they felt it established a de facto protectorate of the United States. Instead, the US government presented its customs collections as a temporary arrangement, an arrangement that was put into effect in March 1905.

US Intervention and Occupation: Part I

The Dominican Republic continued to face political unrest and economic instability. The country's debt was simply too large and many of the claims from creditors were fraudulent. Working with financial analysts from the United States, in 1906 the Dominican Republic negotiated with the country's creditors to cut the debt in half and consolidate the debt under one lender – the United States. President Roosevelt agreed to the plan because it decreased European power in the Caribbean. The US government continued in its role collecting customs receipts to pay off the country's debts. This relationship was codified in the Dominican–American Convention of 1907. Under similar terms to the Platt Amendment, the United States maintained control over Dominican finances and reserved the right to interfere in Dominican politics whenever it believed there was a threat to the customs receivership or compliance with the convention.[23]

The stabilization of the financial system led to a brief period of more stable politics. Under President Cáceres, the Dominican government invested in roads, schools, and other public works, along with agriculture. As a way to encourage sugar exports, Cáceres eliminated taxes on all sugar production. At the same time, he allowed the partition of communal lands. The result was that many foreign sugar producers were able to purchase large tracts of high-quality farmland in the north and south. The resentment these policies fomented led to Cáceres' assassination in November 1911 and a return to political chaos on the island. By September 1912, the situation had deteriorated sufficiently for the United States to consider military intervention, as established by the 1907 convention. Instead, President Taft sent a pacification commission to Santo Domingo to resolve the civil conflict and fix a provisional border with Haiti.

The commission arrived with 750 marines, making clear that the United States would intervene militarily should negotiations fail. Despite ongoing talks and the institution of a number of regimes into power, with US diplomatic and financial support, fighting across the various factions continued. Another insurrection took place in 1913 and the US helped to negotiate a settlement. A US comptroller was selected and presidential elections were scheduled, but they never occurred because of continued intensive armed conflict in 1914. The United States again helped to negotiate a truce under threat of military intervention.

President Woodrow Wilson then laid out his plan for addressing the instability in the Dominican Republic. It included five parts: (1) a US-supervised election for a new Dominican president, who would receive US support and protection during his term in office; (2) a reordering of the Dominican financial system under US administration; (3) the appointment of a US comptroller as a permanent official financial adviser within the Dominican government; (4) the appointment of a US-designated director of public works within the Dominican government; and (5) the creation of a Dominican national guard under the command of US military personnel to replace the existing Dominican armed forces.[24] The Wilson Administration saw the Customs Convention as having failed and that the United States needed to establish economic and political stability in the Dominican Republic in order to ensure that debt payments would continue. The rival Dominican parties agreed to the plan.

As a result, Juan Isidro Jiménes was elected President and took office in December 1914. The United States insisted that he implement points 3, 4, and 5 of the Wilson Plan. Jiménes refused.[25] The US government refused to offer economic assistance until he agreed to its demands. After Jiménes' enemies staged another rebellion, the United States again insisted the Wilson Plan be implemented. In response to the United States' insistence, the various Dominican factions joined together to oppose US policy. This harmony did not last, however. In April 1916, the Minister of War led a rebellion against the Jiménes regime; the rebels convinced the Dominican Congress to impeach Jiménes. The US sent troops into the Dominican Republic to support Jiménes and "protect the lives and interests of the foreigners in the city."[26] Jiménes, uninterested in serving under US military occupation, resigned.

The United States made clear it would not leave the Dominican Republic until a new government was installed, a government which accepted the United States' demands under the Wilson Plan. The United States refused to release any customs duties until the Dominican Republic complied with its demands. Francisco Henríquez y Carvajal, who had been elected President by the Dominican Congress after Jiménes' resignation, accepted the US financial adviser but rejected the other US demands.[27] Without access to its customs duties, the Henríquez government had no funds. Public employees worked with no pay and the country's commerce came to a standstill, but the government did not agree to the United States' terms. The United States had to decide whether to withdraw or to occupy the Dominican Republic outright. Because the United States knew it would be soon entering into the First World War, and that many Dominicans were pro-German, there were concerns that the Dominican Republic could be used as a base for German operations, threatening the Panama Canal. As a result, on November 29, 1916, US Rear Admiral Harry S. Knapp announced that the

Dominican Republic was in a state of military occupation by the United States. Dominican laws would remain in effect as long as they did not conflict with the purposes of the occupation.

The United States military remained in the Dominican Republic until 1924. Under its occupation, Dominicans were banned from possessing weapons and the press was strictly censored. The US military also established the Dominican National Police, a new national guard trained by the US marines and designed to maintain social order once the US troops left the country. Under the US regime a property tax was instituted in 1920 along with a Land Registration Law that eliminated all communal lands in favor of private land ownership. Since trade with Germany was outlawed under the US occupation and trade with the rest of Europe was interrupted due to the First World War, by the end of the occupation most Dominican commerce was oriented toward the United States. The 1919 Customs Tariff Act facilitated this orientation by making many US manufactured items duty-free or establishing drastically reduced tariff rates. The disruption of sugar beet production in Europe after the war resulted in significant prosperity for the Dominican Republic during this period.

Despite that prosperity, from 1917 to 1921, a guerrilla group called *los Gavilleros* fought the occupation and had considerable support from the Dominican people. The US forces were able to defeat the *Gavilleros* by using scorched-earth tactics, and having superior air and fire power, and greater resources. But, in the face of growing resistance, the United States began negotiating the terms of its withdrawal. Most important to the US government was a guarantee that the acts of the military government would be considered valid after the military's withdrawal. The US plan was to hold a general election supervised by the military government. The newly elected President would recognize all the acts of the military government and accept US control over the Dominican police force.

The plan was rejected unanimously by the Dominicans. After much negotiation, the Hughes–Peynado Plan was approved in 1922. It established a provisional government, elected by political and religious leaders, to lay out rules for elections and necessary constitutional reforms. The provisional government would also accept certain acts approved by the military government, specifically the loans the US military had contracted to pay for public works programs and the 1919 customs tariff rules. The 1907 Customs Convention would remain in place until the country paid off its debts (which had only increased under US military rule). The US military occupation officially ended on July 1, 1924, but the United States still administered all the country's customs houses and reserved the right to intervene in Dominican affairs as it deemed necessary. The Dominican Republic also had to obtain the United States' consent before incurring any additional public debt. For all intents and purposes, the Dominican Republic was a US protectorate.

The biggest change wrought by the 8-year US occupation was the establishment of a new highway system that connected all areas of the country for the first time. This facilitated trade, mail service, internal migration, and the country's political unification. Education and sanitation improved under the US military regime. There was also significant growth in the sugar industry, with 438,000 acres of land controlled by sugar interests. This growth in sugar production also meant the island was more vulnerable to price changes for sugar on world markets. Many local manufacturers were also put out of business, unable to compete with US products that entered the Dominican market duty free.

The Trujillo Era

After the end of the US occupation, the Dominican Republic experienced a period of relative economic and political stability. This began to fray as the country neared new elections in 1930. Rafael Trujillo, nicknamed "El Jefe," was chief of the Dominican National Police (whose name changed to the National Army in 1928) and had used the army to serve his political and personal ambitions. He organized a *coup* that resulted in his (fraudulent) election to the presidency in 1930. Through violence and coercion that was mainly carried out by a paramilitary group he formed called "La 42," Trujillo consolidated his position. It is estimated that 50,000 people died during his rule, including 20,000–30,000 Haitians living on the Dominican/Haitian border whose massacre he ordered in 1937. In 1940, Trujillo negotiated the Hull–Trujillo Amendment that finally ended US control over the Dominican customs houses. Under the agreement, the funds from the customs houses had to be deposited in a New York bank and it was from that bank that the funds would be distributed between the Dominican government and its international creditors.

During the Trujillo regime, civil liberties and human rights were mostly nonexistent. Dominicans who dared to oppose Trujillo were imprisoned, tortured, and murdered. Their bodies often disappeared, rumored to have been fed to the sharks. He remained in control of the

Plate 6.1 *First Lady Eleanor Roosevelt with the Trujillos, March 1934.*
Source: www.latinamericanstudies.org/trujillo-1.htm.

country until his assassination in 1961. As a military officer trained by the United States, Trujillo enjoyed US support throughout most of his rule.

One of the hallmarks of Trujillo's regime was his control of particular industries in order to expand his personal fortune. He held monopolies over the country's salt production, slaughterhouses, rice production, and the sale and distribution of milk in Santo Domingo; his business interests only expanded during the course of his rule. At the end of his life, he controlled 80 percent of the country's industrial production and his companies employed 45 percent of the country's labor force. Since he also controlled government employment, it was estimated that 60 percent of Dominican families depended on Trujillo for some aspect of their livelihoods.[28] During his time in office, Trujillo undertook a massive public works and industrialization campaign, fundamentally transforming the Dominican economy.

By the late 1950s, many Dominicans had grown tired of Trujillo's rule. In 1959, a group of Dominican exiles invaded the country in an attempt to overthrow the regime. They were defeated, but their efforts led to increased opposition to the regime. Many dissidents were jailed, tortured, or assassinated. Trujillo's enemies were not limited to those on the island. Venezuelan President Romulo Betancourt was one of Trujillo's greatest critics. Trujillo attempted to have him killed using a car bomb. The bomb exploded, but Betancourt survived. News of the failed assassination attempt led the Organization of American States (OAS) to sever diplomatic ties with the Dominican Republic and impose economic sanctions. International condemnation of the Trujillo regime intensified in 1960 when it assassinated the Mirabal sisters, daughters of a prominent Dominican family, for their opposition to the regime. After these events, even the United States, long Trujillo's supporter, began to think him a problematic ally. In a declassified memo from Associate Deputy Attorney General James A. Wilderotter, dated January 3, 1975, the CIA acknowledges that it plotted Trujillo's assassination. But the agency claims it played "no active part" in the actual event despite the "faint connection" it had with the groups that in fact carried it out.[29]

Trujillo was assassinated on May 30, 1961 by seven members of his armed forces. Trujillo's son, Ramfis, immediately called for the assassins' execution. Six were executed after an extensive manhunt; one survived. Trujillo's Vice-President, Joaquín Balaguer, took over as President of the Republic. In case armed intervention was needed in the days after his death, 40 US navy ships began patrolling the Dominican coast. Their presence there in November 1961, when two of Trujillo's brothers attempted to take power, is credited with ensuring the Trujillo family did not regain power over the Dominican Republic.[30] The day after the *New York Times* and *Wall Street Journal* published reports that the US government was prepared to land marines, if necessary, to keep them out of power, the Trujillo family fled the country.[31]

US Occupation: Part II

The US government was intimately involved in what happened in the Dominican Republic after Trujillo's assassination. As early as 1961, it was clear that the Kennedy Administration was adamant that the Dominican Republic not become "another Cuba."[32] Thus, it is not surprising that the United States kept its navy patrolling the Dominican coast while involving itself in negotiations to establish an interim Council of State that would organize elections to select a new president. President Kennedy pledged to renew diplomatic relations with the Dominican Republic (which had been severed after the Betancourt incident), to increase US sugar purchases, and to provide economic assistance upon the formal installation of the Council. When a *coup* against the Council was attempted shortly after its installation in January 1962, the US government again made clear its willingness to intervene militarily to keep the Council in power. The United States and the OAS oversaw the elections in 1962 and made certain that the new President, Juan Bosch, was successfully sworn into office.

The Bosch election is widely regarded as the first free election in the country's history. Bosch promulgated a new constitution that angered key parts of the Dominican elite: landowners, the church, industrialists, and the military. These sectors quickly labeled Bosch a communist and began to plot his removal. Seven months after taking office, Bosch was removed from power and replaced by a right-wing civilian junta. That junta, in turn, was short-lived, as Bosch's supporters organized a "constitutionalist" movement to return him to power. Early in 1965, the junta fell, leaving a political vacuum in the country. The military forces had split, disintegrating into various factions. As the social unrest and violence grew, the country was moving toward civil war.

In the initial period of the unrest, the pro-Bosch constitutionalists seemed to be gaining control. Their success, in fact, made President Johnson more convinced that the Castro government had infiltrated their ranks. Johnson said to Secretary of Defense Robert McNamara:

> They've already captured tanks now and they've taken over the police and they're marching them down the streets and they've got a hundred of them as hostages and they're saying they're going to shoot them if they don't take over. Now our CIA says that this is a completely led, operated, dominated – they . . . have got men on the inside of it– Castro operation.[33]

Based on these concerns, within days of the fall of the junta President Johnson approved the landing of 500 marines in the Dominican

Republic.[34] Johnson wanted to avoid Bosch regaining power and to place Balaguer in the presidency. Shortly after the US occupation began, Johnson had the following exchange with adviser Thomas Mann, the Assistant Secretary of State for Inter-American Affairs:

> JOHNSON: We're going to have to really set up that government down there and run it and stabilize it some way or other. This Bosch is no good. . ..
> MANN: He's no good at all. . .. If we don't get a decent government in there, Mr. President, we get another Bosch. It's just going to be another sinkhole.
> JOHNSON: Well that's what you ought to do. That's your problem. You better figure it out.
> MANN: . . . The man to get back, I think, is Balaguer. He's the one that ran way ahead in the polls [referring to secret polls the United States had run in the Dominican Republic].
> JOHNSON: Well, try to do it, try to do it.[35]

Administration spokespeople announced that the action was to restore order and to protect American lives. The pro-Bosch forces resisted, but a cease-fire was soon put into place. Eventually, over 40,000 US troops would be involved in the Dominican occupation. The operation was called "Operation Power Pack."[36] In mid-May, an Inter-American Peace Force, made up of troops from a variety of Latin American countries and sponsored by the OAS, arrived in the Dominican Republic to replace some of the US troops. The US forces did not withdraw completely until September 1966. In 1966, former President Joaquín Balaguer was re-elected, defeating Juan Bosch. Balaguer would remain President until 1978 and was re-elected in 1986. This political transition ushered in a period of relative stability in Dominican politics.

The United States retains significant influence over the Dominican economy and is the Dominican Republic's most important trading partner, with half of the island's exports going there.[37] The remittances the island receives from its migrants living in the United States are also important. In 2012, Dominicans in the United States sent $3.16 billion to the Dominican Republic, a number equal to almost 10 percent of the country's gross domestic product (GDP).[38]

Dominican Migration to the United States

Travel and migration had been severely restricted under the Trujillo regime, to the point where the government limited even the issuance of passports to Dominican citizens.[39] Trujillo feared that Dominicans abroad would become exposed to dangerous "democratic" ideas and

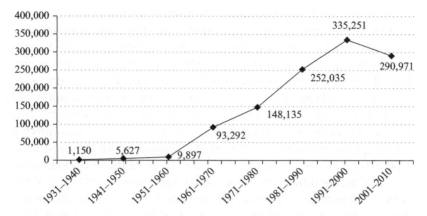

Figure 6.1 *Dominicans Granted Legal Permanent Residence in the United States, 1931–2010*

Source: *US Office of Immigration Statistics, 2010 Yearbook of Immigration Statistics (Washington, DC: US Department of Homeland Security, 2010), table 2, pp. 8 and 10.*

work to oust his regime.[40] Thus, as we see in figure 6.1, Dominican migration to the United States was quite low under Trujillo. A small Dominican community existed in New York City before 1930, but did not experience much growth from 1930 to 1961. The political instability that characterized the four years between the fall of the Trujillo regime and the US occupation in 1965, combined with the removal of restrictions on travel, led to a dramatic increase in Dominican migration. Given the long-term ties between the two countries, it was only logical that a large proportion of those migrants headed to the United States.

During its twelve years in power, the Balaguer regime engaged in a sweeping restructuring of the island's economy, ending Trujillo's import substitution industrialization and opening the Dominican economy to foreign investment. The regime did protect state-owned and some private interests, but in general there was a dramatic liberalization of the Dominican economy. The result was rapid economic growth during the 1970s. But, as we saw in Puerto Rico, the Dominican economic "miracle" did not result in significant increases in employment. In fact, despite this growth, the Dominican economy was characterized by a persistent and growing economic inequality. Those sectors of the poor who spoke out against the government's policies were labeled "communist" and repressed by Balaguer's security forces.

The economic inequality within the Dominican Republic was due in part to the tremendous consolidation of landholding and economic production that had occurred under the Trujillo regime, almost all of which had been geared toward export. In 1960, 1 percent of landowners controlled over one half of the country's farmland; Trujillo alone controlled 35 percent of all cultivated land.[41] The largest export crop was sugar, and two-thirds of sugar production was controlled by Trujillo himself.[42] This meant that little agricultural production was geared toward internal consumption, requiring the Dominican Republic to import most basic food items. This, in turn, raised the cost of these items. Since Dominican peasants' removal from their communal lands, which had begun at the turn of the twentieth century and intensified under Trujillo, there was little subsistence agriculture to produce food for the local market. This, combined with the lack of employment created by Dominican industrialization programs, particularly for the Dominican middle class, formed the economic basis for continued Dominican migration to the United States.

The United States, concerned about communist expansion during the Cold War, supported Balaguer's political and economic policies. It is also suspected that the United States encouraged the migration of Dominican "troublemakers" off the island to the United States in order to shore up the regime and diffuse the island's political situation.[43] As figure 6.1 shows, from 1961 to 1970, the United States granted legal permanent residence to 93,292 Dominicans. Another 636,058 were admitted under temporary visas, which many overstayed. Thousands of others entered the United States without authorization.[44] Those numbers increased dramatically in subsequent decades, partly fueled by the family reunification visas that the 1965 Immigration and Nationality Act made available. Thus, in the initial period during the 1960s, Dominican migration to the United States was driven by Dominicans' response to the removal of the migration restrictions that had been in place under Trujillo and the political upheaval that characterized the island during the Bosch regime and subsequent US occupation. The island's ongoing economic difficulties, combined with political repression and the desire on the part of earlier immigrants to be reunited with family members, fostered the later waves of Dominican immigration to the United States.

Economic developments in the United States also encouraged Dominican migration. Many cities in the US northeast needed unskilled labor to work in factories, construction, and other industries. Thus, Dominican immigrants satisfied important labor force needs in their destination cities. Dominicans' occupational distribution has changed over time, in response to changes in these cities' economies. The shifts in Dominican employment patterns in New York City are indicative of these changes. In 1980, 41 percent of Dominican men and 60 percent of Dominican women worked in New York's manufacturing sector. By 2009, only 24 percent of Dominican men and 9 percent of Dominican women worked in manufacturing. As the New York City economy moved away from manufacturing after 1980, Dominicans found work in service and sales/office jobs, with 48 percent of men and 73 percent of women concentrated in these two sectors by 2009.[45] This occupational distribution, of course, does vary by nativity, with native-born Dominicans more likely to be working in management/professional and sales and office occupations and the foreign-born concentrated in the service sector.[46]

Most Dominicans, particularly in the initial wave, settled in the Washington Heights neighborhood of New York City, which is located in the northern part of Manhattan. Because of the large Dominican community living there, Washington Heights is sometimes referred to as *Quisqueya* Heights or *el Alto* Manhattan. Since 1990, a growing number of New York Dominicans have moved to the Bronx, likely because of the high cost of housing in Manhattan and the (relatively) lower cost of living in the Bronx. More Dominicans now live in the Bronx than in Washington Heights. In 2008, 40 percent of Dominicans in New York lived in the Bronx and only about 29 percent in Manhattan.[47] This has created some tensions with Puerto Ricans who historically have been the largest Latino national-origin group in the Bronx. It also has led to the diversification of the Latino community in Washington Heights, which now includes growing numbers of Ecuadorans and other Latino national-origin groups.

It is important to keep in mind the context of reception that Dominicans faced in New York City in the mid-to-late 1960s. Like Cubans, Dominicans arrived in the United States in large numbers in the midst of the civil rights movement. When Dominicans began exploring their ethnoracial and political identities in this new place, the political space these movements had created there provided them with more opportunities for political self-expression than had been available to the Puerto Ricans who came before them. They were able to insist on an identification as not simply "Black," "Puerto Rican," or "Hispanic." Instead, Dominicans were able to insist on "Dominican" as its own category.[48] This, in turn, facilitated their ability to organize and engage politically. This did not, however, mean that Dominicans in New York did not experience racism.

New Yorkers ascribed many negative characteristics to Dominicans based on their phenotype, accents, and class status, regardless of what they called themselves. It is clear that Dominicans' experiences in the United States reinforced their sense of "blackness." More than 10 percent of Dominicans reported their race as "Black" on the 2000 census. They were much more likely to do so the longer they had been resident in the United States.[49] Through the interaction between new opportunities for identification and political organization in the post-civil-rights era and the existing racial divides in New York City, a new "Dominican" identity and politics were born.[50]

A "Transnational" Migration?

Dominicans in the United States have remained highly involved in the politics of their homeland, to the point that Dominican politicians often campaign in the United States. Because of this cross-national engagement, scholars studying Dominican migration to the United States often describe it as a "transnational" migration. José Itzigsohn sees transnationalism as: (1) a social morphology; (2) a type of consciousness; (3) a mode of cultural production; (4) an avenue of capital; (5) a site of political engagement; and (6) the (re)construction of place and locality.[51] For our purposes, we are most interested in numbers (2) and (5) – the degree to which experiences that cross the boundaries of the nation state affect the development of a transnational Dominican identity and how that identity affects the ways in which Dominicans choose to engage in politics. In his ethnographic study of Dominicans in Washington Heights, Jorge Duany finds

> Dominicans in New York sustained strong cultural, family, and emotional bonds with the Dominican Republic. Most of my key informants felt more connected with their home communities than with the surrounding environment. Many of them did not actively participate in regular activities such as traveling to the Dominican Republic or belonging to Dominican voluntary associations in the United States. Yet they displayed a persistent attachment to a Dominican identity, especially to the traditional food, music, language, and religion of the Dominican Republic . . . I am still struck by how deeply Dominicans felt about their homeland, affectionately calling it *mi país* ("my country"), while remaining distant from the United States, which they usually described as *este país* ("this country"). The transnational identity of Dominicans in Washington Heights was split between "here" and "there" in ways that resonate strongly with other diasporic communities, such as Puerto Ricans.[52]

However, Duany cautions, this identity did not arise out of a vacuum, but rather as a result of discrimination and other difficulties with incorporation that Dominican immigrants have experienced in the United States. Thus, in part, "transnational identities may be interpreted as forms of popular resistance to racialized social structures and cultural practices in the United States."[53]

The most clear example of transnational engagement on the part of Dominican immigrants relates to their efforts to push the Dominican government to allow Dominicans in the United States to retain their Dominican citizenship and have the right to vote in Dominican elections. A number of Dominican organizations were formed in the 1970s to advance this agenda. These groups included the *Concilio de Organizaciones Dominicanas* (Council of Dominican Organizations) and the *Asociación Nacional de Dominicanos Ausentes* (National Association of Absent Dominicans).[54] In 1994, these groups' efforts were successful. The Dominican government formally allowed Dominican dual citizenship. In 2004, Dominicans abroad were given the right to vote in Dominican presidential elections. In that election, 35,042 Dominicans living abroad cast ballots; 30,118 of those votes, or 86 percent, were cast by Dominicans living in the United States.[55] They elected Leonel Fernández to the presidency, a Dominican who had moved with his family to New York City in the 1970s and spent his summers working at his family's *bodega* (corner store) while he was attending law school in Santo Domingo.[56]

In 2008, 76,713 Dominicans living abroad participated in the election, 77 percent of whom resided in the United States. In the 2012 Dominican presidential election, Dominicans abroad comprised 3.2 percent of registered voters, making it clear why Dominican presidential candidates make a point of visiting New York City to campaign and distribute their election advertising in New York neighborhoods like Washington Heights.

As of 2012, Dominicans living abroad also had the opportunity to elect seven migrant representatives to the lower house of the Dominican Congress, comprising 3.7 percent of the 190 representatives in that legislative body.[57] Three of those elected officials represent North America, which includes the United States (minus Florida) and Canada. Almost 55 percent of the Dominican voters registered abroad live in the North American area; 63 percent of those live in New York City. Florida and Puerto Rico comprise another region, which was granted two migrant representatives and includes about 21 percent of Dominican registered voters abroad.[58] Thus, five of the seven diasporic representatives in the Dominican Congress are representing the interests of Dominican migrants in the United States.

Plate 6.2 *Campaign Posters from the Dominican Republic, Posted in Washington Heights in 2012.*
Source: *Reproduced courtesy of El Diairio/Impremedia.*

Dominican Political Engagement in the United States

Even though they are a relatively new immigrant community, Dominicans in the United States have already begun to make their mark politically. Dominican Americans are more dispersed across the United States now than they had been previously, but half of US Dominicans still live in New York City. It is not surprising, therefore, that most Dominican American political activity has been focused in that city. Anthropologist Ana Aparicio argues that there are two types of Dominican political activists: (1) ethnic entrepreneurs – those who appeal to the local political machinery in order to obtain grants and other social supports for the community; and (2) community mobilizers – those who believe community empowerment requires grassroots work to establish the foundation for community demands.[59]

When considering the types of political activity immigrants choose to engage in, we must keep in mind how nativity might influence the options available to them. As we saw in chapter 2, fewer than half of Dominican immigrants are US citizens; over 60 percent have arrived in the United States since 1990. In addition, the Migration Policy Institute estimates that between 13 and 15 percent of Dominican immigrants (around 100,000) are unauthorized.[60] Thus, nativity limits Dominican immigrants' ability to express their political views through formal political channels, such as voting. Those channels are likely to be most important for those activists who are attempting to be ethnic entrepreneurs, according to Aparicio's definition. Those community advocates will be better able to get the demands they make to city leaders met if they can show electoral clout. The community mobilizers, on the other hand, may be able to show their influence by organizing individuals beyond the ballot box, regardless of nativity. It is likely that a combination of these strategies will be necessary to ensure Dominican voices are heard within New York City and state politics.

As we saw with other immigrant groups in this volume, Dominican organizing began with the formation of a number of local political/social clubs, similar to the mutual-aid societies we have seen for other groups. Two of the largest – the *Centro Cívico Cultural Dominicano* (Dominican Cultural and Civic Center) and *Club Juan Pablo Duarte* (the Juan Pablo Duarte Club) – date back to the 1960s. These groups were focused initially on home-country politics, including the dual citizenship concerns discussed above, and on supporting immigrants in their transitions in the United States. Dominican organizations were so prolific that in 1992 Dennis DeLeon, head of New York City's Commission on Human Rights (and not a Dominican), stated, "The Dominicans are the most political community I've ever seen in this city. There are more clubs per square inch in Washington Heights than you will find anywhere in the city. Dominicans bring a lot of the island politics with them, and that creates a structure for how they organize here."[61]

Dominicans' organizational efforts soon turned to the political sphere, starting on the transnational front. Many of the constitutionalists who were exiled by the 1965 US invasion settled in the Dominican *colonia* of Washington Heights and continued their efforts opposing US intervention in the Dominican Republic and the Balaguer regime. As a result, the *Partido Revolucionario Dominicano* (Dominican Revolutionary Party – PRD) became the *colonia*'s most active political and social institution. They organized annual demonstrations and protests to commemorate the constitutionalist uprising against the junta and to express their opposition to the Balaguer regime. Thousands of Dominicans participated, with the female marchers often dressed in black shirts, military pants, and with ammunition belts carrying dummy rifles.[62] The PRD joined forces with other leftist groups in New York that opposed the United

States' foreign policy toward Vietnam and Latin America. PRD activists worked in coalition with activists Norman Thomas, Stokely Carmichael, members of the Students for a Democratic Society (SDS) and the North American Conference on Latin America (NACLA).[63] Their efforts pushed NACLA to take a more critical stance on US policy toward the Dominican Republic, emphasizing Balaguer's human rights abuses. Because of these relationships, other left-wing groups, including the Young Lords, began signing anti-Balaguer petitions and attending anti-Balaguer rallies.[64] The PRD also began to provide basic legal services to Dominicans in New York and protested against the treatment of Dominicans by US immigration services and the Balaguer government when they traveled back to the island.[65] Today, the PRD actively supports Dominican-American participation in island politics while also encouraging naturalization and voter registration among Dominican Americans in the United States.[66] Similarly, the *Partido de los Trabajadores Dominicanos* (Dominican Workers' Party – PTD) raises awareness about worker concerns in the Dominican Republic while also fundraising to support Dominican-American political candidates in the United States. It was the PTD that organized Guillermo Linares' first electoral campaign (discussed below).[67]

Dominican political parties from the right wing also organized in New York. The *Reformista* Party, founded by Joaquín Balaguer, was active in the city. Its main source of support was the Dominican Consul General. The *Reformista* Party worked to defend the images of the Dominican President and the Dominican Republic in the United States. The Party maintained social clubs and domino tables throughout Washington Heights, helping to support the community's collective organization.[68] As the Dominican population in New York grew, the consular office grew in size and importance as well.

One of the first areas Dominican political organizing focused on in New York City was education. Representation on school boards, parent associations, and other institutions responsible for decisions about how to educate children had long been an issue of contention in Washington Heights. In the late 1970s, non-Dominicans controlled the Washington Heights board of education (School District 6) even though the majority of the students in the district were Dominican.[69] The Dominican community organized and was able to elect Sixto Medina, a Dominican community activist, to the school board.[70] What helped to make this success possible was the fact that New York City allowed residents to vote in school board elections regardless of citizenship status. That allowed Dominicans to have a much greater impact on this election than they would have otherwise. From the 1970s to the mid-1980s, María Luna was a district leader for the Democratic Party in the Washington Heights / Inwood area and a member of the community planning board. In 1985, local Dominican activists Julio Hernández and Ivelisse Fairchild also became district leaders.[71] Dominicans' deeper integration into city politics is exemplified by the election of Guillermo Linares, former head of the school board, to the New York City Council in 1991 as the representative for Washington Heights. In the Democratic primary election for what would become Linares' council seat, three of the five candidates were Dominican. María Luna came in second, losing to Linares by 258 votes. After winning the primary, Linares easily won the general election. When talking about his electoral success, Linares emphasized that his victory would not have been possible had he not forged coalitions with the local African American and Puerto Rican communities.[72]

Dominican organizing efforts grew out of local tragedy as well. In July 1992, New York City policeman Michael O'Keefe fatally shot Dominican immigrant José García in the lobby of his apartment building.[73] Police claimed that García was a drug suspect and was armed, and that the police officer acted in self-defense. Witnesses from inside the building claimed that Officer O'Keefe beat García with a police radio and pointed his gun at him "for no good reason."[74] The shooting set off six days of civil unrest that resulted in 1 death, 90 injuries, and 139 arrests. It came on the heels of growing tensions between the New York police and Dominican residents resulting from the police's intensification of efforts to combat the drug trade, which local residents felt resulted in the indiscriminate detainment and harassment of Dominicans in Washington Heights.

In response to the shooting, established Dominican organizations mobilized community members against police violence. During the civil unrest, leaders from these organizations helped to calm the unrest. As Maria Newman of the *New York Times* reported:

> Armed with walkie-talkies and wearing yellow ribbons, a cadre of Dominicans, from homemakers to lawyers to ministers, have constantly been on the streets in these days of rage, mediating between angry crowds of demonstrators and police officers in riot gear who have been posted throughout the Manhattan neighborhood.
>
> They have organized candlelight vigils. They have negotiated with the police to allow demonstrators to burn an effigy of an officer if the organizers could keep the crowd from turning violent. They have asked for, and got, a meeting with Police

Commissioner Lee P. Brown to discuss their complaints with how the 34th Precinct polices an area besieged by drugs, crime and violence.[75]

Here we see how established organizations, like the *Alianza Dominicana*, the Dominican Women's Development Center, and the Union of Young Dominicans, were able to respond to a local crisis, and how that crisis spurred new and deeper political organization within the community.[76]

Quisqueya United is an example of just this sort of evolving Dominican political organization. In the early 1980s, a number of leaders from the various Dominican clubs began to talk about the need to unite these disparate organizations under one roof in order to maximize their impact. The result was the formation of *Quisqueya* United, which in the mid-2000s was the largest Dominican political organization in Washington Heights.[77] *Quisqueya* United focuses on social service provision and operates a number of after-school and youth programs in New York City. It has been able to secure sufficient grants and support to have a number of full-time staff and offer a variety of programs operating under its umbrella. Similarly, Dominican Nation is a political organization founded by a young group of Dominican students from Washington Heights.[78] Operating mainly out of a student union office in the City College of New York (CCNY), in 2000 they organized a conference whose goal was to delineate a Dominican American "national agenda."[79]

Aparicio engaged in an in-depth ethnography of these two groups' work and argues that common ways of understanding identity and transnationalism cannot fully explain Dominican American political engagement. She finds that both organizations engaged in coalition building with African Americans and Puerto Ricans, among other groups, in order to achieve their political goals. Similarly, she argues that characterizations of Dominican American politics as transnational ignores the importance of local issues to Dominican political engagement, particularly for those in the second generation. As Jorge Duany points out, "transnationalism may foster the simultaneous incorporation of Dominicans in their host societies as well as the enduring connection to their country of origin."[80] The two are not, in fact, mutually exclusive. As we saw with Puerto Ricans, the growth of the second generation does not result in the abandonment of concerns about home-country politics, but rather the addition of local issues as motivators driving political engagement.

One key motivator for this engagement came from the business sector. The growth of Dominican electoral involvement in the 1990s was supported by Dominican small business associations, particularly the National Supermarkets Association and the Federation of Taxi Drivers.[81] These organizations supported Dominican politicians who, in turn, helped them get the legislation regarding zoning, taxes, and other issues that were important to the growth and maintenance of their businesses. As we saw with Cuban Americans, the growth of this business sector was another key impetus for Dominican American political incorporation.

That growth in Dominican political and social influence was also reflected in the establishment of the Dominican Studies Institute (DSI) at the City University of New York (CUNY) in 1992. The result of organizational efforts by the Council of Dominican Educators, community activists, and other CUNY faculty, CUNY DSI was the nation's first university-based research institute devoted to the study of people of Dominican descent in the United States and other parts of the world. Its mission is "to produce and disseminate research and scholarship about Dominicans, and about the Dominican Republic. CUNY DSI is the locus for a community of scholars, including doctoral fellows, in the field of Dominican Studies and sponsors multidisciplinary research projects."[82] The Institute has commissioned and published a variety of studies focusing on the Dominican experience in the country. It also houses an archive and library, the only institutions in the United States collecting primary and secondary materials about people of Dominican descent in the United States. As with the other political organizing Dominicans have engaged in in New York City, CUNY DSI would not have been possible without the support of key allies from the African American Studies, Puerto Rican Studies, and Language and Literature departments at CUNY. Again we see the coalitional character of Dominican politics in the United States.

The political maturation of the Dominican community in New York is reflected in the growth of Dominican officeholding in the United States. Dominican political parties from the island have always been active in New York City and those efforts only intensified after the passage of dual citizenship in 1994. While Dominican presidential candidates come to New York City to vie for Dominican votes, Dominican candidates also compete to represent the community within US political institutions. When Guillermo Linares gave up his seat on the New York City Council in 2001, eight Dominican candidates entered the race to replace him.[83] Currently, Dominicans hold political office at all levels of government.

Nationally, Obama's Secretary of Labor in his second term is Dominican Thomas Pérez. During President Obama's first term, he was Assistant Attorney General for the Justice Department's Civil Rights Division.

Plate 6.3 *Normandía Maldonado.*

Source: The Normandia Maldonado Collection, Dominican Studies Institute Archives, City College of New York

Normandía Maldonado: The Politics of Cultural Performance

Normandía Maldonado was a dancer and choreographer who used her art to foster greater recognition of the Dominican community in the United States. Born in the city of Santiago in the Dominican Republic in 1929, she arrived in the United States in 1960. To make ends meet, she began working in a clothing factory but soon began performing with a group she founded with her sister Marina, called the Mambo Girls. The Mambo Girls performed in a variety of venues around the world, including New York's Lincoln Center. In 1966, Normandía co-founded the *Centro Cívico Cultural Juan Pablo Duarte*, an organization that worked to promote Dominican culture in the United States. One of their central goals was to have a statue of the founding father of the Dominican Republic, Juan Pablo Duarte, erected as a landmark for Dominicans living in New York City, a goal they realized in 1978. The statue now sits in New York's Central Park alongside statues of José Martí, Simon de Bolívar, and other Latin American independence leaders. This national symbol has helped to sustain Dominican activism in New York. Under the leadership of the *Club Juan Pablo Duarte*, Dominican parents took over the parent association at PS 132 in the late 1970s. Its first act was to rename the school after Juan Pablo Duarte, making the school a symbol of Dominican cultural pride.[84]

Through her artistic work, Normandía is credited with helping to foster and maintain that cultural pride within the US Dominican community. In 1967, Normandía began the *Central Cultural Ballet Quisqueya*, a folkloric dance troupe for children and adults.[85] The *Ballet Quisqueya* continues to the present day, educating Dominicans, particularly the second generation, about their rich cultural heritage and performing that cultural patrimony on the international stage. In 1982 Normandía founded the Dominican Day Parade, a parade which honors Dominican cultural pride and in which the *Ballet Quisqueya* has always performed. Normandía has received recognition and honors from a variety of Dominican organizations and New York elected officials. She was among the first Dominicans to donate their papers to the Dominican archives at CUNY's Dominican Studies Institute (DSI). According to DSI, Normandía Maldonado "stands as one of the most accomplished activist and community leaders among the Dominican people in the United States."

Dominicans have a great deal of representation at the state and local levels, particularly in New York and New Jersey.[86] In New York, José Peralta and Adriano Espaillat are state senators, while Gabriela Rosa and Rafael L. Espinal serve in the New York State Assembly. Four Dominicans serve on the New York City Council: Julissa Ferreras, Diana Reyna, Fernando Cabrera, and Ydanis Rodríguez. Also at the local level, Vivian Viloria-Fisher is a Legislator for the County of Suffolk, Francisco Batista serves as Deputy Mayor of Haverstraw Village, and Rafael Bueno and Emily Dominguez are both Village Trustees for Haverstraw Village.

In New Jersey, Alex D. Blanco is Mayor of the City of Passaic and Zaida Polanco serves as a Councilwoman. Hector Lora is a Freeholder for Passaic County. In Paterson, Rigo Rodriguez is Councilman-at-Large, and Julio Tavarez is Councilman for the 5th Ward. Wendy Guzmán and Alex Méndez are both Commissioners on the Paterson Board of Education. Carlos Aguasvivas is Mayor of Bergenfield and Rafael Marte a Councilman. Tilo Rivas is a Freeholder for Hudson County. Reynaldo Martinez is a Councilman for the Borough of Haledon. Cristina Peralta is a Councilwoman in the Borough of Prospect Park. Yessenia Frias is a Councilwoman for the Borough of Bogota. Ruben Vargas and Fior D'Aliza are Commissioners for West New York. Milady Tejeda and Samuel Lebrault serve on the Perth Amboy Board of Education. Eric Cedano is Commissioner of the Roselle Board of Education and Sebastian Rodriguez is Commissioner of the Teaneck Board of Education.

Dominicans also have political representation in those localities where they make up a smaller portion of the overall population, a testament to these elected officials' ability to build coalitions with other groups in order to get elected. In Massachusetts, Marcos Devers is a state representative. William Lantigua is Mayor of the City of Lawrence. Frank Moran, Oneida Aquino, Sandy Almonte, Estela Reyes, and Kendrys Vasquez serve on the Lawrence city council, making up five of the council's nine members. In Pennsylvania, Julio Guridy is a Councilman in Allentown. In the

Plate 6.4 *Dominican Day Parade in New York City.*
Source: *Corbis Images.*

Rhode Island State House, Juan Pichardo serves as a state senator and
Grace Diaz as a state representative. Angel Taveras is Mayor of the City of
Providence. Davian Sánchez and Sabina Matos serve on the Providence
city council. As would be expected, we see that Dominicans are much
more likely to achieve political representation at the local level where
they are better able to surpass the majoritarian threshold.

Conclusion

The Dominican Republic has had a long and turbulent history characterized by political unrest and deep economic instability. Since the early twentieth century, the United States was intimately involved in Dominican economics and politics, going as far as invading the country twice in the course of the century. After the 1960s, political upheaval at home, economic dislocation, economic growth in the United States, and encouragement on the part of US immigration officials led to dramatic growth in Dominican migration to the United States. Although large-scale Dominican migration there is a relatively new phenomenon, Dominican migrants have been able to develop the organizational and political resources needed to become a force in US and Dominican politics. This is largely due to the context of reception they faced when they arrived, their ability to build coalitions with African Americans and Puerto Ricans in New York City, and the financial and organizational support Dominican politicians were able to receive from small-business associations. Using that foundation, Dominican Americans play an important role in their home-country politics and are a growing political presence and force in the United States.

QUESTIONS FOR DISCUSSION

1 Why was the Dominican Republic's political and economic history so turbulent?
2 What explains the United States' involvement in the Dominican economy and politics?
3 What role did Trujillo's fall and the subsequent US invasion plan play in fostering Dominican migration to the United States?
4 How did the timing of large-scale Dominican migration and the migrants' settlement in New York City affect the nature of Dominican political activity in the United States?
5 Are US Dominican politics "transnational?" Why or why not?

GUIDE TO FURTHER READINGS

Aparicio, Ana. 2006. *Dominican-Americans and the Politics of Empowerment.* Gainesville: University Press of Florida.
Duany, Jorge. 2008. *Quisqueya on the Hudson: The Transnational Identity of Dominicans in Washington Heights*, 2nd edn. Research Monograph. New York: CUNY Dominican Studies Institute.

Hoffnung-Garskof, Jesse. 2008. *A Tale of Two Cities: Santo Domingo and New York after 1950*. Princeton: Princeton University Press.

Krohn-Hansen, Christian. 2013. *Making New York Dominican: Small Business, Politics, and Everyday Life*. Philadelphia: University of Pennsylvania Press.

Pessar, Patricia. 1995. *A Visa for a Dream: Dominicans in the United States*. Boston: Allyn & Bacon.

CHAPTER SEVEN

Central Americans:
Inequality, War, and Solidarity

Objectives
- Understand the relationship Central America has had with the United States, including with its military and economic interventions in the region
- Understand the role economic inequality has played in the evolution of each country's politics
- Understand the role Cold-War ideology has played in the response of the Central American elites and of the United States to reformist movements in the region
- Understand how violence in the region has affected migration flows
- Understand how US foreign policy goals have influenced Central Americans' migration status in the United States
- Understand how Central Americans were able to change their migration status and to influence US foreign policy in their countries of origin

Introduction

Central America's proximity to the United States has made it a target of US foreign and economic interests. The phrase "Central America" refers to the geographic isthmus stretching from Guatemala to Panamá. As early as the 1850s, US politicians and businessmen began involving themselves in Central American affairs, seeing the region as "the next American frontier."[1] Private American adventurers called *filibusteros*, or filibusters, amassed small armies and attempted to take over parts of Central America through force of arms. Often they were out for personal gain, or they were hired by US business interests to protect US property in the region. One of the most famous filibusters was William Walker, who, after attempting to take over parts of Mexico in 1853, turned his sights to Central America. One of the factions in Nicaragua's civil war hired him as a mercenary and, in 1856, he declared himself President of the Republic of Nicaragua. He then tried to conquer the remaining

Central American countries, but was defeated by the combined Central American forces and executed by Honduran authorities in 1860.

The stories of the filibusters' adventures were very popular in the American press, but the filibusters' actions were in violation of US law. At the turn of the twentieth century these incursions continued, and began to include actions carried out by the US military on behalf of the US government. In 1927, Undersecretary of State Robert Olds described how the United States understood its interests and role in the region:

> The Central American area constitutes a legitimate sphere of influence for the United States, if we are to have due regard for our own safety and protection ... Our ministers accredited to the five little republics ... have been advisors whose advice has been accepted virtually as law ... we do control the destinies of Central America and we do so for the simple reason that the national [US] interest dictates such a course ... There is no room for any outside influence other than ours in this region ... Until now Central America has always understood that governments which we recognize and support stay in power, while those which we do not recognize and support fall.[2]

The United States often expressed its support for or opposition to these regimes through military action. The United States military invaded Nicaragua in 1894, 1896, and 1910, and occupied the country from 1912 to 1933. US troops entered Honduras in 1903, 1907, 1911, 1912, 1919, and 1924, in most cases in response to conflictual elections. In Panamá, the US government was instrumental in making that country separate from Colombia so as to be able to build the Panama Canal, and it was heavily involved in the country's politics in order to ensure the canal's function and defense. United States companies were also heavily invested in many Central American countries, particularly the United Fruit Company. United Fruit developed an integrated production plan, not only producing bananas but also building and controlling the infrastructure necessary to get them to market – for instance roads, railroads, utilities, ports, and so on. In many Central American countries, United Fruit owned the majority of the existing infrastructure; this made it a key player in the countries' internal affairs. Thus US interests were deeply intertwined with Central American politics and economics. That relationship would help to shape the economic development that occurred in the region, the kinds of political leadership that were possible, and the opportunities available to everyday Central Americans. After the mid twentieth century, it would also have important effects on Central American migration patterns and on US immigration policy toward those migrants.

Salvadorans and Guatemalans

Even though the United States is a home for migrants from all the countries of Central America, the two largest groups are those from El Salvador and Guatemala. Table 7.1 summarizes the population of Central American origin in the United States, which numbered 3,998,280 in 2010. Between 2000 and 2010, the US Central-American-origin population grew by 137 percent. Of these, 1,648,968 were from El Salvador and 1,044,209 from Guatemala. Together, these two groups make up over 67 percent of Central Americans living in the United States. Although Central Americans' experiences do vary in important ways by national origin, an examination of these two groups encompasses the experiences of over two-thirds of migrants with origins in this region.

El Salvador

El Salvador declared its independence from Spain in 1821, along with the other countries of Central America. Until 1838, the country formed part of a united Central American federation. When that union dissolved, El Salvador became an independent nation. Its history in the nineteenth century was marked by frequent revolutions and ongoing attempts to form a larger Central American state. Although various agreements were reached, none was able to survive. After the mid nineteenth century, the Salvadoran economy quickly became dependent on the exportation of coffee. The expansion of coffee production led to the government's elimination of communal landholdings in 1881 and to the subsequent concentration of land ownership into a small oligarchy called *las catorce* (the [group of the] fourteen [families]). The country's infrastructure development centered on ensuring the smooth export of coffee. In addition, the Salvadoran government was almost entirely dependent on coffee production for revenue, which ensured that this sector had a tremendous influence on the country's politics. The government passed anti-vagrancy laws to ensure an available work force for coffee production. For example, the 1907 Agrarian Law stated that landless laborers could be arrested for vagrancy and had to carry workbooks listing their work obligations. The law established Agrarian Law judges, who, with the assistance of the army, were appointed in each village to keep lists of all day laborers and to arrange for the capture of any workers who ran away from the estates.[3] In 1912, the state created the rural National Guard to maintain peace and control in the countryside.

Table 7.1 The Central-American-Origin Population in the United States, 2010

Nationality	Population	Percent of total	Percent change, 2000–2010
Costa Rican	126,418	3.2	84.3
Guatemalan	1,044,209	26.1	180.3
Honduran	633,401	15.8	191.1
Nicaraguan	348,202	8.7	96.0
Panamanian	165,456	4.1	80.4
Salvadoran	1,648,968	41.2	151.7
Other Central American	31,626	0.8	−69.5
Total	3,998,280	100.00	137

Source: US Department of the Census, Census Brief, "The Hispanic Population: 2010"

The Salvadoran peasantry did not passively accept this transfer of land and power from the indigenous population to the coffee elite. Between 1870 and 1900, the peasants staged four separate revolts, but they were easily defeated by the military.[4] What had already been a difficult situation for the peasantry worsened significantly during the Great Depression. Growers halved wages for coffee workers and significantly decreased production, leaving thousands of Indian families without work. As a US military attaché described the situation in 1931: "There is practically no middle class between the very rich and the very poor . . . Roughly 90 percent of the wealth in the country is held by one-half of one percent of the population. Thirty or forty families own nearly everything in the country. They live in regal splendor [while] the rest of the country has practically nothing."[5] The Salvadoran peasantry continually protested against this state of affairs. In 1930, 80,000 protesters gathered to celebrate May Day and to denounce deteriorating wages and working conditions for workers. The following year this growing movement of students, peasants, and workers elected liberal Arturo Araujo to the presidency. Shortly afterwards, Araujo announced that the Salvadoran Communist Party would be allowed to participate in the December 1931 municipal elections. The Salvadoran military would not allow this; they deposed Araujo and replaced him with a conservative general, Maximiliano Hernández Martínez.

The peasantry broke out in rebellion. In January 1932, bands of largely Pipil Indians from western El Salvador, armed with machetes and led by Agustín Farabundo Martí, attacked local towns. Within three days they had taken control of several towns and of a number of major supply routes. The Martínez regime responded with brutal repression. All Indians – or anyone looking like an Indian – were targeted. It is estimated that as many as 30,000 Salvadorans were killed, including Martí: this in a country with a population of only 1.4 million. The military tied the Indians' thumbs behind their backs, lined them up, and shot them. Historian Thomas P. Anderson wrote: "The extermination was so great that they could not be buried fast enough, and a great stench of rotting flesh permeated the air of western El Salvador."[6] The US military was alerted during the rebellion. Two destroyers and a naval cruiser were stationed off the coast, in case they were needed by the Salvadoran military. This uprising is remembered as *La Matanza* (the Massacre) and resulted in many Pipil Indians adopting western dress and the Spanish language in order to avoid being targeted by the military. This traumatic event would have far-reaching effects on the future of Salvadoran politics. Martínez stayed in power until he was deposed in 1944 by a general strike called *la huelga de brazos caídos* (the strike of still arms).

The experience of the 1931 elections and of their aftermath led the military to take direct control of the government from that point forward; no other civilian would be elected President in El Salvador until 1984. Throughout this time, the army controlled the government with the complicity of *las catorce*. The presidents were chosen from the military, and civilians from the coffee elite served as cabinet members.[7]

Meanwhile, inequality continued to increase within the Salvadoran economy. The land concentration which had begun with coffee production only intensified after 1950, with the introduction of cotton and sugar as new cash crops. As a result, the number of landless laborers increased from 11 percent of the labor force in 1961 to 40 percent by 1975.[8] The maintenance of this rural economic system rested on an increasing use of security forces and of repression in the countryside. In 1950, the government amended the 1907 Agrarian Law, establishing that National Guard members should be used to maintain order on private estates and that the law enforcement officials should be appointed (and therefore controlled) by the landowners themselves.[9] Unwanted tenant farmers could be summarily evicted from their homes, and local police had the right to destroy the homes of anyone they considered a criminal. Any peasant found out at night could be detained by the police without cause and the National Guard could, at any time, arrest any laborer who was seen as failing to fulfill his obligations to the landowner.[10] A 1991

Americas Watch report on the status of the Salvadoran peasantry during this period found it to be in a state of "virtual serfdom."

The United States also assisted with the expansion of the Salvadoran security apparatus. During the 1960s, the Alliance for Progress was meant to deepen US ties throughout Latin America. In most countries, Alliance programs included assistance with counterinsurgency and support for small-scale land reform. In El Salvador, the elite equated land reform with communism, so the US Alliance for Progress assistance was focused almost exclusively on supporting counterinsurgency and on strengthening the Salvadoran police forces.[11] This investment led to the Salvadoran security forces turning toward the use of paramilitary death squads. Their precursor was the Democratic Nationalist Organization (ORDEN), created in 1968 by General José Alberto Medrano. A highly paid CIA consultant, Medrano created a rural vigilante force which kept watch on progressive peasant organizations. This force, 50,000-strong, was considered the "eyes and ears" of the military in the countryside and worked with the military to eliminate the peasant leadership.[12]

The first major political challenge to the military dictatorship in El Salvador came in 1972. In that year, the *Unión Nacional Opositora* (UNO) Coalition was formed by three political parties: the Christian Democratic Party (CDP), the social democratic National Revolutionary Movement (MNR), and the leftist National Democratic Union (UDN). The UNO chose José Napoleon Duarte, Mayor of San Salvador (1964–70) and founder of the CDP, as their presidential candidate. The coalition was supported by urban intellectuals, professionals, and workers. The development of industry in El Salvador during the 1960s had led to growing political strength among industrial workers. Unlike their rural counterparts, these workers were allowed to form unions and grew in power over the course of the decade. Representing these interests, Duarte ran on a platform in favor of human rights and social justice. Blatant electoral fraud on the part of the military deprived him of victory in the 1972 presidential election. Instead, the military had him arrested, tortured, and exiled, and installed one of their colonels as President. The 1972 elections made clear to many in El Salvador that the army was unwilling to allow reform to occur through electoral means.

After the 1972 elections revealed that the political system could not be used to solve the country's problems, the number of mass organizations in El Salvador began to increase. Students, workers, peasants, and church members joined together to fight the military dictatorship. Their tactics included street demonstrations and the occupation of public buildings, factories, and large estates. As these movements strengthened, the military increasingly responded with violence. For example, in 1975, students in Santa Ana occupied the local campus to protest against the government's spending of $1.5 million to host the Miss Universe pageant. When San Salvador students held a march to show their solidarity with the students from Santa Ana, the National Guard opened fire. Scores of students were wounded or killed and 24 disappeared.[13]

These mass organizations were joined in their opposition to the regime by some sectors within a major institution in Salvadoran society: the Catholic church. Although historically the church had helped to support the regime by encouraging parishioners to focus on the afterlife rather than on any problems in the here and now, the growth of liberation theology among many in the clergy led to a change in the role of the church in Salvadoran society. Liberation theology was a movement within the Catholic church that grew out of the changes in church policy put forth by the Second Vatican Council (1962–5) and the conference of Latin American bishops held in Medellín, Colombia, in 1968. This new theology asserted that poverty and injustice were not God's will and that believers had the right to challenge any oppressive institutions in society. To address inequality, the bishops in Medellín called for more education, increased social awareness, and the creation of *comunidades de base* (faith communities) which encouraged parishioners to meet weekly for Bible readings with a focus on New Testament readings emphasizing social justice.[14] Followers of this theology argued that it was not radical, but rather a reversion back to the original teachings of Jesus Christ. The Salvadoran military and elite, however, saw this movement as a grave threat to their social structure and death squads (*escuadrones de la muerte*) began to target nuns and priests specifically. The White Warriors Union death squad is reported to have circulated flyers in 1977 that read: "Be a Patriot, Kill a Priest!"[15]

Thus, during the 1970s violence continued to increase in El Salvador. A number of death squads were organized by the government after 1975; these included the White Warriors Union mentioned above, the White Hand, the Anticommunist Forces for Liberation (FALANGE), the Organization for Liberation from Communism (OLC), the Secret Anti-Communist Army (ESA), and the Maximiliano Hernández Martínez Brigade, named after the general responsible for *La Matanza*. According to one US official, the death squads were made up of members of the Salvadoran army, of the Treasury Police, of the National Guard, of the

National Police, or of "the sick young sons of affluent Salvadorans."[16] The squads were funded by members of the oligarchy, many of whom resided in Miami.

As the 1970s came to a close, the violence continued. General Carlos Romero was fraudulently elected President in 1977; thousands gathered to protest against his election and the police fired upon the demonstrators, leaving nearly 100 dead.[17] One of Romero's first acts as President was to promote a law to "defend and guarantee public order," and violence and repression increased significantly under his rule.[18] Frustrated with the Romero regime, some reformist members of the military and a few civilians took control of the government in 1979. The new *junta* sought the support of the "popular organizations" and wanted to ensure that El Salvador did not follow the same road as Nicaragua, whose Sandinista rebels had just succeeded in taking control of the country's government. The *junta* declared amnesty for all political prisoners and Salvadorans in exile, dissolved ORDEN, and created a special committee to investigate the "disappeared."[19] The decrees were never carried out. Political prisoners remained in jail, no prosecutions for past crimes occurred, and ORDEN continued to function in the countryside with impunity. El Salvador's mass organizations engaged in protests, strikes, and occupations, in an effort to end the repression. The *junta* responded even more violently than the Romero regime; the protests were repressed, and killings took place at a rate of 1,000 per month.[20] Over the next few months, most of the civilian members of the *junta* resigned and the military took back control of the government.

This only increased the bloodshed. The year 1980 was a particularly violent one. Death squads targeted high-profile leaders as well as the civilian population. In January 1980, to commemorate the 48th anniversary of *La Matanza*, a coalition of mass organizations mounted an enormous demonstration in San Salvador, the largest ever held in the country. Guards and sharpshooters attacked the demonstrators, leaving many dead. There is disagreement about the number of civilians killed. Estimates range from 20 to 52.[21] In February 1980, one of the few progressive civilians remaining in the government, Attorney General Mario Zamora, was assassinated during a dinner party in his home. He was shot in the face a dozen times at point-blank range.[22] In March, Archbishop Oscar Romero, head of the Catholic church in El Salvador and a vocal advocate for social justice, was assassinated while he was saying mass. His funeral procession included 30,000 mourners. The military fired into the procession, killing 30 and wounding hundreds more.[23] In

November, 6 leading members of the Democratic Revolutionary Front, one of the last mass organizations advocating non-violent tactics, were kidnapped and murdered – an act which eliminated some of the last influential reformist Salvadoran politicians.[24] In December 3 US nuns and a Catholic lay worker were kidnapped, raped, and murdered. Their mutilated bodies were found buried in shallow graves. The Carter Administration protested and demanded an investigation, but no real effort was made to identify those responsible. In return, the United States temporarily froze military and economic aid to El Salvador.

In 1980 alone, an estimated 8,000 civilians were murdered, yet no one was ever tried for the killings.[25] Human rights organizations calculated that, between 1979 and 1983, the death squads murdered or kidnapped 36,000 Salvadorans.[26] This violence did not occur privately. Rather, the bodies of the dead were left, often mutilated, in town sewers, roads, plazas, empty lots, garbage dumps, gutters, or shallow graves, so that they could be found easily and therefore serve as a warning for others considering opposing the regime.[27]

The assassination of such prominent leaders as Zamora, and especially Romero, and the extent of the violence served to unite the reformers and the revolutionaries in El Salvador. Many groups demanded an investigation of the individual suspected of ordering the assassinations, Roberto D'Aubuisson, but the government failed to act. In response, virtually all the opposition groups in the country – political parties, religious organizations, trade unions, and peasant groups – joined together in April 1980 to create a new Democratic Revolutionary Front (FDR).[28] They became the political arm of the revolutionary opposition.[29] In October 1980, the various guerrilla armies also came together under one banner, establishing the Farabundo Martí National Liberation Front (FMLN), named after the slain leader of the 1932 *Matanza*. By 1981, the FMLN had 5,000 combatants, compared to 15,000 in the Salvadoran army, and confrontations between the two intensified.[30]

The Salvadoran civil war lasted for 12 years, from 1980 to 1992, during which an estimated 75,000 Salvadorans were killed. Hundreds of thousands were displaced internally, and over 1 million Salvadorans fled to other countries, including the United States.

Guatemala

Like El Salvador, Guatemala also experienced a violent and brutal civil war, although the roots of Guatemala's conflict rested largely in the aftermath of the 1954 CIA-backed overthrow of a freely elected reformist government. Also like El Salvador, Guatemala's economy was based on agriculture, although in this country foreign producers, in particular the United Fruit Company, would play a critical role in the development of the country's economics and politics.

The first major export crop in Guatemala was coffee, just as in El Salvador, and, in similar ways, its production quickly generated a small wealthy oligarchy, many of whose members retain economic and political power in the country today. Unlike in El Salvador, however, the financing, processing, and marketing of Guatemalan coffee was from the beginning in the hands of foreign investors, mostly Germans.[31] These foreign investors remained in control of the Guatemalan coffee market until the Second World War, when the US government forced the Guatemalan government to confiscate the German coffee holdings and to arrest German citizens. This allowed US companies to take control of the Guatemalan coffee industry.

Yet US companies had begun their involvement in the Guatemalan economy much earlier. The United Fruit Company entered the scene in 1904. At that time, the most popular fruit consumed in the United States was the apple. United Fruit set out to change that: it aimed to cultivate a type of banana which could be transported long distances and be available year-round throughout the United States. To do this, the company developed a new business model, one that included not only acquiring large amounts of cheap land and ensuring low-cost labor for production, but also developing the infrastructure – roads, railroads, ports, ships, telegraph, postal service, and utilities – which was necessary in order to carry the product to market. The company painted its ships in white in order to make them reflect the sun's heat (keeping the bananas cool), and named them "the Great White Fleet." In addition to transporting bananas, the ships became major carriers of the materials used to build the Panama Canal. They also carried passengers, mostly American tourists interested in visiting Central America, and US mail. Another aspect of the company's business strategy was that it always owned much more land than it had in cultivation at any one time. That way, if any natural disaster were to strike one area, the company could quickly put the fallow land into production and avoid potential economic losses.

United Fruit was active throughout Latin America, but was particularly influential in Guatemala. In 1904, Guatemalan dictator Estrada Cabrera granted United Fruit a 99-year tax-free concession to construct and maintain the country's main rail line from Guatemala City to Puerto

Barrios, which the company completed in 1906. In return for the rail line's completion, United Fruit received a contract for 170,000 acres of the country's best banana-producing land, located on Guatemala's Atlantic coast.[32] In addition to its railroad investments, United Fruit also purchased controlling shares in the country's utilities, ports, and telegraph services. The company created a new city called Bananera, where it established its headquarters. By the 1930s, United Fruit was the largest landowner, employer, and exporter in Guatemala. By 1944, it owned 42 percent of the country's land. The company owned all the country's ports and charged tariffs to Guatemalan exporters for their use. Because it played such a key role in the Guatemalan economy, the company was exempt from most taxes, import or export duties, and the government provided it with guarantees of low wages for its workers.[33] The company was also a main source of government revenue, which made it difficult for any Guatemalan government to favor policies not supported by the United Fruit Company.

On the political side, during the period immediately after independence, Guatemala was run by a series of dictators. Two of the most important were Manuel Estrada Cabrera, who ruled from 1898 to 1920, and General Jorge Ubico Castañeda, who ran the country from 1931 to 1944. Guatemala at this time was characterized by extreme inequality in terms of income and land distribution. The policies of the Ubico government only served to make that situation worse. Ubico passed harsh vagrancy laws, by which all Indians who owned little or no land were required to work for local landowners for at least 100 days a year. The landowners made the situation even more difficult for the Indians by agreeing among themselves not to compete for the labor force by offering higher wages. Additionally, Ubico made it legal for the landowners to murder stubborn or rebellious Indians. In 1944, he was faced with growing opposition, centered mainly in the country's university. The protesters, made up of a coalition of students, teachers, and professionals, held mass rallies in the capital. Guatemalan security forces, not sure how to respond, resorted to violence on the occasion of breaking up a women's protest. Many of the protesters were injured and one schoolteacher was killed. The army's actions only incensed the opposition, leading to a general strike. Ubico was forced to resign and was replaced by a military triumvirate. This group was quickly overthrown by a group of junior military officers led by Jacobo Arbenz and Francisco Araña. Their action is known as the "October Revolution."[34]

The young officers quickly stepped aside and allowed elections to be held, a first in Guatemala. Former Professor Juan José Arévalo was elected as the country's President by 85 percent of the voters (only literate males). Arévalo began a series of reforms, including dramatically increasing investment in the public schools; he passed labor rights legislation, ended the country's anti-vagrancy laws, and established a state bank designed to help small business owners to gain access to credit.[35] He oversaw the ratification of a new progressive Guatemalan Constitution in 1945. It is estimated that, between 1945 and 1950, industrial wages increased up to 80 percent.[36] The military and oligarchy were not idle during this period. Twenty-two *coups* were attempted during Arévalo's time in office, but none was successful.[37]

Yet, for any substantive change in the Guatemalan economy to be achieved, land reform was a necessity. In 1945, 2.2 percent of the country's population owned 70 percent of the arable land, but only 15 percent of that land was being cultivated. That meant that only 10 percent of the country's land was available for 90 percent of the population to cultivate. Arévalo's government proposed land reform as part of its agenda, but its actual implementation was left to his successor, Jacobo Arbenz. Arbenz, still popular because of his role in the October Revolution, won the 1950 elections in a landslide. He continued Arévalo's reform agenda, legalizing unions and political parties, and passing land-reform legislation. He began the construction of a public port on the Atlantic coast, the building of an east–west highway, and the expansion of public works.[38] He also passed the 1952 Agrarian Reform Law, which was meant to target uncultivated lands. The government would pay for the land in 25-year bonds bearing a 3 percent interest rate, and the price of the land would be based on its taxable worth as of May 1952. The law distributed 1.5 million acres to over 100,000 families. The expropriations included 1,700 acres of Arbenz's own land, which he had received from his wife.[39] All cultivated land, regardless of the size of the plantation, was exempt.

Since the law only applied to uncultivated land, it included a large portion of the property owned by United Fruit; 85 percent of United Fruit land at the time was uncultivated. As the single largest landowner in Guatemala, United Fruit possessed at that time more land than the combined holdings of 50 percent of the Guatemalan population.[40] Clearly, any attempt to reform the Guatemalan economy would lead to a direct confrontation with United Fruit. The law proposed to expropriate 387,000 acres of United Fruit's fallow land. The government offered to pay the company $1.2 million. That figure was based on United Fruit's own declaration of the land's value, which the company had used for tax purposes. Instead, United Fruit and the US State Department demanded that the Guatemalan government pay the company $16 million for the land.[41]

United Fruit sought additional help from the US government and tried to convince President Truman that the United States should overthrow the Arbenz regime. When the plan fell apart, the company hired a public relations firm to create the perception in the US popular press that the Arbenz regime was a communist front with links to the Soviet Union. In Guatemala, the land reform was strongly opposed by landowners and by the military, a situation leading to growing civil unrest. When the Eisenhower Administration took office in the United States, the United Fruit Company found the new regime much more sympathetic to its concerns. This was partly due to the fact that the company had important, high-level connections within the Eisenhower Administration. Secretary of State John Foster Dulles had been a senior partner at Sullivan and Cromwell, which was United Fruit's law firm and its principal source of advice on foreign affairs. His brother, Allen Dulles, the head of the CIA, served on United Fruit's board of directors. John Moors Cabot, the assistant Secretary of State for Inter-American Affairs, was the brother of Thomas Dudley Cabot, former President of United Fruit. Ed Whitman, the company's top public relations officer, was married to Ann Whitman, President Eisenhower's private secretary.[42] These connections meant United Fruit officials had the ear of very high-level US government officials and made the administration take the company's claims about the Arbenz regime more seriously. Those US officials with ties to United Fruit would become the key architects of the US plan to overthrow the regime.

In the face of growing US hostility, President Arbenz turned to the eastern-bloc countries to purchase arms to defend the country. This action was used by the United States as proof of his regime's ties to the Soviet bloc. Starting in 1953, the CIA began to plan a covert operation designed to topple the Arbenz government. The plan, called Operation PBSUCCESS, was to have the country invaded by a small group of Guatemalan exiles, led by ousted Colonel Carlos Castillo Armas and trained and equipped by the CIA. The United Fruit Company provided the rebel troops with a plantation in Honduras to conduct their training exercises and furnished the boats they used for the invasion.[43] The rebels were supported by a CIA-operated radio station which, falsely, announced large troop movements and the surrender of successive areas of Guatemala, and by a few Second World War fighter planes which were used to strafe Guatemala City. The planes also dropped pamphlets claiming rebel victory and urging the Guatemalan people to surrender. Duped into thinking that a large invading force was nearing the capital, Arbenz surrendered without a fight. The rebels rolled into Guatemala City practically unopposed.[44]

The *coup* marked the end of progressive reform in Guatemala. During and after the *coup*, 9,000 people were arrested and many were tortured. The agrarian reform was reversed, with over 1.5 million acres returned to large landowners, including United Fruit. The Castillo Armas government abolished unions and signed a mutual defense pact with the United States.[45] The main result of the *coup* was the elimination of the political center in Guatemala. Reform within the political system was now impossible. The country's governments from that point forward consisted of military dictatorships, each more repressive and brutal than the last. The country's economy remained in the hands of the wealthy oligarchy and those who paid the price were the country's indigenous majority.

About 60 percent of the Guatemalan population is of Maya origin, stemming from about 23 different Mayan ethnic groups. These people have been subject to officially sanctioned discrimination in Guatemala since the Spanish colonial period, but they maintain their language and many of their cultural practices. The remainder of the Guatemalan population consists of *ladinos*: individuals of Spanish origin, or with a mixture of Spanish and indigenous backgrounds. Most of the Maya population did not have access to education, electricity, running water, sanitation, or other forms of basic infrastructure. As a result, in the 1960s only 19 percent of Maya were literate, compared to over 50 percent of the rest of the population. Infant mortality among the Maya was also very high: 134 per 1,000 live births, compared to 80 per 1,000 among *ladinos*. Not surprisingly, the life expectancy of the Maya was also low – 16 years lower than for *ladinos*.[46] Because of the land concentration policies mentioned above, most of the Maya were landless, being forced to work on plantations focused on export agriculture. The largest part of the population had to work for less than 2 dollars a day, with no right to organize or to protest against their working conditions. Half the population survived on only about half of the calories needed on a daily basis to avoid malnutrition.[47] Any attempts at unionization were repressed with extreme violence.[48]

With reform within the political process closed off after 1954, the Guatemalan opposition turned to armed revolt. The various guerrilla groups operated independently through the 1960s and 1970s, and then in 1982 the four largest groups joined to form the Guatemalan National Revolutionary Unity (URNG). Their platform included support for agrarian reform and price controls, equality between the Maya and the *ladinos*, democracy and respect for civil liberties.[49] Starting in the 1960s, the Guatemalan army organized an offensive in response and received significant assistance from the United States. The Pentagon established a counterinsurgency base in the Guatemalan highlands and brought in 1,000 US Special Forces troops to train the Guatemalan army in counterinsurgency. The campaign used aerial bombings of the countryside and burned villages suspected of supporting the guerrilla rebels.[50] With the encouragement of US army officers, the Guatemalan army and landowners also created death squads during this period, to root out the "subversives."[51] These squads included groups such as MANO (the National Organized Action Movement), also known as *Mano Blanca* (the White Hand) because of its logo; NOA (the New Anti-Communist Organization); CADEG (the Anti-Communist Council of Guatemala); *Ojo por Ojo* (the Eye for an Eye); *Jaguar Justiciero* (Jaguar of Justice); and ESA (the Secret Anti-Communist Army). These were the transient names of the clandestine military units whose purpose was to eliminate the alleged members, allies, or collaborators of "subversion."

Assuming that the indigenous population was a probable source of support for the guerrillas, the army moved into the countryside, targeting indigenous communities with brutal repression. Between 1966 and 1976, 50,000 people were murdered, and tens of thousands more were subjected to arrest and torture.[52] A good example of the attitude of the Guatemalan military leadership at the time is Colonel Carlos Arana Osorio, who earned the nickname of "Butcher of Zacapa" after the massacres of *campesinos* (peasants) which took place during his 1966–8 counterinsurgency campaign. Arana, who became President in 1970, is reported to have said: "If it is necessary to turn the country into a cemetery in order to pacify it, I will not hesitate to do so."[53] According to Amnesty International, even after the guerrillas were crushed, the military continued to engage in killings for purposes of general intimidation.[54]

It is difficult to overstate the sheer brutality of what occurred in Guatemala during almost four decades of civil war. The army worked methodically across the Maya region, attacking over 600 villages and forcibly conscripting many of the youths. These atrocities were documented by Guatemala's Commission for Historical Clarification in 1999. In its final report, the commission noted:

Particularly serious cruelty in many acts committed by agents of the State, especially members of the Army, in their operations against Mayan communities. The counterinsurgency strategy not only led to violations of basic human rights, but also to the fact that these crimes were committed with particular cruelty, with massacres representing their archetypal form. In the majority of massacres there is evidence of multiple acts of savagery, which preceded, accompanied or occurred after the deaths of the victims. Acts such as the killing of defenceless children, often by beating them against walls or throwing them alive into pits where the corpses of adults were later thrown; the amputation of limbs; the impaling of victims; the killing of persons by covering them in petrol and burning them alive; the extraction, in the presence of others, of the viscera of victims who were still alive; the confinement of people who had been mortally tortured, in agony for days; the opening of the wombs of pregnant women, and other similarly atrocious acts, were not only actions of extreme cruelty against the victims, but also morally degraded the perpetrators and those who inspired, ordered or tolerated these actions. During the armed confrontation the cultural rights of the Mayan people were also violated. The Army destroyed ceremonial centres, sacred places and cultural symbols. Language and dress, as well as other elements of cultural identification, were targets of repression.[55]

The army targeted these villages because the inhabitants were Maya, which led many in the human rights community to describe what happened in Guatemala as genocide. The Commission for Historical Clarification report concluded that

the reiteration of destructive acts, directed systematically against groups of the Mayan population, within which can be mentioned the elimination of leaders and criminal acts against minors who could not possibly have been military targets, demonstrates that the only common denominator for all the victims was the fact that they belonged to a specific ethnic group and makes it evident that these acts were committed "with intent to destroy, in whole or in part" these groups,

making it, in fact, a case of genocide. After murdering the villagers, the army employed a "scorched earth" policy, which including destroying the buildings and crops, fouling the water supply, slaughtering all livestock, and desecrating all sacred cultural sites and symbols.[56]

The violence in Guatemala was so great that, during the 1980s, Mexican *campesinos* in Chiapas reported that the rivers from Guatemala contained so many corpses that it was impossible to bury them all. During this period, the smell of burning and rotting corpses was a permanent fact of life along the Mexico–Guatemala border.[57] In the end, the Commission for Historical Clarification determined that over 200,000 persons were killed or disappeared during Guatemala's civil war: 83 percent of the identified victims were Maya and 17 percent were *ladino*. The commission found that the Guatemalan army and death squads committed 93 percent of the atrocities; the guerrillas were responsible for 3 percent.[58] The report also showed that US officials in Guatemala and Washington, DC, were well aware of the occurrence of these atrocities, and in fact "lent direct and indirect support to some illegal state operations."

Those Maya who survived the massacres were forcibly moved to live in "model villages" organized by the Guatemalan government. In these villages, their activities were strictly monitored. They were allowed to speak only Spanish and were discouraged from practicing Catholicism or any sort of indigenous religious ritual. They were encouraged instead to engage in a form of evangelical Protestantism which emphasized subservience to authority. While living in the villages, the Maya were forced to assist with public works projects which often involved rebuilding the very structures the army had recently destroyed.[59] This upheaval in the countryside led to significant internal displacement – an estimated 750,000 Guatemalans had to flee their homes. Another quarter of a million are estimated to have fled the country.[60]

Salvadoran and Guatemalan Migration

By the late 1970s, then, both El Salvador and Guatemala were in the throes of civil war and were the sites of extreme violence. This situation led to both economic and political dislocations. Many fled their country of origin because of political repression, but also because the civil unrest made it impossible for them to survive in their homelands. Historically, there had always been migration between the countries of Central America. In particular, there had continually been a large number of Salvadoran migrant workers in Honduras. In addition, the Mayan communities of Guatemala had maintained ties with Mayan communities in Mexico, particularly in Chiapas, and had worked there as seasonal labor. As these groups found themselves displaced, they followed these established social networks to settle in those areas. Due to the scale of the new migration and refugee crisis, however, the Mexican and Honduran communities were quickly overwhelmed, and the migrants were compelled to choose less traditional destinations.

One of the most popular new destinations was the United States. Although there had been small Central American populations living in cities like San Francisco, Washington, DC, Miami, Los Angeles, Houston, and New York during much of the twentieth century, large-scale Central American migration to the United States did not begin until the 1970s. According to the 1980 census, 94,447 Salvadorans and 63,073

Guatemalans were living in the United States, and about half of these had arrived within the previous five years.[61] Many of the new arrivals settled in those areas where friends, family, or other network members were living. In California, most Central Americans had migrated to San Francisco during the 1940s and 1950s; but some went to southern California as part of the *Bracero* Program, in which they participated by convincing program officials that they were Mexican.[62] During the 1970s, the size of this small community mushroomed, and Los Angeles became the settlement area of choice for the vast majority of Salvadoran and Guatemalan immigrants to the United States.[63]

Some Central American migrants arrived in the United States on student or tourist visas and simply remained after these permits expired. The vast majority entered the United States illegally, by crossing the US–Mexico border. Starting in the late 1970s, the US Border Patrol began reporting the detention of growing numbers of OTMs (other than Mexicans). These Central American migrants posed a legal dilemma for the Reagan Administration. Although not every migrant had experienced violence directly, it was the growing violence and instability in their countries that had pushed them to migrate. So were they to be considered economic migrants or political refugees? The Reagan Administration, for largely political reasons, insisted that they were economic migrants.

When Reagan won the presidency in 1980, he did so on a strongly anti-communist platform. The leftist Sandinista revolution had just occurred in Nicaragua, and Reagan made it a key focus of his Administration's foreign policy to keep communism from spreading in Central America. Reagan argued: "The national security of all Americans is at stake in Central America. If we cannot defend ourselves here, we cannot expect to prevail elsewhere."[64] The administration dramatically increased its military and economic assistance to the region. This assistance consisted of three main parts: (1) counterinsurgency training for the region's police and military; (2) increased aid for the armed forces; and (3) military and civic action programs coordinated with US economic aid.[65] The aid to El Salvador increased initially under President Jimmy Carter and this expansion accelerated under Reagan. Throughout the 1980s, El Salvador was one of the top five recipients of US military aid. In total, the United States provided $6 billion in economic and military aid to El Salvador during its 12-year civil war.[66] Given the country's estimated population of about 2.5 million people in 1980, this sum is the equivalent of $2,400 for each Salvadoran individual. US economic and military aid to Guatemala was not at the same level, with direct military aid there during the 1980s totaling only $30 million. Most of the aid to Guatemala was in the form of training military personnel, which was conducted in Guatemala, in the United States' School of the Americas located in Panamá, or on bases in the United States. Some of the most notorious human rights abusers – including Generals Castillo Armas and Ríos Montt in Guatemala and General Humberto Romero in El Salvador – received US counterinsurgency training.[67] Over one-third of the graduates of the School of the Americas came from Central America. Under Reagan, enrollment in the school, and in particular the number of Salvadoran officers receiving training there, increased dramatically.[68]

Thus the Reagan Administration had important political reasons to deny the violence and repression that characterized the Salvadoran and Guatemalan regimes. After the high-profile murders of Archbishop Romero and the US nuns, the US Congress began demanding that the administration show improvements in the Salvadoran human rights situation before approving aid. Because of this, the Reagan Administration spent much of the 1980s downplaying the atrocities carried out by these regimes, and also implying that the victims were not so "innocent." For example, when discussing the four US churchwomen who had been raped and murdered in El Salvador, UN Ambassador Jeane Kirkpatrick claimed that the women may have run a roadblock, and that, in any case, "The nuns were not just nuns" – they were also "political activists on behalf of the *Frente* [the Democratic Revolutionary Front]."[69] Any political violence acknowledged by the administration was presented as the product of the left.[71] As one US diplomat who served during the Reagan Administration put it: "Unless they [administration officials] see a guy like D'Aubuisson running a machete through somebody, they're inclined to ignore it . . . There is absolutely zero conception of what these people are really like, how evil they really are."[71]

Given the Reagan Administration's unwillingness to acknowledge the repression occurring in El Salvador and Guatemala, it is not surprising that it also refused to define Salvadoran and Guatemalan migrants as political refugees eligible for asylum. To do so would have undermined its support of these regimes and would have required the US to provide assistance and benefits to the hundreds of thousands of migrants who arrived in the United States from these two countries during the 1980s. Instead, Salvadoran and Guatemalan migrants spent much of the decade in a political limbo, many being forcibly deported to their country of origin (and subsequently tortured and killed). To support its arguments against refugee status, the Reagan Administration pointed out that

Plate 7.1 *Luisa Moreno.*
Source: courtesy of Vicki L. Ruiz.

Luisa Moreno: from Privileged Daughter to Transcontinental Union Organizer

Luisa Moreno's story reflects the longstanding presence of Central American immigrants in the United States.[72] Born Blanca Rosa Rodríguez López on August 30, 1907, Moreno was the daughter of a wealthy Guatemalan family. As an adolescent in Guatemala, Moreno organized a group of elite women to push the government to allow women to attend college; she was successful. Instead of enrolling, however, Moreno decided to leave Guatemala for Mexico City, where she wrote poetry and became part of the social circle of artists Diego Rivera and Frida Kahlo. After marrying and giving birth to a daughter, she moved to New York City. She and her husband had difficulty finding work; Moreno ended up working long hours in a sweatshop to support her family. In New York, her radicalizing moment was arriving with a co-worker at her home and discovering that a rat had eaten off half of her friend's baby's face; the baby died shortly thereafter. In later writings, Moreno said that was the moment she knew she had to do something to improve her fellow workers' material conditions. She joined the Communist Party (CP) in 1930 and began to mobilize workers on the shop floor. She became a full-time organizer with the International Ladies Garment Workers Union (ILGWU) and then moved to Florida to organize Latino, African American, and Italian cigar rollers for the American Federation of Labor (AFL). It was in Florida that she changed her name to Luisa Moreno, choosing Moreno (or "dark") – the opposite of her given name Blanca (or "light") – a move historian Vicki Ruiz argues reflected her identification with working-class people of color, rather than the light-skinned elite world that she came from. Unhappy with how the AFL supported the needs of workers of color, she resigned from the Federation in 1937 to join the newly established Congress of Industrial Organizations (CIO). She joined a small branch of the CIO – the United Cannery, Agricultural, Packing, and Allied Workers of America (UCAPAWA), where she would remain for the rest of her career. She was elected Vice-President of UCAPAWA in 1941, making her the first Latina to be elected to a national high-ranking union post. With UCAPAWA, she organized pecan shellers in San Antonio, Texas, Mexican migrant workers in Texas' Río Grande Valley, southern California cannery workers, and started a school for beet workers in Colorado. Along the way, she helped to organize *El Congreso de Pueblos de Habla Española*, held in Los Angeles in 1939 (see chapter 3). In addition to its liberal stances on immigration and social issues, the Los Angeles chapters of *El Congreso* created a women's committee and women's platform to bring attention to the "double discrimination" faced by Mexican American women in the United States. She continued to organize, rising to the state leadership of the CIO. In 1948, she was subpoenaed by the California State Senate Committee on Un-American Activities, headed by Jack B. Tenney, which accused her of communist subversion. The transcript of her questioning before the committee was sent to the INS (the Immigration and Naturalization Service), where her citizenship application was pending. The INS ordered her deportation. The FBI offered Moreno citizenship in exchange for her testimony against legendary longshoreman union leader Harry Bridges; she refused. Saying she did not want to be "a free woman with a mortgaged soul," Moreno left the United States in 1950. Her exit was defined by the US government as "voluntary departure under warrant of deportation," on the grounds that she had once been a member of the Communist Party. She never entered the United States again and died in Guatemala on November 4, 1992.

Central American migrants most often traveled through Mexico, a country which did not persecute the refugees and allowed them to settle. Since the migrants continued on to the United States, the logic ran, they clearly were traveling farther north for economic opportunities, rather than simply to escape political persecution and violence.

As a result of this policy, fewer than 5 percent of the Central American petitions for asylum were approved, and, unlike in the Cuban case, the government provided no assistance to facilitate their settlement in the

United States.[73] In 1981, the United Nations High Commissioner for Refugees (UNHCR) criticized US policy, arguing that the United States was not living up to its international responsibilities. As a signatory to the UN Protocol on refugees, the United States had agreed not to force the return of refugees to their home country. According to the UNHCR, "the United States had failed to grant asylum to any significant number of Salvadorans and was engaged in a 'systematic practice' of deporting Salvadorans to their country regardless of the merits of their claims of asylum."[74] The UNHCR urged the United States at least to grant the refugees temporary status, thus allowing them to avoid deportation. US immigration law did include such a category, called Extended Voluntary Departure (EVD). The application of this status is under State Department discretion, and is implemented when an administration determines that conditions in the home country make it unsafe to send migrants home. The Reagan Administration refused to acknowledge that those conditions existed in Central America, and also balked at the prospect of granting this status to Salvadoran and Guatemalan migrants given the sheer scope of the migration – already estimated by 1983 to have reached over half a million people.[75] The Administration worried that granting EVD to the refugees already on US territory would only encourage more migration. Thus, from 1983 to 1990, only 2.6 percent of Salvadoran asylum applicants were successful, and only 1.8 percent of those from Guatemala.[76]

The Central American Peace and Solidarity Movement

Yet these Central American migrants, despite their uncertain legal status in the United States, did not accept their situation quietly. Over the course of the 1980s, these refugees, along with actors still in Central America and progressive groups within the United States, would build a transnational social movement, which became known as the Central American Peace and Solidarity Movement (CAPSM), and would challenge Reagan's foreign policy toward the region, pushing the administration to provide some regularization of their migration status.

Within the Salvadoran community, the movement began with exiles organizing themselves so as to call attention to the situation at home. The first such effort occurred in San Francisco in 1975, when a group called El Comité de Salvadoreños Progresistas (the Committee of Progressive Salvadorans) was formed in response to the July 1975 government massacre of protesting students from the National University in San Salvador. The group organized the first march in the United States ever to denounce human rights violations on the part of the Salvadoran government.[77] Within a year, the group had established connections with student organizations in El Salvador, which sent them news, updates, and bulletins on a regular basis. The *Salvadoreños Progresistas* used this information to publish a newspaper called *El Pulgarcito* (Tom Thumb), which they used to inform Salvadorans and Americans about the situation in El Salvador. By 1978, the group had grown large enough to occupy the Salvadoran consulate in order to protest against and draw attention to the growing number of disappearances in El Salvador.[78]

The most successful and influential of the CAPSM groups was the Committee in Solidarity with the People of El Salvador (CISPES), founded in 1980. From its inception, CISPES included members of the Salvadoran exile community and home-country activists with links to the popular movement in El Salvador. Just prior to its founding, a few key activists had met with the newly formed Democratic Revolutionary Front and agreed to help to initiate a US-based solidarity effort.[79] The hope was that the US solidarity groups would help in fomenting US popular opposition to the US military aid and intervention in support of the Salvadoran regime. CISPES' strategy for creating this opposition was to bring attention to the situation on the ground in El Salvador. To do so, they relied on a network of home-country activists and grassroots organizations which coordinated visits of American journalists, human rights workers, and church workers to the region and provided the visitors with first-hand accounts and other evidence of their claims of human rights abuses. Similarly, CISPES coordinated the travel of Salvadoran witnesses to the United States, so that these could speak directly to American audiences about their experiences of death squad activity and government repression.[80] This direct contact with the victims of government abuses helped to raise the profile of the situation in El Salvador among the general US population.

These visits, both in Central America and in the United States, received coverage in the US mainstream media, which resulted in increasing pressure on the Reagan Administration to change US policy toward the region. At the start of the 1980s, few Americans were aware of what was happening in Central America. By the end of the same decade, thanks largely to this political strategy, the situation had transformed significantly. Changing US foreign policy in Central America had become one of the main political goals of US progressives and was part of US political discourse. This being said, the movement was not successful in stopping US funding to El Salvador and Guatemala. The movement did succeed in cutting off funding to the *Contra* rebels in Nicaragua, which occurred in 1982, with the unanimous passage of the Boland Amendment in Congress. It was this refusal of funding by the US Congress that led to the Iran *Contra* affair. The Reagan Administration, unwilling to stop its *Contra* support, covertly sold arms to Iran in order to raise the funds needed. This became one of the biggest political scandals of the decade, and ten administration officials were found guilty for their participation in the subterfuge. Later in the decade, Congress resumed funding to the *Contras*.

But what the CAPSM movement did achieve was the creation of a narrative about what was happening in Central America which was very different from the one espoused by the Reagan Administration. The movement managed to make Central American funding highly controversial and pushed Congress to require the administration to prove that these regimes were making progress on human rights. American presidents have the greatest amount of power in foreign policy, and during the Cold War the tendency was to defer to the commander-in-chief on issues seen as being related to national security. In the case of Central America, CAPSM activities ensured at least that Reagan was not given a blank check and that the atrocities committed in the region were brought to the attention of US lawmakers and of the American public.

In addition to focusing on foreign policy issues, CAPSM worked toward having a positive impact on the political status of Central American refugees in the United States. An important nationwide US-based CAPSM organization which focused on these issues was the Salvadoran Humanitarian Aid, Relief, and Education Foundation (SHARE), created in 1981. SHARE worked directly with the mainstream US religious community to provide assistance and support for the growing refugee population in the United States.[81] The organization "served as an ecumenical clearinghouse of information and coordination, linking US parishes with Salvadoran parishes and communities, especially those devastated or displaced by the war."[82] SHARE's goal was to help to repopulate and restore the war zones. To do so, groups of US activists would travel to El Salvador and act as human shields, literally walking with their Salvadoran counterparts to help them to begin the rebuilding process.[83]

Many of the parishes affiliated with SHARE were also instrumental in the creation of the sanctuary movement, in which Salvadoran exiles also played a key role. Initially, Salvadoran migrants were taken in by their kinship networks and assisted to integrate into life in the United

States. But, given the scope of the migration, the activists quickly real-ized that they needed additional assistance in addressing their compatri-ots' needs. As a result, a number of the immigrant-based organizations which had been striving to stop the war in El Salvador created special branches to deal exclusively with the refugee crisis. One such group was the Central American Refugee Center (CARECEN), now called the Central American Resource Center, with offices in Los Angeles, San Francisco, and Washington, DC. CARECEN was founded in 1983 by a group of Central American refugees in order to help their compatriots to achieve legal status in the United States. CARECEN provided free legal aid to refu-gees, engaged in community education, and coordinated with the other CAPSM groups to lobby the US Congress to address the migration-status issues facing Central American migrants. Today CARECEN continues to lobby Congress on behalf of Central American refugees and to provide legal and educational services to the community.

These organizations would end up building a multinational move-ment which involved thousands of individuals across nations and religions in providing sanctuary to Central American refugees. These participants engaged in civil disobedience – by transporting, harbour-ing, and assisting refugees – in order to protest against the inhuman-ity of US foreign policy.[84] The sanctuary movement began officially in 1982, when a church in Tucson, Arizona, and five churches in Berkeley, California, agreed to make a public declaration that they would provide sanctuary to Central American refugees. In an open letter to the US Attorney General, they stated:

> We take this action because we believe the current policy and practice of the US government with regard to Central American refugees is illegal and immoral. We believe our government is in violation of the 1980 Refugee Act and international law by continuing to arrest, detain, and forcibly return refugees to terror, persecu-tion, and murder in El Salvador and Guatemala.[85]

Modeling themselves after the underground railroad, sanctuary activ-ists facilitated the transportation of migrants from Central America, provided them with housing and financial assistance, and facilitated their establishment in the United States or their settlement in Canada, which had a more liberal refugee policy. At its height, the movement included over 400 churches, temples, and synagogues in the United States, who coordinated with religious and activist organizations in Central America, Mexico, the United States, and Canada in order to accomplish their work.[86]

The Reagan Administration was strongly opposed to the movement's work, and the Justice Department emphasized that anyone participating in it would be prosecuted to the full extent of the law. A number of sanctuary workers were arrested and tried. The most high-profile prosecution was that of 16 activists in Tucson, Arizona, who were charged with 71 counts of conspiracy and harboring illegal aliens. In 1984 and 1985, the FBI used four informants to infiltrate the church and to record meetings and conversations over a 10-month period. The FBI codenamed the effort "Operation Sojourner." On the basis of the FBI's findings, the US government brought charges against the 16 sanctuary movement activists. Of these, 8 were found guilty and were given suspended sentences of 3 to 5 years' probation. The Justice Department claimed victory, yet from a public relations standpoint the prosecutions largely backfired. The trial was covered by national news agencies and by international networks such as the BBC. Dozens of magazines and newspapers reported the stories, and much of the coverage was highly sympathetic to the refugees' plight and supportive of the sanctuary movement's work. One editorial cartoon even showed the Border Patrol arresting Jesus Christ and his apostles.[87]

Many people credit this publicity with invigorating and expanding the sanctuary movement. By 1987 the movement comprised 450 sanctuaries, spread over 28 cities which had pronounced themselves officially sanctuaries for refugees. Some 430 distinct religious bodies, located in 39 states, had joined the movement, along with over 70,000 active participants.[88] Although the sanctuary movement did not provide direct assistance to the vast majority of Central American refugees, it did raise public awareness about the migration status of these individuals and pushed the US public and the US Congress to consider the moral implications of US foreign policy toward the region and of US policies toward the migrants. The result was the securing of some regularization of the migration status of Salvadoran and Guatemalan immigrants.

Salvadorans, Guatemalans, and US Immigration Policy

Most Central American migrants who arrived before 1990 entered the United States without documentation. Central American activists and their allies continually objected to this state of affairs. In response to the 1985 arrest of the Tucson sanctuary workers, a group of 80 churches and refugee assistance groups sued the American government, arguing that the government was discriminating against Salvadoran and Guatemalan asylum applicants.[89] The case, *American Baptist Churches in the USA, et al. v. Edwin Meese III and Alan Nelson*, combined two plaintiffs' suits. The first group was made up of sanctuary workers who sought an injunction against government interference in their sanctuary work, which they argued was protected by the First Amendment. The second group was a set of refugee assistance organizations which wanted an injunction against deportations of Salvadorans and Guatemalans and a declaratory judgment that they would be granted temporary status until the situations in their home countries improved sufficiently for them to return home.[90] The US government moved that the suit be dismissed, but the court disagreed and the suit was allowed to move forward; it became known as the *ABC* lawsuit. The plaintiffs reached a settlement with the US government in 1991. The settlement required that: (1) Salvadorans and Guatemalans still in the United States, whether they had applied for political asylum previously or not, would be given a new adjudication process, which was to be examined by a newly trained set of asylum officers; (2) petitioners would be provided with work authorization while they waited for their cases to be resolved; and (3) asylum officers would not be allowed to consider past denials of asylum in their deliberations, nor the petitioners' country of origin, nor the State Department's opinions or recommendations. Asylum officers were, however, allowed to consider human rights reports from non-governmental agencies such as Amnesty International.[91] As a result of this settlement, 150,000 asylum refusals were overturned and new trials were granted to Salvadorans who had entered the United States before September 19, 1990 and to Guatemalans who had entered before October 1, 1990.[92] This settlement was a major victory for Central American immigrants and activists.

Another legal change to affect the migration status of Central Americans in the United States was the 1986 passage of the Immigration Reform and Control Act (IRCA). Intended to address the problem of unauthorized migration, this law allowed for individuals who were present in the United States without documentation, but who could prove they had entered the country prior to January 1, 1982, to regularize their status. As a consequence of this law, 227,642 Central Americans were able to regularize their status, 60 percent of whom were Salvadoran and 25 percent of whom were Guatemalan.[93] Unfortunately, since most Central American refugees arrived in the United States after 1982, they did not fall under the IRCA amnesty.

In 1990 Congress engaged in another immigration reform which created a new category: Temporary Protected Status (TPS).[94] TPS was intended to apply to aliens in the United States who are temporarily unable to return safely to their home country because of ongoing armed conflict, an environmental disaster, or other extraordinary and temporary conditions. Salvadorans were the first group designated to be eligible for this status, which was scheduled to expire in 1992. Over 200,000 Salvadorans living in the United States registered for TPS.[95] As their TPS was about to expire, a new status, Deferred Enforced Departure (DED), was created, which delayed their deportation for another year. The Salvadorans' DED was extended twice more, until March 1996. Salvadorans who were covered under the *ABC* lawsuit could then apply for asylum after their DED expired. Thus, over the course of the 1990s, Congress passed a number of laws designed to deal with the Central American migration in a piecemeal fashion. In 1996, Congress passed the Illegal Immigration Reform and Immigrant Responsibility Act (IIRIRA), which, among other things, removed many of the potential remedies which would have been available to members of the ABC class in the event that their asylum petitions were denied. Central American activists protested vehemently, and this led to the 1997 passage of the Nicaraguan and Central American Relief Act (NACARA), which gave some Nicaraguans a preferential migration status much like that of Cubans. Salvadorans and Guatemalans under the Act are permitted to apply for US residency under the pre-IIRIRA terms.[96] Yet their petitions would be adjudicated on a case-by-case basis, with no guarantee of success.

The result of these legal changes was that many Central Americans were able to regularize their status and become legal permanent residents in the United States. This being said, today many Salvadoran and Guatemalan immigrants remain in a legal limbo, waiting for the final resolution of their cases. As an example, in May 2013, the US Citizenship and Immigration Services (USCIS) announced another extension of TPS for Salvadorans, which will last through 2015 (Guatemala is no longer a designated TPS country). The Migration Policy Institute estimated that just over 300,000 Central Americans were in the United States under TPS in 2011.[97] Yet at the start of the 1980s, few observers would have thought that the US government would address their concerns at all. This group of political refugees, made up of non-citizens, many of whom did not have legal status, was able to help to create a multinational social movement which not only restricted the US government's foreign policy activities in their home countries but also moved the US Congress to attempt to address their migration status. As political scientist Hector Perla points out, these Central American activists "relied on symbolic politics that used personal testimonies, stories, revolutionary and religious narratives, movies, art, posters, poetry, and music to frame their plight in a viscerally tangible way for North American audiences."[98] That strategy was successful and allowed them, together with their allies, to change US policies in very important ways.

Traditional Political Engagement

Since their arrival in the United States, much of Central American immigrants' political activism has been focused on ending the wars in their home countries and on regularizing their status in the United States. In this process, Central Americans have formed a variety of organizations, such as CARECEN, the Salvadoran Leadership and Education Fund (SALEF), and the Salvadoran American National Association (SANA), among others. Like Mexican Americans and Dominican Americans, Central Americans also participate in a growing number of hometown associations (HTAs) which provide charitable aid and investments in their communities of origin. It is estimated that there are about 164 Guatemalan HTAs in the United States, most of which have been focused on responding to the many natural disasters that have hit Guatemala since 1991. There are an estimated 200 Salvadoran HTAs.[99] Most focus on assisting one town and hold dinners, pageants, and other events to raise funds for community-based development projects. Scholars argue that HTAs are important not only because of their contributions to local development but also because they help to foster and support positive ethnoracial identities within immigrant communities in the United States.

In terms of electoral participation, because it took so many years to address their legal status, it is only recently that large numbers of Central Americans have begun to naturalize. This helps to explain why, as we saw in chapter 2, more than three-quarters of foreign-born Salvadorans and Guatemalans are not US citizens. It is likely that, as their legal situation normalizes, more Central Americans will choose to naturalize, which is the first step toward engaging in US electoral politics. Given the high level of activism already in the community, it seems likely that, once they naturalize, their formal participation levels will be high as well. This can already be seen among elected officials, a growing proportion of which are of Central American origin, including Salvadorans Walter Tejada, Chair of the Arlington County Board in Virginia, and Ana Sol Gutiérrez and Victor Ramírez, both of whom serve in county-level government in Maryland. Liz Figueroa, a former Democratic California state senator, is of Salvadoran origin. Norma Torres, a Democratic member of the California State Senate, is of Guatemalan origin. At the national level, former US Labor Secretary and US congressperson Hilda Solís is half Nicaraguan.

Conclusion

Salvadorans and Guatemalans comprise a growing and important segment of the Latino population in the United States. Their journeys to the United States have been strongly influenced by the role the US government played in their countries' political and economic development. The key role which Central America was seen as playing in the Cold War was also important and affected the ability of reformist political movements to address the extreme economic and political inequality present in both countries. As a result, both countries experienced extremely violent civil wars. These structural factors had an important impact on Salvadoran and Guatemalan immigrants' decision to leave their home countries and on the legal status they were granted when they arrived in the United States.

Despite the end of the civil wars in both countries, many of the political and economic problems that drove these groups' migration persist. Paramilitary groups continue to operate in both countries, and there continue to be important human rights violations. Since the 1992 peace accord was signed, the two main political parties in El Salvador are the conservative Alianza Republicana Nacionalista (ARENA) and the liberal FMLN. The FMLN currently holds power in El Salvador and has been working to reform the country's economic structures. But El Salvador still faces significant economic and political challenges. Similarly, Guatemala's guerrilla forces and government signed peace accords in 1996. Since then, the country has held four consecutive democratic elections, a first in its history. There are many political parties; no party has won the presidency more than once since 1996. The current President, Otto Pérez Molina, is a former military officer who has been accused of human rights abuses during the civil war. His is not an isolated case. After the 1999 UN Commission for Historical Clarification report found widespread human rights abuses by the military during the civil war, few of the perpetrators were brought to justice. That changed in May 2013 when former General Efraín Ríos Montt was found guilty of genocide and crimes against humanity by a panel of three Guatemalan judges. A week later, the Guatemala Supreme Court of Justice overturned the ruling, citing technical problems with how the trial was carried out. Ríos Montt's fate remains unclear, but the fact that he was brought to trial was a surprise to many human rights advocates. The controversy over his conviction, however, shows that Guatemalan society is still coming to terms with its bloody and violent political history.

Economic inequality remains a significant problem in both countries, and it has only been exacerbated by the neo-liberal economic restructuring which intensified under the Central American Free Trade Agreement with the United States. In response, as we saw in the Mexican case, Central American migrants play an important role in the economic development of their home countries through the provision of remittances. In 2011, Salvadorans sent almost $4 billion in remittances to El Salvador, which the World Bank estimates constitutes about 16 percent of the country's GDP.[100] It is estimated that over one-fifth of Salvadoran families receive remittances from their relatives in the United States. This is one of the country's largest sources of hard currency. Similarly, in 2011 Guatemalan emigrants sent over $4.9 billion home in remittances. This is the equivalent of about 10 percent of the country's GDP. Given the current political and economic pressures, it is unlikely that Central American migration patterns to the United States will change in the near term and likely that Central American immigrants in the United States will continue to play a positive role in their home countries' economic development.

But the Central American story is not solely about structural limitations. These migrants, despite their poverty and uncertain legal status, were able to help to organize a unique, transnational social movement which would not only change their situation in the United States, but also influence international public sentiment toward what was occurring in their countries of origin. From this point forward, human rights would become an important consideration in evaluating US activity abroad. Central American activism helped to change the structural situation faced by new migrants who arrived in the United States later in the 1980s, and shows that minority groups without voting rights can still influence the US political system in important ways.

Yet the movement's aspirations have not been fully realized. Many Central Americans in the United States remain in a legal limbo, under threat of deportation. Their countries of origin continue to struggle economically and politically, which makes it difficult for them to integrate these potential returnees back into their homelands. And Central

American communities in the United States continue to face poverty, lack of access to education, and discrimination. Resolving these issues will continue to be the focus of Central American social service organizations and political organizing for the foreseeable future.

QUESTIONS FOR DISCUSSION

1 Why did the economic and political problems in El Salvador and Guatemala result in civil wars?
2 What role did the United States play in the civil wars in El Salvador and Guatemala?
3 Why was the US government unwilling to grant political asylum to refugees from El Salvador and Guatemala?
4 What is CAPSM and what makes it a unique political movement?
5 What is the current legal status of many Central American migrants living in the United States? How does their legal status affect their political incorporation?

GUIDE TO FURTHER READINGS

Coutin, Susan Bibler. 2003. *Legalizing Moves: Salvadoran Immigrants' Struggle for US Residency*. Ann Arbor: University of Michigan Press.
García, María Cristina. 2006. *Seeking Refuge: Central American Migration to Mexico, the United States, and Canada*. Berkeley: University of California Press.
Hamilton, Nora, and Norma Stoltz Chinchilla. 2001. *Seeking Community in a Global City: Guatemalans and Salvadorans in Los Angeles*. Philadelphia: Temple University Press.
Perla, Hector. 2008. "*Si Nicaragua Venció, El Salvador Vencerá*: Central American Agency in the Creation of the US–Central American Peace and Solidarity Movement," *Latin American Research Review*, 43 (2): 136–58.

CHAPTER EIGHT

Conclusion:
Context and Latino Migration
and Mobilization

Objectives

- Understand what unauthorized migration is, its causes, and why it is an important issue for Latinos in the United States
- Understand the structural factors that generated the 2006 immigration marches
- Understand the racialized attitudes underlying the anti-immigrant movement in the United States
- Understand the broader context framing the political engagement of all Latino national-origin groups

Introduction

We have seen that the different national-origin Latino groups discussed in this volume have engaged in a variety of political activities in order to address their social, economic, and political concerns. Mexican Americans created social service organizations, engaged in labor organizing, brought legal challenges to segregation, and fomented a mass political movement. Similarly, Puerto Ricans engaged in New York City politics, formed organizations to support community needs, and used non-traditional methods to get local, state, and national officials to pay greater attention to the status of Puerto Rico and of Puerto Ricans living in the United States. Cubans developed a shared political identity which allowed them to achieve political and economic success and to ensure the successful integration of subsequent waves of Cuban migrants. Dominicans established a robust organizational life in New York City and have engaged in transnational political activity since the 1970s. Central American refugees formed a transnational political movement which curtailed US foreign policy activity and regularized the migration status of millions of Central American migrants. We have seen that the tactics and effectiveness of each group have been affected by their time of migration, geographic location, and the opportunity structures available to them within those contexts. We have also seen the important ways in which US immigration policy affects the reception and incorporation of Latino migrants to the United States. The 2006 wave of Latino pro-immigrant mobilization provides yet another example of this kind of political engagement in response to government policies affecting Latinos' migration status. Yet this mobilization should not be understood in isolation, but rather as a continuation of the kinds of collective activity and engagement we have seen throughout this volume.

The 2006 Marches and Unauthorized Migration

On March 25, 2006, between 500,000 and 1 million immigrant supporters marched in Los Angeles to protest against HR 4437. The bill, passed by the House of Representatives in December 2005, made illegal presence in the United States a felony (currently illegal *entry* into the United States is a misdemeanor, but to remain in the country without authorization is not a crime). The law would also have made it illegal for anyone to provide aid or assistance to unauthorized immigrants. The sheer size of the March 25 demonstration took the media and lawmakers by surprise. Over the next few months, millions of immigrants and their supporters would take to the streets in cities across the United States to protest against HR 4437 and to demand a fair and humane reform to the nation's immigration laws. This constitutes the largest mass mobilization to have occurred in the United States since the civil rights movement and the anti-Vietnam war movement.

The passage of HR 4437, and the pro- and anti-immigrant political mobilization it fomented, brought the issue of unauthorized migration to the forefront of US political discourse. Unauthorized migration refers to the migration of individuals to the United States without legal documentation. In many cases, individuals arrive on tourist or student visas and overstay the amount of time allowed them, which makes them "unauthorized." In other cases, individuals cross the international border between the United States and Mexico, or between the United States and Canada, without visas or other legal permission to be present in the United States. For these migrants, the act of entering the country illegally is a misdemeanor, but being in the country without authorization is not a crime.

As we have seen in the previous chapters, whether or not an individual is authorized to be in the United States depends on that individual's status in the eyes of US immigration authorities. For migrants from the western hemisphere, before 1965 there were no restrictions on migration to the United States. The US government used administrative rules to deny individuals entry. Some migrants, because they did not want to subject themselves to often invasive health examinations, circumvented the administrative authorization process, making them de facto unauthorized migrants. But these numbers were relatively small. In 1965, the United States passed the Immigration and Nationality Act. This Act removed the national quota system which had been passed under the 1924 National Origins Act. The 1924 Act was designed to limit migration from southern and eastern Europe and restricted the allocation of visas to countries from those areas, while encouraging northern European migration. The 1965 Act awarded all eastern-hemisphere countries an equal number of visas. It also placed restrictions on western-hemisphere migration for the first time: it granted 120,000 visas to western-hemisphere countries, to be allotted on a "first come, first served" basis. The law also provided for an unlimited number of visas for family reunification, which allowed naturalized US citizens and permanent residents to petition for permission to bring their family members to the United States.

The 1965 Act had a number of unintended consequences. First, it fundamentally changed the ethnoracial make-up of US migration flows. After its passage, European countries did not send large numbers of migrants. Instead, immigrants already present in the United States, most of whom were Latino or Asian American, petitioned to bring their family members, dramatically changing the ethnoracial make-up of immigrants to the United States.[1] Second, the Act created the phenomenon of large-scale unauthorized western-hemisphere migration. Up until that point, there had been no numeric restriction on these migration flows, and those flows, particularly from Mexico, well exceeded the 20,000 visas per year allotted to each country under the 1965 Act. As we have seen in this volume, migration flows are the product of complex geopolitical factors, not simple individual choice. Without any changes in the broader economic and political factors that had driven Mexican (and later Central American) migration to the United States since 1900, individuals continued to come, and, because the cap was set so low, often without the documentation now required under the new law.

In the 1980s, US politicians began to express concern about this phenomenon. This led to discussions in Congress about how to curb unauthorized migration. The result was the passage of the Immigration Reform and Control Act (IRCA) in 1986. This Act contained two parts. The first part made it illegal for employers knowingly to hire unauthorized workers. It required employers to verify their workers' migration status. Second, it allowed for the legalization of two categories of unauthorized immigrants: (1) all immigrants who could prove continuous residence in the United States since January 1, 1982; and (2) seasonal workers employed in agricultural work for at least 60 days of the year prior to May 1986. Of the 3 million immigrants who applied for legalization under IRCA, 2.7 million, or nine out of ten applicants, had their petitions approved. Of those 2.7 million immigrants, over 2 million, or 75 percent, were of Mexican origin.[2]

Although IRCA did curb unauthorized migration to the United States for the first few years after it was passed and reduced the aggregate number of unauthorized migrants present in the United States through the legalization program, in the long term it did not fundamentally change unauthorized migration flows to the United States.[3] As a result, Congress and sectors of the US public continued to see unauthorized migration as a problem and, in response, Border Patrol funding is now almost 15 times what it was in 1990. These funds have gone toward hiring more Border Patrol agents and toward providing them with manned and unmanned technology for monitoring the border. The Border Patrol is currently made up of more than 21,000 agents, who constitute almost half of all federal law enforcement officials. Congress also passed two other immigration reform bills in the 1990s – the 1990 Immigration Act and the 1996 Illegal Immigration Reform and Immigrant Responsibility Act. The 1990 law increased the number of legal immigrant visas available, in the hope that this would decrease the need for immigrants to resort to unauthorized entry into the United States. The 1996 law was more extensive and, among other things, it doubled the size of the Border Patrol, decreased immigrants' opportunities for appeal against deportation orders, required the mandatory detention of criminal aliens, and allowed for the retroactive deportation of non-citizens previously convicted of crimes. Yet these laws seem to have had little impact on the levels of unauthorized migration to the United States. Instead, it was the Great Recession, combined with economic growth in Mexico, that seems to have brought Mexican migration rates to historic lows. Critics argue that US attempts to curb unauthorized migration through changes in its immigration laws failed because these changes did not address the structural causes of migration flows. Instead, they focus on policing the behavior of individual migrants. Without addressing the causes underlying migration, it is unlikely that unilateral US legal action will significantly change migratory flows.

As a result, it is estimated that currently there are about 11 million unauthorized immigrants living in the United States. Even though there are non-trivial numbers of unauthorized Canadian, Irish, and Asian immigrants in the United States, about 58 percent of the unauthorized are of Mexican origin and another 23 percent are from other countries in Latin America.[4] Therefore the unauthorized immigrant problem is often characterized as a "Mexican" or "Latino" problem. The presence of these unauthorized migrants, and the significant demographic change which has occurred in the United States since the passage of the 1965 Act, have resulted in waves of anti-immigrant backlash targeting Latino immigrants. Groups like the Minuteman Project, a vigilante group formed to patrol the border and guard against illegal crossings, or the Federation for American Immigration Reform (FAIR), a group which lobbies Congress to tighten restriction on all types of immigration, or Save our State (SOS), a group which sponsored a series of ballot initiatives aimed at denying public services to unauthorized immigrants and their children, were formed in response to a perceived immigration crisis and work to lobby state governments and the US Congress to restrict immigration to the United States severely. A look at some of the comments by the leaders of these groups shows the degree to which a lack of differentiation across types of immigrants, documented or unauthorized, and racialized assumptions about Latinos in general are often included in their rhetoric:

> We need the National Guard to clean out all our cities and round them [immigrants] up . . . They have no problem slitting your throat and taking your money or selling drugs to your kids or raping your daughters, and they are evil people.
> (Chris Simcox, co-founder of the Minuteman Project and President of the Minuteman Civil Defense Corps)[5]

> Mexican men have a reputation for leering and worse at little girls, which shouldn't surprise us, since sex with children is socially acceptable in Mexico.
> (Brenda Walker, Californian anti-immigrant leader and publisher)[6]

Other commentaries by anti-immigration advocates also point to their authors' conceptualization of this fight as a "war," with echoes of manifest destiny and the need to control conquered territories:

> My message to them [Mexicans] is, not in two weeks, not in two months, not in two years, never! We must be clear that we will not surrender America and we will not turn the United States over to the invaders from south of the border.
> (United States Representative Virgil Goode (R-VA))[7]

> Our enemies are bloodied and beaten. We cannot relent. Our boot is on their throat and we must have the willingness to crush their "throat" so that we can put our enemy down for good. The sovereignty of our nation and the future of our culture

and civilization is [*sic*] at stake. The United States is a beacon of salvation unto the rest of the world. Our freedoms, our culture is man's salvation. If we perish, man perishes.

(Joseph Turner, organizer of Save Our State, now a staff member in the Federation for American Immigration Reform)[8]

Many of the comments, particularly from those involved with the Minutemen, also include calls to violence, such as this one: "What we'll do is randomly pick one night every week where we will kill whoever crosses the border . . . step over there and you die. You get to decide whether it's your lucky night or not. I think that would be more fun" (Brian James, anti-immigrant talk radio host with KFYI–AM on the air in Phoenix in 2006, proposing his solution to the immigration problem in Arizona). Given this kind of rhetoric, it is not surprising that, according to the FBI, from 2003 to 2007 hate crimes against Latinos increased by 40 percent, reaching the highest level ever reported since the agency began compiling data on these types of crimes. The perpetrators of those crimes rarely distinguished between US citizen and unauthorized Latinos. The number of hate crimes against Latinos decreased in 2008 and 2009, a drop that experts attribute to a decrease in anti-immigrant-related speech in the public sphere. A recent spike in Latino-focused hate crimes in California in 2011, however, suggests that this decline may have been temporary.[9]

Thus US-born Latinos understand that anti-immigrant rhetoric affects them, even if they themselves are not immigrants. Given this larger context, the 2006 immigration marches were not so surprising. The first major march was in Los Angeles, the site of a previous wave of anti-immigrant backlash during the 1990s. In 1994, Proposition 187 was on the California ballot, an initiative that called for denying health care and social services to unauthorized immigrants and their children. It was approved by over 60 percent of California voters. The months leading up to the November 1994 election were marked by heated demonstrations on both sides, which resulted in protest marches and school walkouts that constituted the largest mass protests Latinos in California had engaged in since the Chicano Movement mobilization in the late 1960s. Even though the proposition passed (it was never implemented because it was found to be unconstitutional), this experience, and the mobilization surrounding it, led to increased rates of naturalization and voting among Latinos who engaged in this activity. The experience also laid the groundwork for how Latino organizations and community members understood the threat of HR 4437 and how they framed their reactions to it.

Although not all the protesters who engaged in the 2006 marches were themselves immigrants, many of them were, and many were unauthorized. These are not individuals who would normally be expected to engage in the political process. Unauthorized immigrants, because of their vulnerable position, generally try not to draw attention to themselves, and certainly do not often take to the streets demanding their rights. So what happened in the spring of 2006 to change their behavior? The greatest impetus was simply the harshness of the House Bill. It was easy for these activists to see that criminalizing immigrants would do nothing to solve the United States' immigration problems and would only make life more difficult for people who often live in the shadows of US society. In this case, the offending legislation was so extreme that it was easy for people to see why they should be protesting against it.

The other factor that made this mobilization possible was the organizational infrastructure, in terms both of advocacy organizations and of ethnic media, which now exists in Latino communities across the United States. As we saw in the previous chapters, one of the main outcomes of the social mobilizations which occurred in Latino national-origin communities during the late 1960s and early 1970s was the establishment of Latino-oriented civil rights organizations such as MALDEF, Latino Justice, the National Council of La Raza, and the Southwest Voter Registration Education Project (SVREP), together with the revitalization of long-term organizations such as LULAC. These bodies were joined by Central American social service organizations like CARECEN in putting together a response to HR 4437. Many analysts saw these protests as spontaneous, but in fact they were the product of months of meetings and planning on the part of community activists.[10] As early as February 2006, groups of community leaders were meeting to discuss the best ways to respond to the House Bill. Before the Los Angeles march was held, about 30,000 immigrant supporters had marched in Washington, DC, and an estimated quarter of a million had taken to the streets in Chicago. At the same time, using text messaging and MySpace, students across the country began coordinating school walkouts to protest against the bill.

The tendency in the popular media was to see these actions as spontaneous, spurred by popular Spanish-language radio personalities such as "El Piolín" and "El Cucuy" in Los Angeles and "El Pistolero" in Chicago. While it is true that these radio hosts played an important role in educating the community about the bill and in mobilizing people to get out and express opposition, the marches would not have been possible without the organizational and financial support of Latino civil rights and social service organizations. For example, for the Los Angeles event to happen, these groups had to take out permits to hold the march, set up a stage and provide audio equipment for the day's speakers, and work with the Los Angeles police in mapping out the march's route and required street closures; and they had to ensure that there were additional trash receptacles and portable toilets available for the marchers to use. All this required significant coordination, effort, and funding. Without this organizational infrastructure in place, the community could never have responded to HR 4437 in such an immediate and dramatic way. Yes, the movement needed the people; but it also needed this infrastructure and logistical support.

The political implications of organization often get underestimated. Many of those who look at the post-civil rights United States lament the lack of any ongoing mass mobilization to address issues of social justice. But there is a great deal going on behind the scenes, as became clear with the 2006 immigration marches. The organizational development which came out of the 1970s can be seen as an important structural change that increases the Latino community's ability to lobby Congress and to inform lawmakers about issues important to their constituencies. These organizations also represent an important social network, one that, as we saw in 2006, can be activated when there are issues of great importance to the community. This being said, the marches of 2006 were an exceptional circumstance and a response to an extreme piece of legislation. But the fact that they were possible shows the tremendous political potential of the Latino community and the significant structural resources that have been developed within it since the 1970s.

Only time will tell whether this unprecedented level of activism on the part of pro-immigrant Latinos will have long-term effects on their engagement in other kinds of politics. Attending a march is very different from contacting an elected official or from voting. As we saw in chapter 2, Mexicans and Puerto Ricans in particular are more likely to engage in this kind of activity than in voting. Political scientists like to distinguish between *expressive* and *instrumental* forms of civic engagement. Expressive forms constitute activity that is solely meant to express an opinion about an issue. Instrumental engagement is activity meant to address a particular policy question or to solve a particular problem. The marches clearly were expressive; the question is whether that momentum can be shifted toward focusing on more instrumental activities.

The preliminary evidence suggests that this transition may be occurring. After the marches, the participating groups began the "*Hoy*

Marchamos, Mañana Votamos / Today we march, tomorrow we vote," campaign, which was meant to focus on registering Latinos to vote and on mobilizing them to turn out to vote in the 2008 and 2012 elections. For many, the first step in this process is naturalization, and naturalization applications have increased significantly since 2006. Of course, this may be because immigrants feel insecure in the current anti-immigrant environment; or the rise may be due to USCIS significantly increasing the fees for naturalization in 2008: many people may have been rushing to get their applications in before the fee increases took effect. Again, only time will tell. But results from studies undertaken in California during the 1990s show that Latinos who naturalized and registered to vote after 1994, when an anti-immigrant proposition was on the state ballot, remain more likely to vote than Latinos who registered during less politically charged periods. The question is whether the current environment will provide the same type of political socialization for Latinos at the national level.

The marches also showed other structural limitations when one considers issues of immigration reform. Since immigration law is under the jurisdiction of the federal government, any changes to current law have to be passed by Congress. The fate of the congressional immigration reform bill during the spring and summer of 2006 shows the difficulty Latinos have in significantly influencing the national debate on this issue. A bi-partisan group of congressional reformers, led by Senators Edward Kennedy and John McCain, attempted to craft a bill that would provide a path to citizenship for the estimated 11 million unauthorized immigrants residing in the United States, while still providing sufficient border enforcement and security provisions to earn the support of lawmakers who were vehement about maintaining a hard line against unauthorized migration. Even though all the members of the Congressional Hispanic Caucus were in favor of immigration reform, the bill failed to pass, largely because Republican lawmakers defined any path to citizenship as "amnesty," and few in Congress were willing to say that they were in support of such a measure. This experience shows the difficulty which Latino lawmakers have in influencing what happens in Congress. Even though this is an issue which affects the Latino community more than any other, the votes of Latino lawmakers make up only a small proportion of the 218 votes needed to pass legislation in the House of Representatives, and only 3 of the 51 votes needed for a bill to pass the Senate.

With the failure of reform in Congress, localities across the nation began implementing their own measures, some of which make it illegal for anyone to rent housing to an unauthorized person, or to ask local police to enforce federal immigration law. The courts have deemed some of these laws unconstitutional, but others remain in effect. The most famous of these is Arizona's SB 1070. Passed in 2010, the law required all resident aliens over the age of 14 to register with the government and to have their registration documents with them at all times. It also required law enforcement officials to check an individual's immigration status during any "lawful contact" with said individual. The law sparked protests in cities across the country. In *Arizona v. United States*, the US Supreme Court struck down much of the law but upheld the provision requiring immigration checks in law enforcement stops. Thus, the 2006 marches not only failed to move lawmakers to pass comprehensive reform, many now argue that the show of strength caused fear and retrenchment among anti-immigrant groups, leading to a backlash against Latino immigrant political engagement.[11]

The DREAMers

One group that has continued to engage in political activism despite this backlash is the DREAMers: youth eligible for the Development, Relief, and Education for Alien Minors (DREAM) Act, a bill first introduced in 2001 that provides a path to citizenship for youth that were brought to the United States without authorization before the age of 16. Under the Act, youth who have lived in the United States for more than five years, graduate from a US high school, attend two years of college or join the military, and maintain good moral character, can achieve permanent residency. Even though not all DREAM-eligible youth are Latino, Latino youth have made up the majority of DREAM activists. After the failure of comprehensive immigration reform in 2007, bill sponsor Senator Dick Durbin (D-IL) tried to bring the DREAM Act to a vote in the US Senate. It garnered 59 votes, 1 vote shy of the 60 needed to overcome a Republican filibuster, and so the bill never made it to the Senate floor. The bill has been reintroduced each year, but has never again come to a vote.

Frustrated with a lack of movement within Congress, DREAM activists have engaged in a variety of collective protest activities, including expressing their concerns through social media, film, comedy, and performing arts, and engaging in a variety of political actions. On June 7, 2008, DREAMers held a sit-in at Obama's presidential campaign headquarters in Denver to protest against the President's deportation policies.

Under his Administration, Obama has deported over 1.5 million immigrants. Mexicans are overrepresented among deportees. Even though Mexicans make up only about 58 percent of unauthorized migrants in the United States, 73 percent of deportees under Obama have been of Mexican origin.[12] Activists from the Campaign for an American Dream (CAD) wanted to bring attention to these policies. While other CAD members waited outside, two members, Javier Hernández and Verónica Gómez, entered the President's campaign office and delivered a 100-page petition with more than 2,000 signatures asking that the President stop the deportations of unauthorized youth.[13] Hernández and Gómez then began a hunger strike, effectively closing the office to visitors and volunteers.[14] The youths left the following day, but their action received national press attention and led the National Immigrant Youth Alliance (NIYA) to pledge to stage similar actions at Obama offices throughout the country until the November presidential elections. A similar protest was held in Detroit a few days later. On June 15, 2013, the Obama Administration announced Deferred Action for Childhood Arrivals (DACA), which allows DREAM Act-eligible youth to apply for a two-year temporary regularization of their status. Although DACA does not provide applicants with an opportunity to gain permanent residency, it does offer them the right to work and protection from deportation for two years, with possibilities for renewal. As of June 2013, more than half a million young people had applied for DACA. Many believe it was the DREAMers' organizing and threat of ongoing protests during an election year that pushed President Obama to take this executive action.

DREAM activists continue to organize and to advocate for comprehensive immigration reform. One of the critiques of the DREAM movement is that it is too narrow, deeming DREAMers "worthy" of citizenship based on their personal (usually academic) accomplishments and on the fact that they violated US immigration law "through no fault of their own" because they were brought by their parents as children. This narrative implies that their parents are therefore not "worthy" and are the true "lawbreakers." It is also estimated that two-thirds of unauthorized youth in the United States would be ineligible for the DREAM Act because they would not meet its strict requirements. In advocating for comprehensive immigration reform, DREAM activist groups have rejected these frames, emphasizing the need for a humane and just reform of the nation's immigration laws, one that includes their parents and DREAM-ineligible youth, thus broadening established definitions of belonging and citizenship. As an example, in June 2013, United We Dream (UWD), the largest of the DREAM organizations, held a rally in Washington, DC, spotlighting mothers of DREAM-eligible youth. The activists took over the US Capitol's Visitor Center, singing "The Star Spangled Banner" and reciting the Pledge of Allegiance, as part of a week of actions to support comprehensive immigration reform. As of this writing, it is unclear what will happen with the comprehensive immigration bill that passed the US Senate, with a vote of 68 to 32, in June 2013. The House of Representatives seems unlikely to act on the bill as it stands, showing the difficulty a minority group like Latinos has in getting important legislation enacted within a majoritarian body like the US House of Representatives.

The November 2012 Election and the Latino Vote

Barack Obama's re-election in November 2012 was historic for a number of reasons. Not only did the country re-elect its first African American president, but he was re-elected despite losing the white vote. Obama is estimated to have won 71 percent of the Latino vote in 2012. In 1980, whites comprised 88 percent of the electorate; in 2012, they made up 73 percent. Whites are still overrepresented in the US electorate relative to their share of the population, but their proportion of the electorate is decreasing. This helps to explain why in 1980 Ronald Reagan won the white vote over Jimmy Carter by 20 points – 56 to 36 percent – and was able to win the White House in a landslide, while in 2012 Mitt Romney won the white vote over Barack Obama by the same 20-point margin – 59 to 39 percent – and lost the election. It is also important to consider the role of gender in support for Obama. Much of the news coverage of the 2012 election talked about "women and minorities" as key to Obama's re-election. Few of these stories specified *which* women supported Obama. In fact, according to exit polls, 56 percent of white women voted for Governor Romney. That is still less than the 62 percent of white men who supported Romney, but a significantly lower level of support for Obama than the 96 percent of Black women and 76 percent of Latina women who voted for him.[15] For a variety of reasons, Black women and Latinas, on average, turn out at much higher rates than Black and Latino men. It was these women's higher turnout, combined with their overwhelming support for Obama, which made it possible for Obama to win the election without winning the white vote.

Many Republican political consultants, such as Dick Morris and Karl Rove, were surprised by the outcome. They assumed the demographics of the 2008 electorate were an anomaly, and that the white proportion of US voters would return to 2004 levels in 2012. As long as whites were significantly overrepresented among voters, appealing to whites, and therefore winning them by large margins, could be a winning strategy for Republicans. This calculus largely explains why the Republican Party spent a great deal of political capital in 2011 and 2012 working within state legislatures to pass laws that would suppress the votes of Democratic-leaning constituencies, specifically Blacks and Latinos. Since 2011, 19 states have passed laws that restrict voter registration efforts and establish voter identification requirements – laws that the Brennan Center for Justice estimates will disenfranchise the 11 percent of eligible voters who do not have a government-issued photo identification. In Texas, a three-judge federal panel struck down the state's voter identification law, citing its disproportionate impact on poor and minority voters.[16] In the ruling, the panel emphasized the fact that the State of Texas had found about 800,000 persons on its voter rolls whose names did not match Department of Motor Vehicles (DMV) records, and therefore could be presumed not to possess identification. Almost 40 percent of those voters were Latino. In addition, given 81 of Texas' 254 counties have no operational DMV office, many of these low-paid voters would have to travel up to 250 miles in order to obtain the required identification. Analysis of other states' laws showed they also would have a disproportionate impact on voters of color.

The significant weakening of the Voting Rights Act that will be a consequence of the Supreme Court's *Shelby* ruling will likely lead to an intensification of these efforts in 2014 and beyond. Many of the voter identification laws that had been nullified under the VRA were reinstated after the ruling. After *Shelby*, Texas, as we saw in chapter 2, will now be implementing the very law that was previously struck down on VRA grounds. Other voter suppression efforts, such as Pennsylvania's voter identification law, passed legal muster and were simply on hold for the November 2012 election because the courts felt there was insufficient time to implement them before Election Day. When they take effect in 2014, those laws already on the books are expected to disenfranchise 5 million US voters, over 800,000 of whom are Latino. Given Republican strength within state legislatures, it is highly likely more states will pass these sorts of laws in order to suppress the Latino and African American vote in 2014 and beyond. Thus, getting Latino voters to flex their demographic muscle at the ballot box will only become more difficult, at least in the short term.

Because of that, the stability of the Obama coalition remains an open question. Many pundits discussing the November 2012 election's outcome quoted the refrain "demography is destiny." Yet American history has shown that not to be the case. Through the elaboration of Jim Crow laws, as an example, many southern states were able to maintain white control of all levels of government despite the fact that African Americans comprised a majority or near-majority of the population. In the current era, voting rates among youth and ethnoracial groups may be increasing, but significant portions of these populations are still choosing to stay home on Election Day. Among Latino voters, one of the voting blocs most discussed after the election, even though 11.2 million turned out to vote in November 2012, almost 10 million eligible Latino voters decided not to cast a ballot on Election Day. In Texas alone, 2.6 million eligible Latinos chose not to vote in this presidential election. That is a significant portion of the Latino electorate that is not having its voice heard.

Stories from two of the places that showed real change in 2012 are suggestive of what will be necessary for the Obama coalition to be maintained. In Colorado, Obama's Latino vote share increased by 14 points between 2008 and 2012. Organizers on the ground argue this change was possible because they went into the field early, coordinated efforts across various organizations, had an extensive field campaign, and maintained a continual presence on Spanish-language media. Similarly, in California's Riverside County, community organizations capitalized on the implementation of online voter registration to dramatically expand the voter rolls, particularly among Latinos; more than 77 percent of Latino online registrants in Riverside County in November 2012 were new voters. This registration opportunity, combined with the direct mobilization of these and other new voters, is credited with helping to secure the election of Mark Takano – the first openly gay person of color to be elected to the US Congress. Similar efforts occurred across the country and demonstrate the importance of direct organization and mobilization in order to ensure Latinos are sufficiently represented at the ballot box.[17]

In line with what we have seen throughout this book, the "demographic destiny" that "happened" on election night in November 2012 was in reality the product of years of organizing and coordination on the ground within Latino communities across the United States. Among Latinos, that organizing was facilitated by Republican candidate Mitt Romney's extreme positions on immigration – including advocacy of self-deportation as an immigration policy solution. Also critical was the funding available for this work, including the Democratic Party's establishment of the Futuro Fund, which put $30 million into supporting the Latino vote, the largest investment of this kind in the party's history. Various Latino national and local organizations also invested resources and coordinated their activities to expand the Latino vote, targeting their efforts in those areas where the Latino vote is most likely to have an impact on electoral outcomes. In 2012, Latino voters were mobilized directly and indirectly by the political context. As we saw in the 2006 marches, that mobilization was supported by the existing Latino organizational infrastructure. If this momentum is to continue, it is important that these groups' funding and coordination continue as well. The lesson from November 2012 is that only through sustained organization, mobilization, and coordination can Latinos realize their full electoral potential.

Latino Political Engagement in Context

With each national electoral cycle in the United States, the popular media discuss the "Sleeping Giant" and whether Latinos will "wake up" and flex their political muscle. Although it is true that Latinos have yet to exercise their power at the ballot box at a level commensurate with their numbers, the national-origin groups we have studied clearly have not been idle in terms of their political organizing. Time and again, we see groups engaging in union organizing, community organizing, and political protest, most often targeted at very specific issues which are key to the quality of life within each community. So it clearly is not the case that Latinos do not engage in collective political activity, but rather that that activity is often of the type that flies beneath the radar of politicians and the popular media. Within this context, the large-scale mobilization that happened in the spring of 2006 is not so surprising.

This being said, Latinos, because they are a minority group with relatively low SES and high levels of non-citizenship, face important structural barriers in US politics. Given the majoritarian nature of the electoral system, they will need to build political coalitions in order to achieve electoral success. Those coalitions will continue to be necessary within the legislative institutions themselves, and may limit the degree to which Latino elected officials can implement their preferred policy agendas. Although past organizing within the community has changed a number of structural factors – including the group members' migration status and ability to exercise the vote – the majoritarian orientation of the US political system is here to stay. This means that Latino political influence will vary significantly at the local, state, and national levels, and that Latinos will continue to engage in traditional and nontraditional forms of politics in order to address the pressing needs of their communities.

Appendix

Table A.1 Reported Voter Registration by Race and Nativity, 1978–2012 (%)

Year	White, Non-Latino Total population[a]	Citizens	African American Total population	Citizens	Asian American Total population	Citizens	Latino Total population	Citizens
2012	72.4	73.7	68.5	73.1	37.2	56.3	38.9	58.7
2010	67.0	68.2	58.8	62.8	34.1	49.3	33.8	51.6
2008	72.0	73.5	65.5	69.7	37.3	55.3	37.6	59.4
2006	69.7	71.2	57.4	60.9	32.9	49.1	32.1	53.7
2004	73.5	75.1	64.4	68.7	34.9	51.8	34.3	57.9
2002	67.9	69.4	58.5	62.4	30.7	49.2	32.6	52.5
2000	70.0	71.6	63.6	67.5	30.7	52.4	34.9	57.4
1998	67.9	69.3	60.2	63.6	29.1	48.9	33.7	55.2
1996	71.6	73.0	63.5	66.4	32.6	57.2	35.7	58.6
1994	68.1	69.4	58.5	61.3	28.7	51.9	31.3	52.9
1992	73.5	77.1	63.9	70.0	31.2	61.6	35.0	62.5
1990	66.7	69.9	58.8	63.5	28.4	56.0	32.3	55.2
1988	70.8	73.6	64.5	68.8	NA[b]	NA	35.5	59.1
1986	67.7	70.2	64.0	67.3	NA	NA	35.9	56.4
1984	71.6	75.1	66.3	72.0	NA	NA	40.1	61.4
1982	67.5	70.1	59.1	62.6	NA	NA	35.3	53.7
1980	70.3	74.1	60.0	64.1	NA	NA	36.4	56.0
1978	65.4	68.2	57.1	60.6	NA	NA	32.9	50.1

a 'Total population' refers to the population over 18. 'Citizens' refers to the citizen population over 18.

b Data not available.

Source: US Department of the Census, Current Population Survey, November 2012 and earlier reports.

Table A.2 Reported Voting by Race and Nativity, 1978–2012 (%)

Year	White, Non-Latino		African American		Asian American		Latino	
	Total population[a]	Citizens	Total population	Citizens	Total population	Citizens	Total population	Citizens
2012	63.0	64.1	62.0	66.2	31.3	47.3	31.8	48.0
2010	47.8	48.6	40.7	43.5	21.3	30.8	20.5	31.2
2008	64.8	66.1	60.8	64.7	32.1	47.6	31.6	49.9
2006	50.5	51.6	38.6	41.0	21.8	32.4	19.3	32.3
2004	65.8	67.2	56.3	60.0	29.8	44.1	28.0	47.2
2002	48.0	49.1	39.7	42.3	19.4	31.2	18.9	30.4
2000	60.4	61.8	53.5	56.8	25.4	43.4	27.5	45.1
1998	46.5	47.4	39.6	41.8	19.3	32.4	20.0	32.8
1996	59.6	60.7	50.6	53.0	25.7	45.0	26.8	44.0
1994	50.1	51.0	37.1	38.9	21.8	39.4	20.2	34.0
1992	66.9	70.2	54.1	59.2	27.3	53.9	28.9	51.6
1990	49.0	51.4	39.2	42.4	20.3	40.0	21.0	36.0
1988	61.8	64.2	51.5	55.0	NA	NA	28.8	48.0
1986	48.9	50.7	43.2	45.5	NA	NA	24.2	38.0
1984	63.3	66.4	55.8	60.6	NA	NA	32.7	50.0
1982	51.5	53.4	43.0	45.5	NA	NA	25.3	38.5
1980	62.8	66.2	50.5	53.9	NA	NA	29.9	46.1
1978	48.6	50.6	37.2	39.5	NA	NA	23.5	35.7

Source: US Department of the Census, Current Population Survey, November 2012 and earlier reports.

Table A.3 Mexican Migration to the United States, 1900–1997

Year	Number of migrants	Year	Number of migrants	Year	Number of migrants
1900	237	1933	1,936	1966	47,217
1901	347	1934	1,801	1967	43,034
1902	709	1935	1,560	1968	44,716
1903	528	1936	1,716	1969	45,748
1904	1,009	1937	2,347	1970	44,821
1905	2,637	1938	2,502	1971	50,324
1906	1,997	1939	2,640	1972	64,209
1907	1,406	1940	2,313	1973	70,411
1908	6,067	1941	2,824	1974	71,863
1909	16,251	1942	2,378	1975	62,552
1910	18,691	1943	4,172	1976	74,449[a]
1911	19,889	1944	6,598	1977	44,646
1912	23,238	1945	6,702	1978	92,681
1913	11,926	1946	7,146	1979	52,479
1914	14,614	1947	7,558	1980	56,680
1915	12,340	1948	8,384	1981	101,268
1916	18,425	1949	8,083	1982	56,106
1917	17,869	1950	6,744	1983	59,079
1918	18,524	1951	6,153	1984	57,820
1919	29,818	1952	9,079	1985	61,290
1920	52,361	1953	17,183	1986	66,753
1921	30,758	1954	30,645	1987	72,511
1922	19,551	1955	43,702	1988	95,170
1923	63,768	1956	61,320	1989	405,660
1924	89,336	1957	49,321	1990	680,186
1925	32,964	1958	26,791	1991	947,923
1926	43,316	1959	22,909	1992	214,128
1927	67,721	1960	32,708	1993	126,642
1928	59,016	1961	41,476	1994	111,415
1929	40,154	1962	55,805	1995	90,045
1930	12,703	1963	55,986	1996	163,743
1931	3,333	1964	34,448	1997	146,680
1932	2,171	1965	40,686		

a Includes 58,354 entrants, plus 16,095 added due to changes in recordkeeping (transitional quarter).

Source: Susan B. Carter, Scott Sigmund Gartner, Michael R. Haines, Alan L. Olmstead, Richard Sutch, and Gavin Wright, eds., *Historical Statistics of the United States. Millennial Edition Online.* New York: Cambridge University Press, 2006, Series. Ad162–Ad175, 1–571–1–576, available at http://hsus.cambridge.org/HSUSWeb/HSUSEntryServlet (last accessed March 2, 2014).

Table A.4 Puerto Rican Migration to the United States, 1900–2000

Decade	Number of migrants
1900–1910	2,000
1911–1920	11,000
1921–1930	42,000
1931–1940	18,000
1941–1950	151,000
1951–1960	470,000
1961–1970	214,000
1971–1980	65,817
1981–1990	116,571
1991–2000	96,327

Source: Acosta-Belén and Santiago, 2006, p. 81.

Notes

Preface to the second edition

1 As cited by IowaWatchdog.org: http://watchdog.org/97513/ia-stevekingquotes (last accessed February 23, 2014).

Chapter 1

1 *Merriam Webster's Collegiate Dictionary*, 11th edn. (Springfield, MA: Merriam-Webster Inc., 2003.)

2 Thus individuals from Haiti, for example, or Brazil, would not be included in the definition of "Latino" used in this book.

3 Nicolas DeGenova and Ana Y. Ramos-Zayas, "Latino Racial Formations in the United States: An Introduction," *Journal of Latin American Anthropology* 8(2003): 2–16, p. 4.

4 Iris Marion Young, "Structure, Difference and Hispanic/Latino Claims of Justice," in Jorge J. E. Gracia and Pablo De Greiff, eds., *Hispanics/ Latinos in the United States: Ethnicity, Race, and Rights* (New York: Routledge, 2000), 147–65, p. 153.

5 Omi and Winant, *Racial Formation in the United States from the 1960s to the 1990s* (New York: Routledge, 1994).

6 Linda Alcoff, "Is Latina/o Identity a Racial Identity?" in Jorge J. E. Gracia and Pablo DeGreiff, eds., *Hispanics/Latinos in the United States: Ethnicity, Race and Rights* (New York: Routledge, 2000), p. 246.

7 For an overview of whiteness, law, and the prerequisite cases, see Ian Haney-López, *White by Law: The Legal Construction of Race* (New York: New York University Press, 1997).

8 New Orleans did have a racial system which included quadroons and other categories of *mulatto*, but this was the exception rather than the rule.

9 George Lipsitz, *The Possessive Investment in Whiteness: How White People Profit from Identity Politics* (Philadelphia: Temple University Press, 1998).

10 See Dalton Conley, *Being Black, Living in the Red: Race, Wealth, and Social Policy in America* (Berkeley: University of California Press, 1999).

11 For an overview of gender and migration trends in the United States, see Richard Fry, *Gender and Migration* (Washington, DC: Pew Hispanic Center, 2006), available at: www.pewhispanic.org/2006/07/05/gender-and-migration (last accessed July 12, 2013).

12 For an overview of these findings, see Cecilia Menjívar and Olivia Salcido,

"Gendered Paths to Legal Status: the Case of Latin American Immigrants in Phoenix, Arizona" (Washington, DC: Immigration Policy Center, 2013), available at: www.immigrationpolicy.org/sites/default/files/docs/genderedpaths052813.pdf (last accessed July 12, 2013).

13 See Pat Zavella, *I'm Neither Here Nor There: Mexican Migrants' Quotidian Struggles with Migration and Poverty* (Raleigh, NC: Duke University Press, 2011), and Jacqueline Maria Hagan, "Social Networks, Gender, and Immigrant Incorporation: Resources and Constraints," *American Sociological Review* 63 (1998): 55–67.

14 As quoted in Martha S. Hewson, *John Quincy Adams* (New York: Chelsea House Publishers, 2004), 41.

15 The full text of the original speech can be found at www.ourdocuments.gov/doc_large_image.php?doc=56 (last accessed February 9, 2014).

CHAPTER 2

1 For a description of the Futuro Fund, see www.nytimes.com/2013/03/08/us/politics/3-fund-raisers-show-latinos-rising-clout.html?_r=0 (last accessed November 30, 2013).

2 Source: US Census Quick Facts, http://quickfacts.census.gov/qfd/states/00000.html (last accessed July 12, 2013).

3 Pew Hispanic Center, "Hispanic Population Trends" (based on the 2011 American Community Survey): www.pewhispanic.org/2013/02/15/hispanic-population-trends/ph_13–01–23_ss_hispanics1/ (last accessed July 12, 2013).

4 Populations numbers for all groups other than Dominicans based on the US Department of the Census, "The Hispanic Population in the United States: 2011," tab. 2, "Hispanic Population by Sex, Age, and Hispanic Origin Type: 2011," available at: www.census.gov/population/hispanic/data/2011.html (last accessed July 12, 2013). Dominican population figures found at the Pew Hispanic Center, "Hispanic Population Trends."

5 Katherine Tate, *From Protest to Politics: The New Black Voters in American Elections* (Cambridge, MA: Harvard University Press, 1993); F. Chris García, Angelo Falcón and Rodolfo de la Garza, "Ethnicity and Politics: Evidence from the Latino National Political Survey," *Hispanic Journal of Behavioral Sciences* 18(1996): 91–103; and John A. García, "Political Participation: Resources and Involvement among Latinos and the American Political System," in F. Chris García, ed., *Pursuing Power: Latinos and the Political System* (Notre Dame, IN: University of Notre Dame Press, 1997), 44–71.

6 For linked fate, see Michael C. Dawson, *Behind the Mule: Race and Class in African American Politics* (Princeton, NJ: Princeton University Press, 1995); for political alienation, see Marvin E. Olsen, "Two Categories of Political Alienation," *Social Forces* 47(1969): 288–99; for group identity, see Tate, 1993, and Carol Hardy-Fanta, *Latina Politics, Latino Politics: Gender, Culture and Political Participation in Boston* (Philadelphia, PA: Temple University Press, 1993); for group conflict, see Henri Tajfel and J. Turner, "The Social Identity Theory of Intergroup Behavior," in Stephen Worchel and William Austin, eds., *Psychology of Intergroup Relations* (Chicago: Nelson-Hall, 1986), 7–24.

7 Cristina Beltrán, *The Trouble with Unity: Latino Politics and the Creation of Identity* (New York: Oxford University Press, 2010).

8 The other US immigrant group least likely to be naturalized is that of Canadians, which leads scholars to suggest that geographic proximity may have a negative impact on immigrants' decision to naturalize.

9 NALEO Educational Fund, *National Directory of Latino Elected Officials, 2013* (Los Angeles, CA: NALEO Educational Fund, 2013).

10 For more detail on the law, see www.justice.gov/crt/about/vot/intro/intro_b.php. Sections 4(e) and 4(f) contain provisions specific to the protection of language minorities: www.justice.gov/crt/about/vot/misc/sec_4.php (website last accessed February 23, 2014).

11 Travis Crum, "The Voting Rights Act's Secret Weapon: Pocket Trigger Litigation and Dynamic Preclearance," *Yale Law Journal* 119(2010): 1992–2038.

12 www.justice.gov/crt/about/vot/sec_5/tx_obj2.php (last accessed February 23, 2014).

13 They are the cities of: San Joaquín, 63.5%; Maywood, 59.5%; Cudahy, 58.9%; Bell Gardens, 56.5%; Huron City, 55.9%; Huntington Park, 55.9%; Bell, 53.9%; Arvin, 53.8%; Mendota, 53.5%; King City, 52.3%; Santa Ana, 51.9%; Orange Cove, 51.6%. From Joaquín Avila, "Political Apartheid in California: Consequences of Excluding a Growing Noncitizen Population," in *Latino Policy and Issues Brief* (Los Angeles: UCLA Chicano Studies Research Center, 2003).

14 Granted, both systems were quite exclusionary in terms of who was accorded "citizenship," particularly in terms of gender and class, and both systems allowed for slavery; but they did, despite their flaws, allow all their "citizens" to have a say.

15 The full text of *Federalist* 10 can be found at: http://thomas.loc.gov/home/histdox/fed_10.html (last accessed February 23, 2014).

CHAPTER 3

1 John C. Calhoun, speech on the floor of the Senate, 1848, available at www.teachingamerican history.org/library/index.asp?document=478 (last accessed December 11, 2008).

2 Library of Congress, "A Century of Lawmaking for a New Nation: Congressional Documents and Debates, 1774–1875," pp. 929–30, available at http://memory.loc.gov/ cgi-bin/ampage (last accessed February 23, 2014).

3 Chapter XLVII, "An Act for the Protection of Actual Settlers and to Quiet Land Titles in this state. Approved March 26, 1856," in *Statutes of California passed at the Seventh Session of the Legislature, Begun on the Seventh Day of January, One Thousand Eight Hundred and Fifty-six, and Ended on the Twenty-first Day of April, One Thousand Eight Hundred and Fifty-six, at the City of Sacramento* (Sacramento, CA: James Allen, 1856), 54–7.

4 New Mexico's population was almost evenly split between Mexicans, Anglos, and Native Americans until the early twentieth century, which made multi-racial power-sharing more the norm there than it was in other parts of the southwest. See M. Menchaca, *Recovering History, Constructing Race: The Indian, Black, and White Roots of Mexican Americans* (Austin: University of Texas Press, 2001).

5 Raúl E. Fernández and Gilbert G. González, *A Century of Chicano History: Empire, Nations, and Migration* (New York: Routledge, 2003), 37.

6 Ibid., p. 38.

7 Mae Ngai, *Impossible Subjects: Illegal Aliens and the Making of Modern America* (Princeton: Princeton University Press), p. 55.

8 Gilbert G. González, *Guest Workers or Colonized Labor? Mexican Labor Migration to the United States* (Boulder, CO: Paradigm, 2006), 2.

9 Since 1993, more than 400 women and girls have been murdered and more than 70 remain missing in Ciudad Juárez and Chihuahua, Mexico. Very few individuals have been prosecuted for these crimes.

10 Foreign Direct Investment (FDI) info.: www.reuters.com/article/2013/02/23/mexico-fdi-idUSL1N0BN0IE20130223 (last accessed February 23, 2014).

11 Jeffrey Passel, D'Vera Cohn, and Ana Gonzalez Barrera, "Net Migration from Mexico Falls to Zero – Perhaps Less" (Washington, DC: Pew Hispanic Center, 2013), available from: www.pewhispanic.org/files/2012/04/Mexican-migrants-report_final.pdf (last accessed July 22, 2013).

12 Rogers M. Smith. "Living in a Promised Land? Mexican Immigration and American Obligations," *Perspectives on Politics* 9.3(2011): 545–57.

13 This is what occurred in the case of the Bernal family in Fullerton, California, who were sued by their neighbors when they moved into a home in a neighborhood that had restrictive covenants. The family fought the lawsuit and, in 1943, the state court judge ruled that they be allowed to stay in their home. An overview of the Bernal case may be found in Gustavo Arrellano's "Mi Casa es Mi Casa," published in the *OC Weekly* in May 2010: www.ocweekly.com/2010–05–06/news/alex-bernal-housing-discrimination (last accessed November 30, 2013).

14 I should note that these restrictions were not enforced in south Texas, where landowners would, through coercion and bribery, "deliver" their Mexican workers' votes to whichever political candidate they supported. See Julie Leininger Pycior, *LBJ and Mexican Americans: The Paradox of Power* (Austin: University of Texas Press, 1997).

15 Ibid., p. 7.

16 William T. Carrigan and Clive Webb, "The Lynching of Persons of Mexican Origin or Descent in the United States, 1848 to 1928," *Journal of Social History* 37(2003): 411–38.

17 As quoted in Pycior, 1997, pp. 7–8.

18 For men, the style entailed wearing wide-brimmed hats, broad-shouldered long coats, high-waisted peg-legged trousers, and long dangling watch chains, often in bright colors. For women, the style included tight sweaters, short or long flared skirts, and large earrings.

19 One policeman was quoted as saying, after the riots: "You can say that the cops had a 'hands-off' policy during the riots. Well, we represented public opinion. Many of us were in the First World War, and we're not going to pick on kids in the service."

20 Taxi drivers offered free trips to soldiers wishing to travel to the riot areas. A Los Angeles newspaper published instructions on how to "de-zoot" a zoot suiter.

21 Vicki L. Ruiz, "Tapestries of Resistance: Episodes of School Segregation and Desegregation in the U.S. West," in Peter Lau, ed., *From Grassroots to the Supreme Court: Exploration of Brown v. Board of Education and American Democracy* (Durham: Duke University Press, 2004), 44–67.

22 *Méndez v. Westminster School District*, 64 F. Supp. 544 (D.C.CAL. 1946).

23 Vicki L. Ruiz, *From Out of the Shadows: Mexican American Women in Twentieth Century*

America (New York: Oxford University Press, 1998), 89.

24 We will see, with the advent of the United Farm Workers Union, that these laws were often not enforced. That being said, these actions at least got the statutes put on the books.

25 This is a standard practice of parliamentary procedure used to run meetings (how people make motions, second them, etc.). A history of Robert's Rules may be found at www.robertsrules.com/history.html (last accessed February 23, 2014).

26 See Cynthia Orozco, "Regionalism, Politics, and Gender in Southwest History: The League of United Latin American Citizens' Expansion into New Mexico from Texas, 1929–1945," *Western Historical Quarterly* 29(1998): 459–83.

27 Vicki L. Ruiz, "*Una mujer sin fronteras*: Luisa Moreno and Latina Labor Activism," *Pacific Historical Review* 73(2004): 1–20.

28 Clare Sheridan, "'Another White Race': Mexican Americans and the Paradox of Whiteness in Jury Selection," *Law and History Review* 21(2003): 109–44.

29 Margaret Rose, "Dolores Huerta: The United Farm Workers Union," in Eric Arnesen, ed., *The Human Tradition in American Labor History* (Wilmington, DE: SR Books, 2004), 211–30.

30 Lisa García Bedolla, *Fluid Borders: Latino Power, Identity, and Politics in Los Angeles* (Berkeley: University of California Press, 2005).

31 Armando Navarro, *Mexicano Political Experience in Occupied Aztlán* (Lanham, MD: AltaMira Press, 2004), p. 277.

32 John David Skrentny, *The Minority Rights Revolution* (Cambridge, MA: Harvard University Press, 2002), p. 198.

33 Julie Leininger Pycior, "From Hope to Frustration: Mexican Americans and Lyndon Johnson in 1967," *Western Historical Quarterly* 24(1993): 469–94, p. 477.

34 As quoted in ibid., p. 478.

35 Ibid.

36 Peter Nabokov, *Tijerina and the Courthouse Raid* (Albuquerque: University of New Mexico Press, 1969).

37 Individuals of Mexican descent living in New Mexico often refer to themselves as Hispanos rather than Hispanics, Latinos, or Mexican Americans.

38 Reies López Tijerina, *They Called Me "King Tiger": My Struggle for the Land and Our Rights*, trans. José Angel Gutiérrez (Houston, TX: Arte Público Press, 2001).

39 Matt S. Meier and Margo Gutiérrez, *Encyclopedia of the Mexican American Civil Rights Movement* (Westport, CT: Greenwood Press, 2000).

40 As quoted in George Mariscal, *Brown-Eyed Children of the Sun: Lessons from the Chicano Movement, 1965–1975* (Albuquerque: University of New Mexico Press, 2005).

41 Carlos Muñoz, *Youth, Identity, Power: The Chicano Movement*, 2nd edn. (New York: Verso, 2007), p. 60.

42 Juan Gómez-Quiñones, *Chicano Politics: Reality and Promise, 1940–1990* (Albuquerque: University of New Mexico Press, 1990), p. 118.

43 Muñoz, 2007, p. 64.

44 Sal Castro continued his advocacy of Chicano educational access until his death in April 2013. His experiences are recorded in Mario García's book, *Blowout! Sal Castro and the Chicano Struggle for Educational Justice* (Raleigh: University of North Carolina Press, 2011).

45 Muñoz, 2007, p. 65.

46 Ibid., p.68.
47 Dolores Delgado Bernal, "Grassroots Leadership Reconceptualized: Chicana Oral Histories and the 1968 East Los Angeles School Blowouts," *Frontiers: A Journal of Women Studies* 19(1998): 113–42.
48 José Angel Gutiérrez, *The Making of a Chicano Militant: Lessons from Cristal* (Madison: University of Wisconsin Press, 1998), pp. 187–8.
49 Gómez-Quiñones, 1990, p.130.
50 Ibid., p.132.
51 Alma M. García, *Chicana Feminist Thought: The Basic Historical Writings* (New York: Routledge, 1997).
52 Denise A. Segura, "Challenging the Chicano Text: Toward a More Inclusive Contemporary Causa," *Signs* 26(2001): 541–50.
53 Aida Hurtado, "*Sitios y lenguas*: Chicanas Theorize Feminisms," *Hypatia* 13(1998): 134–61; Alma García, 1997.
54 In 1996, the University of Texas at Arlington interviewed Rosie Castro as part of its *Tejano Voices* series. She describes her early life, work in the Chicano Movement, and subsequent political efforts in San Antonio. The full audio of the interview is available at: http://library.uta.edu/tejanovoices/interview.php?cmasno=123 (last accessed August 21, 2013).
55 Gisele Henriques and Raj Patel, "NAFTA, Corn, and Mexico's Agricultural Trade Liberalization," Special Report. Interhemispheric Resource Center (IRC) Americas Program, 2004, available at http://americas.irc-online.org/reports/2004/0402nafta.html (last accessed December 14, 2008).
56 Fred Krissman, "'Them' or 'Us'? Assessing Responsibility for Undocumented Migration from Mexico," Working Paper, UC San Diego: Center for Comparative Immigration Studies (2001).
57 Passel et al., 2013.
58 Interhemispheric Resource Center, "Mexican Hometown Associations," *Citizen Action in the Americas*, 5, available at www.cipamericas.org/archives/1179 (last accessed March 2, 2014).

CHAPTER 4

1 Nuclear DNA, or the genetic material present in a gene's nucleus, is inherited in equal proportions from one's father and mother. Mitochondrial DNA is inherited only from one's mother and does not change or blend with other materials over time. See www.centrelink.org/KearnsDNA.html (last accessed February 23, 2014).
2 There are seven ways in which a US-born individual may lose her citizenship: (1) by being naturalized in a foreign country, upon the person's own application, made after reaching 18 years of age; (2) by making an oath or other declaration of allegiance to a foreign country or division thereof – again, after reaching 18 years of age; (3) by serving in the armed forces of a foreign country, if those armed forces are engaged in hostilities against the US, or if the person serves as an officer; (4) by working for the government of a foreign country, if the person also obtains nationality in that country, or if, in order to work in such a position, an oath or some other declaration of allegiance is required; (5) by making a formal

renunciation of US citizenship before a US consular officer or diplomat in a foreign country; (6) by making a formal written statement of renunciation during a state of war, if the US Attorney General approves the renunciation as being not contrary to US national defense; and (7) by committing an act of treason against the US, or by attempting by force or the use of arms to overthrow the government of the US. Renunciation by this means can be accomplished only after a court has found the person guilty.

3 Statehood and independence were not given as options in this plebiscite.

4 Both major US political parties do allow Puerto Rican delegates to participate in their nominating conventions, but Puerto Ricans on the island have no formal say in the general election.

5 There was a referendum in 1991, but this vote was to amend the island's constitution, and was not a referendum on the status of the island.

6 These referenda are non-binding. Although they do provide important information about Puerto Rican opinion on the subject, if Puerto Rico were to vote in favor of either statehood or independence, the US Congress is under no obligation to act so as to support that decision.

7 Brett Wallach, "Puerto Rico: Growth, Change, Progress, Development," *Focus* 39(1989): 27–33.

8 Pedro A. Cabán, "Industrial Transformation and Labour Relations in Puerto Rico: From 'Operation Bootstrap' to the 1970s," *Journal of Latin American Studies* 21(1989): 559–91, p. 565.

9 Wallach, 1989.

10 Cabán, 1989, p. 566.

11 James L. Dietz, *Economic History of Puerto Rico: Institutional Change and Capitalist Development* (Princeton, NJ: Princeton University Press, 1984), p. 297.

12 As quoted in José Ramón Sánchez, *Boricua Power: A Political History of Puerto Ricans in the United States* (New York: New York University Press, 2007), p. 57.

13 Felix Padilla, *Puerto Rican Chicago* (Notre Dame, IN: University of Notre Dame Press, 1987).

14 Much of this discussion of early political life in New York City is taken from Virginia Sánchez-Korrol, *From Colonia to Community: The History of Puerto Ricans in New York City* (Berkeley: University of California Press, 1994), ch. 6.

15 Ibid., p. 26.

16 Angelo Falcón, "A History of Puerto Rican Politics in New York City: 1860s to 1945," in James Jennings and Monte Rivera, eds., *Puerto Rican Politics in Urban America* (Westport, CT: Greenwood Press, 1984), 15–42, p. 23.

17 This account relies heavily on Nancy A. Hewitt, "Luisa Capetillo: Feminist of the Working Class," in Vicki L. Ruiz and Virginia Sánchez-Korrol, eds., *Latina Legacies: Identity, Biography, and Community* (New York: Oxford University Press, 2005), 120–34, p. 132.

18 Sánchez, 2007, p. 70.

19 Falcón, 1984, p. 26.

20 As quoted in Sánchez-Korrol, 1994, p. 183.

21 Ibid., p. 184.

22 "Introduction," in Jennings and Rivera, 1984, p. 3.

23 Falcón, 1984, p. 32.

24 Sánchez-Korrol, 1994, p. 184.
25 Ibid., p. 177.
26 Sherrie Baver, "Puerto Rican Politics in New York City: The Post-World War II Period," in Jennings and Rivera, 1984, 43–59, p. 45.
27 Ibid.
28 Sánchez-Korrol, 1994, p. 191.
29 Sánchez, 2007, p. 197.
30 Baver, 1984, p. 49.
31 Ibid., p. 47.
32 The Black power movement was a movement advocating violence and led by the Black Panthers; it was very influential in US leftist politics in the late 1960s.
33 Sánchez-Korrol, 1994, p. 214.
34 Iris Morales, "¡Palante, Siempre Palante! The Young Lords," in Andrés Torres and José E. Velásquez, eds., *The Puerto Rican Movement: Voices from the Diaspora* (Philadelphia: Temple University Press, 1998), 210–27, p. 218.
35 Ibid., p. 213.
36 Ibid., p. 216.
37 Torres, "Introduction," in Torres and Velázquez, 1998, p. 9.
38 Ibid.

CHAPTER 5

1 This account relies heavily on Nancy A. Hewitt, *Southern Discomfort: Women's Activism in Tampa, Florida, 1880s–1920s* (Urbana and Chicago: University of Illinois Press, 2001). See also www.thetampariverwalk.com/userfiles/files/RW%20 HMT%20PAULINA%20PEDROSO_Long%20Bio_Draft.pdf (last accessed August 21, 2013).
2 It is now suspected that the explosion of the USS *Maine* was an accident, the result of an overheated boiler. But at the time, the US military and most government officials felt certain the explosion was the result of Spanish sabotage. Regardless of the facts, this explosion did set the stage for the United States' declaration of war against Spain.
3 "Gomez to Write on the War," *New York Times*, November 1, 1899, p. 5.
4 "Cubans Define Relations," *New York Times*, February 28, 1901, p. 2.
5 Louis A. Pérez, *Cuba between Empires, 1878–1902* (Pittsburgh, PA: University of Pittsburgh Press, 1998), p. 325.
6 H. W. Brands, *T. R.: The Last Romantic* (New York: Basic Books, 1998), p. 569.
7 Terence Cannon, *Revolutionary Cuba* (New York: Crowell, 1981), p. 94.
8 Jeffrey J. Safford, "The Nixon–Castro Meeting of 19 April 1959," *Diplomatic History* 4(1980): 425–31, p. 431.
9 This ban remains in place despite a 1958 Supreme Court ruling to the effect that US citizens have a constitutional right to travel abroad. In *Rockwell Kent and Walter Briehl* v. *John Foster Dulles*, the court held that "the right to travel is a part of the 'liberty' of which the citizen cannot be deprived without due process of law under the Fifth Amendment": Jane Franklin, *The Cuban Revolution and the United States: A Chronological History* (Melbourne: Ocean Press, 1997), p. 17.

10 María Cristina García, *Havana USA: Cuban Exiles and Cuban Americans in South Florida, 1959–1994* (Berkeley: University of California Press, 1997), p. 121.

11 Darío Moreno, "The Cuban Model: Political Empowerment in Miami," in F. Chris García, ed., *Pursuing Power: Latinos and the Political System* (Notre Dame, IN: University of Notre Dame Press, 1996), 208–26.

12 Félix Roberto Masud-Piloto, *From Welcomed Exiles to Illegal Immigrants: Cuban Migration to the US, 1959–1995* (Lanham, MD: Rowman & Littlefield, 1995).

13 Ibid., p. 54.

14 During 1961, commercial flights continued between the US and Cuba, even though both countries had ended diplomatic relations. After the Cuban missile crisis in 1962, direct flights were canceled, and were restarted only as part of the Camarioca airlift.

15 Dick Russell, "Little Havana's Reign of Terror," *New Times*, October 29, 1976.

16 Moreno, 1996, p. 219.

17 US Census Bureau, 'The Hispanic Population: Census 2000 Brief," May, 2001.

18 "Cuban Emigré Wins Election to US House," *New York Times*, August 31, 1989.

19 Bendixen & Amandi International, "Exit Poll of Hispanic Voters in Florida, 2012." Full report available at: http://bendixenandamandi.com/wp-content/uploads/2011/05/ElectionResults-ExitPoll.pdf (last accessed July 23, 2013).

20 Jorge Más Canosa passed away in 1997. The organization is now run by his son, Jorge Más Santos.

21 For more detailed information on the Free Cuba PAC and its financial disclosures, see www.opensecrets.org/pacs/lookup2.php?strID=C00142117&cycle=2004 (last accessed November 21, 2013).

22 Chris McGreal, "America's Hardline against Cuba Softens as Obama Lifts Restrictions," *The Guardian*, April 13, 2009, available at: www.guardian.co.uk/world/2009/apr/13/obama-ends-cuba-restrictions (last accessed July 23, 2013).

23 Cuban American National Foundation, "A New Course for U.S.–Cuba Policy: Advancing People-Driven Change" (2009), available at: http://69.89.31.192/~canforg/wp-content/uploads/2013/03/A-New-Course-for-US-Cuba-Policy.pdf (last accessed July 23, 2013).

24 Benjamin G. Bishin and Casey A. Klofstad, "The Political Incorporation of Cuban Americans: Why Won't Little Havana Turn Blue?" *Political Research Quarterly* 65.3 (2012): 586–99.

25 Ibid.

26 Cuban political expert Darío Moreno, in comments made at a conference sponsored by Florida International University's Cuban Research Institute, "Revisiting the Cuban American Vote," held in November 2013. Professor Moreno's comments may be found here: http://cri.fiu.edu/news/2013/presentations-on-revisiting-the-cuban-american-vote/ (last accessed November 21, 2013).

27 María Cristina García, *Havana USA: Cuban Exiles and Cuban Americans in South Florida, 1959–1994* (Berkeley: University of California Press, 1996), p. 79.

28 White House Press Release, "Fact Sheet: Reaching Out to the Cuban People," April 13, 2009, available at: www.whitehouse.gov/the_press_office/Fact-Sheet-Reaching-out-to-the-Cuban-people (last accessed July 23, 2013).

29 Damien Cave, "Raúl Castro Says this 5-Year Term Will Be His Last," *New York Times*, February 24, 2013, available at: www.nytimes.com/2013/02/25/world/americas/

raul-castro-to-step-down-as-cubas-president-in-2018.html?_r=0 (last accessed 23 July 2013).

30 US Department of State, Daily Press Briefing Transcript, February 25, 2013, available at: www.state.gov/r/pa/prs/dpb/2013/02/205179.htm#CUBA (last accessed July 23, 2013).

CHAPTER 6

1 Frank Moya Pons, *The Dominican Republic: A National* History, 3rd edn. (Princeton, NJ: Marcus Wiener, 2010), p. 38.
2 Ibid., p. 40.
3 Ibid., p. 47.
4 Ibid., p. 48.
5 Ibid., p. 58.
6 Ibid., p. 76.
7 Under French law, the offspring of unions between white colonists and their Black slaves were automatically free upon birth. They also could inherit their father's property if formally acknowledged by him. The lack of white women in the colony made these types of unions common, and resulted in a large number of wealthy *mulatto* landowners. White colonists, however, did not see the *mulattos* as their social equals and passed a number of laws to limit their political rights.
8 Moya Pons, 2010, p. 106.
9 Ibid., p. 109.
10 Ibid., p. 123.
11 Ibid., p. 132.
12 Ibid., p. 162.
13 As cited in ibid., p. 163.
14 Ibid., p. 222.
15 "Samana Bay," *New York Times*, January 19, 1873.
16 Ibid.
17 "Samana Bay. Work of the Company. Active Operations in Progress – New and Interesting Facts – Political Conditions of Santo Domingo," *New York Times*, September 6, 1873.
18 "Meeting of Directors of Samana Bay Company," *New York Times*, April 15, 1874.
19 Moya Pons, 2010, p. 260.
20 US State Department, "U.S. Relations with the Dominican Republic," available at: www.state.gov/r/pa/ei/bgn/35639.htm (last accessed August 21, 2013).
21 Moya Pons, 2010, p. 271.
22 Michael Waibel, *Sovereign Debts before International Courts and Tribunals* (Cambridge: Cambridge University Press, 2013), 47–8.
23 Moya Pons, 2010, p. 295.
24 G. Pope Atkins and Larman C. Wilson, *The Dominican Republic and the United States: From Imperialism to Transnationalism* (Athens: University of Georgia Press, 1998), p. 46.
25 Ibid., p. 47.
26 As cited in Moya Pons, 2010, p. 317.
27 Atkins and Wilson, 1998, p. 49.

28 Moya Pons, 2010, p.365.
29 The full text of the declassified memo is available at: www2.gwu.edu/~nsarchiv/NSAEBB/NSAEBB222/family_jewels_wilderotter.pdf. The portion referring to the Trujillo assassination may be found in section 11 (last accessed August 22, 2013).
30 Abraham F. Lowenthal, *The Dominican Intervention* (Baltimore, MD: Johns Hopkins University Press, 1995), p. 11.
31 Ibid.
32 Ibid., p.26.
33 Alan McPherson, "Misled by Himself: What the Johnson Tapes Reveal about the Dominican Intervention of 1965," *Latin American Research Review* 28(2003): 127–46, p.140.
34 Lowenthal, 1995, p.103.
35 McPherson, 2003, p.136.
36 Brendon J. O'Shea, "Operation Power Pack: U.S. Military Intervention in the Dominican Republic" (2010), available at: www.army.mil/article/37660 (last accessed August 22, 2013).
37 Clare Ribando Seelke, "Dominican Republic: Background and U.S. Relations" (Washington, DC: Congressional Research Service, 2012).
38 www.dominicantoday.com/dr/opinion/2013/6/28/48126/Remittances-underpin-the-Caribbean-economy (last accessed August 21, 2013).
39 Sherri Grasmuck and Patricia R. Pessar, *Between Two Islands: Dominican International Migration* (Berkeley: University of California Press, 1991), p. 19.
40 Ernesto Sagás and Sintia E. Molina, eds., *Dominican Migration: Transnational Perspectives* (Gainesville: University Press of Florida, 2004), p. 12.
41 Grasmuck and Pessar, 1991, p.30.
42 Ibid., pp.28–9.
43 Sagás and Molina, 2004, p.14; Grasmuck and Pessar, 1991, p.3.
44 Sagás and Molina, 2004, p.14.
45 Stephen Ruszczyk, "How do Latino Groups Fare in a Changing Economy? Occupation in Latino Groups in the Greater New York Area, 1980–2009," Report 48, Latino Data Project (City University of New York, Center for Latin American, Caribbean, and Latino Studies, 2010), p. 5.
46 Ibid., p.13.
47 Howard Caro-López and Laura Limonic, "Dominicans in New York City, 1990–2008," Report 31, Latino Data Project (City University of New York, Center for Latin American, Caribbean, and Latino Studies, 2009), 8.
48 Jesse Hoffnung-Garskof, *A Tale of Two Cities: Santo Domingo and New York after 1950* (Princeton, NJ: Princeton University Press, 2008), p. 99.
49 Ibid., p.118.
50 Ibid., p.131.
51 José Itzigsohn, "Immigration and the Boundaries of Citizenship: The Institution of Immigrants' Political Transnationalism," *International Migration Review* 34(2000): 1126–54.
52 Jorge Duany, *Quisqueya on the Hudson: The Transnational Identity of Dominicans in Washington Heights*, 2nd edn. Research Monograph (New York: CUNY Dominican Studies Institute, 2008), p. 5.
53 Ibid., p.6.

54 www.everyculture.com/multi/Bu-Dr/Dominican-Americans.html#ixzz2cjzDLLij_ (last accessed November 30, 2013).

55 Yamil Vargas, "Dominicanos en el exterior: la participación y la representatividad" (Santo Domingo: Observatorio Político Dominicano, Unidad de Partidos Políticos), available at: www.opd.org.do/index.php?option=com_content&view=article&id=592 (last accessed August 22, 2013).

56 Hoffnung-Garskof, 2008, p. 5.

57 Ibid.

58 Ibid.

59 Ana Aparicio, *Dominican-Americans and the Politics of Empowerment* (Gainesville: University Press of Florida, 2006), p. 10.

60 Migration Policy Institute, "The Dominican Population in the United States: Growth and Distribution" (Washington, DC: Migration Policy Institute, 2004), 1, available at: www.migrationpolicy.org/pubs/mpi_report_dominican_pop_us.pdf (last accessed August 22, 2013).

61 As quoted in Maria Newman, "New Leadership Forms in a Crucible of Violence," *New York Times*, July 11, 1992, available at www.nytimes.com/1992/07/11/nyregion/new-leadership-forms-in-a-crucible-of-violence.html (last accessed August 22, 2013).

62 Hoffnung-Garskof, 2008, p. 120.

63 Ibid., p. 123.

64 Ibid., p. 123.

65 Ibid., p. 123.

66 Milagros Ricourt, *Dominicans in New York City: Power from the Margins* (New York: Routledge: 2002), p. 66.

67 Ibid.

68 Hoffnung-Garskof, 2008, p. 125.

69 Luis E. Guarnizo, "Los Dominicanyorks: The Making of a Binational Society," *Annals of the American Academy of Political and Social Science* 533(1994): 70–86, p. 84.

70 Ricourt (2002), p. 80.

71 Ibid., p. 81.

72 Ibid., p. 77.

73 Ronald Sullivan, "New York Officer Said to be Cleared in Fatal Shooting," *New York Times*, September 10, 1992, available at www.nytimes.com/1992/09/10/nyregion/new-york-officer-said-to-be-cleared-in-fatal-shooting.html (last accessed August 22, 2013).

74 Ibid.

75 Newman, 1992.

76 www.everyculture.com/multi/Bu-Dr/Dominican-Americans.html#ixzz2cjyaBzP7 (last accessed February 23, 2014).

77 Aparicio, 2006, p. 47.

78 Ibid., p. 48.

79 Ibid., p. 34.

80 Duany, 2008, p. 13.

81 Krohn Hansen, 2013, p. 203.

82 www.ccny.cuny.edu/dsi/about-cuny-dsi.cfm (last accessed August 27, 2013).

83 Jonathan P. Hicks, "A Vigorous and Clamoring Campaign in the City's Dominican

Heartland," *New York Times*, August 21, 2011, available at: www.nytimes. com/2001/08/21/nyregion/a-vigorous-and-clamoring-campaign-in-the-city-s-dominican-heartland.html (last accessed August 22, 2013).

84 Hoffnung-Garskof, 2008, p. 130.

85 For more information about Maldonado, see: http://iarchives.nysed.gov/xtf/ view?docId=DSI_Maldonado.xml;query=;brand=default and http://www1.ccny. cuny.edu/ci/dsi/archives/archives-maldonado.cfm (last accessed August 27, 2013).

86 Elected-official information gathered from the Dominican American National Roundtable's list of Dominican elected officials, available at: http://danr.org/ elected-officials (last accessed August 22, 2013).

CHAPTER 7

1 Tom Barry and Deb Preusch, *The Central America Fact Book* (New York: Grove Press, 1986), p. 3.

2 Ibid., p. 4.

3 Americas Watch, *El Salvador's Decade of Terror: Human Rights Since the Assassination of Archbishop Romero* (New Haven, CT: Yale University Press, 1991), p. 2.

4 Thomas E. Skidmore and Peter H. Smith, *Modern Latin America*, 3rd edn. (New York: Oxford University Press, 1992), p. 333.

5 As quoted in ibid., p. 333.

6 As quoted in Barry and Preusch, 1986, p. 201.

7 Americas Watch, 1991, p. 3.

8 Ibid., p. 4.

9 Ibid.

10 Ibid.

11 Ibid.

12 Ibid, p. 5; Barry and Preusch, 1986, p. 204.

13 Barry and Preusch, 1986, p. 201.

14 Skidmore and Smith, 1992, p. 334; María Cristina García, *Seeking Refuge: Central American Migration to Mexico, the United States, and Canada* (Berkeley: University of California Press, 2006), p. 21.

15 Barry and Preusch, 1986, p. 201.

16 Ibid., p. 205.

17 Americas Watch, 1991, p. 6.

18 Skidmore and Smith, 1992, p. 335; Americas Watch, 1991, p. 6.

19 Americas Watch, 1991, p. 7.

20 Skidmore and Smith, 1992, p. 335.

21 Americas Watch, 1991, p. 8.

22 García, 2006, p. 23.

23 Ibid.

24 Americas Watch, 1991, p. 10; Skidmore and Smith, 1992, pp. 335–6.

25 García, 2006, p. 23.

26 Anthony Lewis, "A Bloody Joke," *New York Times*, October 17, 1983, p. A1.

27 García, 2006, p. 22.

28 Ibid., p. 23.

29 Americas Watch, 1991, p. 9.
30 Ibid.
31 Barry and Preusch, 1986, p. 226.
32 Ibid.
33 Ibid.
34 Skidmore and Smith, 1992, p. 339.
35 Barry and Preusch, 1986, p. 227.
36 Skidmore and Smith, 1992, p. 339.
37 Ibid.
38 Ibid.
39 Ibid., p. 340.
40 Barry and Preusch, 1986, p. 228.
41 Skidmore and Smith, 1992, p. 340.
42 Barry and Preusch, 1986, p. 228.
43 Ibid.
44 Ibid., p. 341.
45 Ibid.
46 García, 2006, p. 27.
47 Barry and Preusch, 1986, p. 225.
48 García, 2006, p. 26.
49 Ibid., p. 27.
50 Barry and Preusch, 1986, p. 229.
51 Ibid.
52 García, 2006, p. 27.
53 Barry and Preusch, 1986, p. 229; García, 2006, p. 27.
54 Barry and Preusch, 1986, p. 230.
55 "Guatemala Memory of Silence," Report of the Commission for Historical Clarification: Conclusions and Recommendations, pp. 34–5.
56 Ibid.
57 García, 2006, p. 28.
58 "Guatemala Memory of Silence," p. 42.
59 García, 2006, p. 29.
60 Ibid.
61 Ibid., p. 31.
62 Hamilton and Stoltz Chinchilla, 2001, p. 44.
63 Ibid., p. 45.
64 Barry and Preusch, 1986, p. 83.
65 Ibid.
66 García, 2006, p. 26.
67 Barry and Preusch, 1986, p. 88.
68 Ibid., p. 89.
69 Quoted in Americas Watch, 1991, p. 120, and in García, 2006, p. 25.
70 Americas Watch, 1991.
71 As quoted in García, 2006, p. 25.
72 This account relies heavily on Vicki L. Ruiz, "Luisa Moreno and Latina Labor Activism," in Vicki L. Ruiz and Virginia Sánchez-Korrol, eds., *Latina Legacies: Identity, Biography, and Community* (New York: Oxford University Press, 2005),

175–92. See also: www.sandiegohistory.org/journal/95fall/moreno.htm (last accessed July 25, 2013).

73 García, 2006, p.x.

74 Ibid., p.89.

75 Ibid., p.90.

76 Ibid.

77 Hector Perla, '*Si Nicaragua Venció, El Salvador Vencerá*: Central American Agency in the Creation of the US–Central American Peace and Solidarity Movement," *Latin American Research Review* 4.2(2008): 136–58.

78 Ibid.

79 Ibid.

80 Ibid.

81 Ibid.

82 Ibid.

83 Ibid.

84 García, 2006, p.98.

85 Quoted in ibid., p.99.

86 García, 2006, p.100; Perla, 2008.

87 García, 2006, p.107.

88 Ibid.

89 Susan Bibler Coutin, *Legalizing Moves: Salvadoran Immigrants' Struggle for US Residency* (Ann Arbor: University of Michigan Press, 2003), p.4.

90 García, 2006, p.111.

91 Ibid.

92 Ibid., p.112.

93 Ibid., p.91.

94 Coutin, 2003, p.5.

95 García, 2006, p.112.

96 Coutin, 2003, p.xiv.

97 Aaron Terrazas, "Central American Immigrants in the United States" (Washington, DC: Migration Policy Institute, 2011), available at: www.migrationinformation.org/usfocus/display.cfm?ID=821 (last accessed July 23, 2013).

98 Perla, 2008, pp.136–58.

99 Manuel Orozco and Eugenia García Zanello "Hometown Associations: Transnationalism, Philanthropy, and Development," *Brown Journal of World Affairs* 15(2) (2009): 57–73.

100 Based on the World Bank's remittance data, available at: http://econ.worldbank.org/WBSITE/EXTERNAL/EXTDEC/EXTDECPROSPECTS/0,,contentMDK:22759429~pagePK:64165401~piPK:64165026~theSitePK:476883,00.html#Remittances (last accessed July 23, 2013).

CHAPTER 8

1 Charles B. Keely, "Effects of the Immigration Act of 1965 on Selected Population Characteristics of Immigrants to the United States," *Demography*, 8(1971): 157–69.

2 Nancy Rytina, "IRCA Legalization Effects: Lawful Permanent Residence and Naturalization through 2001," paper presented at the "Effects of Immigrant

Legalization Programs on the United States" conference, Mary Woodward Lasker Center, NIH Main Campus, October 2002.

3 Pia M. Orrenius and Madeline Zavodny, "Do Amnesty Programs Reduce Undocumented Migration? Evidence from IRCA," *Demography* 40(2003): 437–50.

4 Jeffrey S. Passel and D'Vera Cohn, "Unauthorized Immigrant Population: National and State Trends, 2010" (Washington, DC: Pew Hispanic Center, 2011), available at: www.pewhispanic.org/files/reports/133.pdf (last accessed July 24, 2013).

5 As quoted in the Southern Poverty Law Center's *Intelligence Report* magazine, Summer 2005.

6 From VDARE.com, article titled "Top Ten Reasons Why the US Should not Marry Mexico," January 1, 2007, available at: www.vdare.com/articles/top-ten-reasons-why-the-us-should-not-marry-mexico (last accessed November 21, 2013).

7 Speech given at the March for America, Washington, DC, June 18, 2007.

8 Message sent to Save Our State supporters on October 7, 2006.

9 As reported by the Southern Poverty Law Center: www.splcenter.org/get-informed/intelligence-report/browse-all-issues/2011/winter/anti-latino-hate-crimes-spike-in-cali (last accessed August 29, 2013).

10 Ted Wang and Robert C. Winn, 'Groundswell Meets Groundwork: Preliminary Recommendations for Building on Immigrant Mobilizations" (New York: Four Freedoms Fund, 2006).

11 Kim Voss and Irene Bloemraad, eds., *Rallying for Immigrant Rights: The Fight for Inclusion in 21st Century America* (Berkeley: University of California Press, 2010).

12 Mark Hugo López, Ana González-Barrera, and Seth Motel, "As Deportations Rise to Record Levels, Most Latinos Oppose Obama's Policy" (Washington, DC: Pew Hispanic Center, 2011).

13 www.latinorebels.com/2012/06/06/dreamers-stage-sit-in-at-obama-campaign-office-to-protest-presidents-deportation-policies (last accessed November 30, 2013).

14 www.huffingtonpost.com/2012/06/13/dream-act-protesters-who-_n_1593739.html (last accessed November 30, 2013).

15 2012 National Election Poll. I understand that Asian American and Native American women are also women of color. Unfortunately, the exit polls did not include them in their reporting so they cannot be included here. Results from the National Asian American survey show no gender gap in Obama support among Asian American women (42 percent male support; 43 percent female), suggesting that this phenomenon may be limited to Latina and African American women.

16 *State of Texas* v. *Holder*. The full text of the ruling is available at: www.washingtonpost.com/wp-srv/politics/documents/texas-voter-id-law/index.html (last accessed November 27, 2012).

17 Lisa García Bedolla and Melissa R. Michelson, *Mobilizing Inclusion: Transforming the Electorate through Get-Out-the-Vote Campaigns* (New Haven: Yale University Press, 2012).

Bibliography

Acosta-Belén, E., and C. E. Santiago. 2006. *Puerto Ricans in the United States: A Contemporary Portrait*. Boulder, CO: Lynne Rienner.

Alcoff, Linda. 2000. "Is Latina/o Identity a Racial Identity?" in Jorge J. E. Gracia and Pablo DeGreiff, eds., *Hispanics/Latinos in the United States: Ethnicity, Race and Rights*. New York: Routledge, pp. 23–44.

Americas Watch. 1991. *El Salvador's Decade of Terror: Human Rights Since the Assassination of Archbishop Romero*. New Haven, CT: Yale University Press.

"An Act for the Protection of Actual Settlers and to Quiet Land Titles in this state. Approved March 26, 1856." 1856. In *Statutes of California passed at the Seventh Session of the Legislature, Begun on the Seventh Day of January, One Thousand Eight Hundred and Fifty-six, and Ended on the Twenty-first Day of April, One Thousand Eight Hundred and Fifty-six, at the City of Sacramento*. Sacramento, CA: James Allen, pp. 54–7.

Aparicio, Ana. 2006. *Dominican-Americans and the Politics of Empowerment*. Gainesville: University Press of Florida.

Arrellano, Gustavo. 2010. "Mi Casa es Mi Casa," *OC Weekly*, May, available at: www.ocweekly.com/2010–05–06/news/alex-bernal-housing-dis crimination (last accessed November 30, 2013).

Atkins, G. Pope, and Larman C. Wilson. 1998. *The Dominican Republic and the United States: From Imperialism to Transnationalism*. Athens: University of Georgia Press.

Avila, Joaquín. 2003. "Political Apartheid in California: Consequences of Excluding a Growing Noncitizen Population," in *Latino Policy and Issues Brief*. Los Angeles: UCLA Chicano Studies Research Center.

Barry, Tom, and Deb Preusch. 1986. *The Central America Fact Book*. New York: Grove Press.

Baver, Sherrie. 1984. "Puerto Rican Politics in New York City: The Post-World War II Period," in James Jennings and Monte Rivera, eds., *Puerto Rican Politics in Urban America*. Westport, CT: Greenwood Press, pp. 43–59.

Beltrán, Cristina. 2010. *The Trouble with Unity: Latino Politics and the Creation of Identity*. New York: Oxford University Press, 2010.

Brands, H. W. 1998. *T. R.: The Last Romantic*. New York: Basic Books.

Briggs, Laura. 2002. *Reproducing Empire: Race, Sex, Science, and US Imperialism in Puerto Rico*. Berkeley: University of California Press.

Cabán, Pedro A. 1989. "Industrial Transformation and Labour Relations in Puerto Rico: From 'Operation Bootstrap' to the 1970s," *Journal of Latin American Studies*, 21: 559–91.

Cannon, Terence. 1981. *Revolutionary Cuba*. New York: Crowell.

Caro-López, Howard, and Laura Limonic. 2009. "Dominicans in New York City, 1990–2008," Report 31, Latino Data Project. City University of New York, Center for Latin American, Caribbean, and Latino Studies.

Carrigan, William T., and Clive Webb. 2003. "The Lynching of Persons of Mexican Origin or Descent in the United States, 1848 to 1928," *Journal of Social History*, 37: 411–38.

Carter, Susan B., Scott Sigmund Gartner, Michael R. Haines, Alan L. Olmstead, Richard Sutch, and Gavin Wright, eds., *Historical Statistics of the United States: Millennial Edition Online* (New York: Cambridge University Press, 2006), available at http://hsus.cambridge.org/HSUSWeb/HSUSEntryServlet (last accessed March 2, 2014).

Conley, Dalton. 1999. *Being Black, Living in the Red: Race, Wealth, and Social Policy in America*. Berkeley: University of California Press.

Coutin, Susan Bibler. 2003. *Legalizing Moves: Salvadoran Immigrants' Struggle for US Residency*. Ann Arbor: University of Michigan Press.

Dawson, Michael C. 1995. *Behind the Mule: Race and Class in African American Politics*. Princeton, NJ: Princeton University Press.

Delgado Bernal, Dolores. 1998. "Grassroots Leadership Reconceptualized: Chicana Oral Histories and the 1968 East Los Angeles School Blowouts," *Frontiers: A Journal of Women Studies*, 19: 113–42.

Dietz, James L. 1984. *Economic History of Puerto Rico: Institutional Change and Capitalist Development*. Princeton, NJ: Princeton University Press.

Duany, Jorge. 2008. *Quisqueya on the Hudson: The Transnational Identity of Dominicans in Washington Heights*, 2nd edn. Research Monograph. New York: CUNY Dominican Studies Institute.

Falcón, Angelo. 1984. "A History of Puerto Rican Politics in New York City: 1860s to 1945," in James Jennings and Monte Rivera, eds., *Puerto Rican Politics in Urban America*. Westport, CT: Greenwood Press, pp. 15–42.

Fernández, Raúl E., and Gilbert G. González. 2003. *A Century of Chicano History: Empire, Nations, and Migration*. New York: Routledge.

Franklin, Jane. 1997. *The Cuban Revolution and the United States: A Chronological History*. Melbourne: Ocean Press.

García, Alma M. 1997. *Chicana Feminist Thought: The Basic Historical Writings*. New York: Routledge.

García, F. Chris, Angelo Falcón, and Rodolfo de la Garza. 1996. "Ethnicity and Politics: Evidence from the Latino National Political Survey," *Hispanic Journal of Behavioral Sciences*, 18: 91–103.

García, John A. 1997. "Political Participation: Resources and Involvement among Latinos and the American Political System," in F. Chris García, ed., *Pursuing Power: Latinos and the Political System*. Notre Dame, IN: University of Notre Dame Press, pp. 44–71.

García, María Cristina. 1996. *Havana USA: Cuban Exiles and Cuban Americans in South Florida, 1959–1994*. Berkeley: University of California Press.

García, María Cristina. 2006. *Seeking Refuge: Central American Migration to Mexico, the United States, and Canada*. Berkeley: University of California Press.

García, Mario. 2011. *Blowout! Sal Castro and the Chicano Struggle for Educational Justice*. Raleigh: University of North Carolina Press.

García Bedolla, Lisa. 2005. *Fluid Borders: Latino Power, Identity, and Politics in Los Angeles*. Berkeley: University of California Press.

García Bedolla, Lisa, and Melissa R. Michelson. 2012. *Mobilizing Inclusion: Transforming the Electorate through Get-Out-the-Vote Campaigns*. New Haven: Yale University Press.

Gómez-Quiñones, Juan. 1990. *Chicano Politics: Reality and Promise, 1940–1990*. Albuquerque: University of New Mexico Press.

González, Gilbert G. 2006. *Guest Workers or Colonized Labor? Mexican Labor Migration to the United States*. Boulder, CO: Paradigm.

Grasmuck, Sherri, and Patricia R. Pessar. 1991. *Between Two Islands: Dominican International Migration*. Berkeley: University of California Press.

Guarnizo, Luis E. 1994. "Los Dominicanyorks: The Making of a Binational Society," *Annals of the American Academy of Political and Social Science*, 533: 70–86.

Gutiérrez, José Angel. 1998. *The Making of a Chicano Militant: Lessons from Cristal*. Madison: University of Wisconsin Press.

Hagan, Jacqueline Maria. 1998. "Social Networks, Gender, and Immigrant Incorporation: Resources and Constraints," *American Sociological Review*, 63: 55–67.

Hamilton, Nora, and Norma Stoltz Chinchilla. 2001. *Seeking Community in a Global City: Guatemalans and Salvadorans in Los Angeles*. Philadelphia, PA: Temple University Press.

Haney-López, Ian. 1997. *White by Law: The Legal Construction of Race*. New York: New York University Press.

Hardy-Fanta, Carol. 1993. *Latina Politics, Latino Politics: Gender, Culture and Political Participation in Boston*. Philadelphia, PA: Temple University Press.

Henriques, Gisele, and Raj Patel. 2004. "NAFTA, Corn, and Mexico's Agricultural Trade Liberalization," Special Report. Interhemispheric Resource Center (IRC) Americas Program, available at http://americas. irc-online.org/ reports/2004/0402nafta.html (last accessed December 14, 2008).

Hewitt, Nancy A. "Luisa Capetillo: Feminist of the Working Class," in Vicki L.

Ruiz and Virginia Sánchez-Korrol, eds., *Latina Legacies: Identity, Biography, and Community*. New York: Oxford University Press, 2005, pp. 120–34.

Hewitt, Nancy A. 2001. *Southern Discomfort: Women's Activism in Tampa, Florida, 1880s–1920s*. Urbana and Chicago: University of Illinois Press.

Hewson, Martha S. 2004. *John Quincy Adams*. New York: Chelsea House Publishers.

Hoffnung-Garskof, Jesse. 2008. *A Tale of Two Cities: Santo Domingo and New York after 1950*. Princeton, NJ: Princeton University Press.

Hurtado, Aida. 1998. "*Sitios y lenguas*: Chicanas Theorize Feminisms," *Hypatia*, 13: 134–61.

Interhemispheric Resource Center. 2003. "Mexican Hometown Associations," *Citizen Action in the Americas*, 5, available at www.cipamericas.org/archives/1179 (last accessed March 2, 2014).

Itzigsohn, José. 2000. "Immigration and the Boundaries of Citizenship: The Institution of Immigrants' Political Transnationalism," *International Migration Review*, 34: 1126–54.

Jennings, James, and Monte Rivera, eds. 1984. *Puerto Rican Politics in Urban America*. Westport, CT: Greenwood Press.

Keely, Charles B. 1971. "Effects of the Immigration Act of 1965 on Selected Population Characteristics of Immigrants to the United States," *Demography*, 8: 157–69.

Krissman, Fred. 2001. "'Them' or 'Us'? Assessing Responsibility for Undocumented Migration from Mexico," Working Paper, UC San Diego: Center for Comparative Immigration Studies.

Krohn-Hansen, Christian. 2013. *Making New York Dominican: Small Business, Politics, and Everyday Life*. Philadelphia: University of Pennsylvania Press.

Lewis, Anthony. 1983. "A Bloody Joke," *New York Times*, October 17, p. A1.

Lipsitz, George. 1998. *The Possessive Investment in Whiteness: How White People Profit from Identity Politics*. Philadelphia, PA: Temple University Press.

López, Mark Hugo, Ana González-Barrera, and Seth Motel. 2011. "As Deportations Rise to Record Levels, Most Latinos Oppose Obama's Policy." Washington, DC: Pew Hispanic Center.

Mariscal, George. 2005. *Brown-Eyed Children of the Sun: Lessons from the Chicano Movement, 1965–1975*. Albuquerque: University of New Mexico Press.

Masud-Piloto, Félix Roberto. 1995. *From Welcomed Exiles to Illegal Immigrants: Cuban Migration to the US, 1959–1995*. Lanham, MD: Rowman & Littlefield.

McPherson, Alan. 2003. "Misled by Himself: What the Johnson Tapes Reveal about the Dominican Intervention of 1965," *Latin American Research Review*, 28: 127–46.

Meier, Matt S., and Margo Gutiérrez. 2000. *Encyclopedia of the Mexican American Civil Rights Movement*. Westport, CT: Greenwood Press.

Menchaca, Martha. 2001. *Recovering History, Constructing Race: The Indian, Black, and White Roots of Mexican Americans*. Austin: University of Texas Press.

Menjívar, Cecilia, and Olivia Salcido, "Gendered Paths to Legal Status: the Case of Latin American Immigrants in Phoenix, Arizona" (Washington, DC: Immigration Policy Center, 2013), available at: www.immigration-policy.org/sites/default/files/docs/genderedpaths052813.pdf (last accessed July 12, 2013).

Montejano, David. 2010. *Quixote's Soldiers: A Local History of the Chicano Movement, 1966–1981*. Austin: University of Texas Press.

Morales, Iris. 1998. "¡Palante, Siempre Palante! The Young Lords," in Andrés Torres and José E. Velásquez, eds., *The Puerto Rican Movement: Voices from the Diaspora*. Philadelphia, PA: Temple University Press, pp. 210–27.

Moreno, Darío. 1996. "The Cuban Model: Political Empowerment in Miami," in F. Chris García, ed., *Pursuing Power: Latinos and the Political System*. Notre Dame, IN: University of Notre Dame Press, pp. 208–26.

Moya Pons, Frank. 2010. *The Dominican Republic: A National History*, 3rd edn. Princeton, NJ: Marcus Wiener.

Muñoz, Carlos. 2007. *Youth, Identity, Power: The Chicano Movement*, 2nd edn. New York: Verso.

Nabokov, Peter. 1969. *Tijerina and the Courthouse Raid*. Albuquerque: University of New Mexico Press.

NALEO Educational Fund. 2013. *National Directory of Latino Elected Officials, 2013*. Los Angeles, CA: NALEO Educational Fund.

Navarro, Armando. 2004. *Mexicano Political Experience in Occupied Aztlán*. Lanham, MD: AltaMira Press.

Newman, Maria. 1992. "New Leadership Forms in a Crucible of Violence," *New York Times*, July 11, available at www.nytimes.com/1992/07/11/nyregion/new-leadership-forms-in-a-crucible-of-violence.html (last accessed August 22, 2013).

O'Shea, Brendon J. 2010. "Operation Power Pack: U.S. Military Intervention in the Dominican Republic," available at www.army.mil/article/37660/ (last accessed August 22, 2013).

Olsen, Marvin E. 1969. "Two Categories of Political Alienation," *Social Forces*, 47: 288–99.

Omi, Michael, and Howard Winant. 1994. *Racial Formation in the United States from the 1960s to the 1990s*. New York: Routledge.

Orozco, Cynthia. 1998. "Regionalism, Politics, and Gender in Southwest History: The League of United Latin American Citizens' Expansion into New Mexico from Texas, 1929–1945," *Western Historical Quarterly*, 29: 459–83.

Orozco, Manuel, and Eugenia García Zanello. 2009. "Hometown Associations: Transnationalism, Philanthropy, and Development," *Brown Journal of World Affairs*, 15 (2): 57–73.

Orrenius, Pia M., and Madeline Zavodny. 2003. "Do Amnesty Programs Reduce Undocumented Migration? Evidence from IRCA," *Demography*, 40: 437–50.

Padilla, Felix. 1987. *Puerto Rican Chicago*. Notre Dame, IN: University of Notre Dame Press.

Passel, Jeffrey S. and D'Vera Cohn. 2011. "Unauthorized Immigrant Population: National and State Trends, 2010." Washington, DC: Pew Hispanic Center, available at: www.pewhispanic.org/files/reports/133.pdf (last accessed July 24, 2013).

Passel, Jeffrey, D'Vera Cohn, and Ana Gonzalez Barrera. 2013. "Net Migration from Mexico Falls to Zero – Perhaps Less." Washington, DC: Pew Hispanic Center, available from: www.pewhispanic.org/files/2012/04/Mexican-migrants-report_final.pdf (last accessed July 22, 2013).

Pérez, Louis. 1998. *Cuba between Empires, 1878–1902*. Pittsburgh, PA: University of Pittsburgh Press.

Pérez, Louis A. 2003. *Cuba and the United States: Ties of Singular Intimacy*, 3rd edn. Atlanta: University of Georgia Press.

Perla, Hector. 2008. "*Si Nicaragua Venció, El Salvador Vencerá*: Central American Agency in the Creation of the US–Central American Peace and Solidarity Movement," *Latin American Research Review*, 43 (2): 136–58.

Pessar, Patricia. 1995. *A Visa for a Dream: Dominicans in the United States*. Boston: Allyn & Bacon.

Pycior, Julie Leininger. 1993. "From Hope to Frustration: Mexican Americans and Lyndon Johnson in 1967," *Western Historical Quarterly*, 24: 469–94.

Pycior, Julie Leininger. 1997. *LBJ and Mexican Americans: The Paradox of Power*. Austin: University of Texas Press.

Rose, Margaret. 2004. "Dolores Huerta: The United Farm Workers Union," in Eric Arnesen, ed., *The Human Tradition in American Labor History*. Wilmington, DE: SR Books.

Ruiz, Vicki L. 1998. *From Out of the Shadows: Mexican American Women in Twentieth Century America*. New York: Oxford University Press.

Ruiz, Vicki L. 2004. "Tapestries of Resistance: Episodes of School Segregation and Desegregation in the U.S. West," in Peter Lau, ed., *From Grassroots to the Supreme Court: Exploration of Brown v. Board of Education and American Democracy*. Durham: Duke University Press, pp. 44–67.

Ruiz, Vicki L.. 2004. "*Una mujer sin fronteras*: Luisa Moreno and Latina Labor Activism," *Pacific Historical Review*, 73: 1–20.

Ruiz, Vicki L. 2005. "Luisa Moreno and Latina Labor Activism," in Vicki L. Ruiz and Virginia Sánchez-Korrol, eds., *Latina Legacies: Identity, Biography, and Community*. New York: Oxford University Press, pp. 175–92.

Ruiz de Burton, María Amparo. 1997. *The Squatter and the Don*, 2nd edn. Houston, TX: Arte Público Press.

Russell, Dick. 1976. "Little Havana's Reign of Terror," *New Times*, October 29.

Ruszczyk, Stephen. 2012. "How do Latino Groups Fare in a Changing Economy? Occupation in Latino Groups in the Greater New York Area, 1980–2009," Report 48, Latino Data Project (City University of New York, Center for Latin American, Caribbean, and Latino Studies).

Rytina, Nancy. 2002. "IRCA Legalization Effects: Lawful Permanent Residence and Naturalization through 2001," paper presented at the "Effects of Immigrant Legalization Programs on the United States" conference, Mary Woodward Lasker Center, NIH Main Campus, October.

Safford, Jeffrey J. 1980. "The Nixon–Castro Meeting of 19 April 1959," *Diplomatic History*, 4: 425–31.

Sagás, Ernesto, and Sintia E. Molina, eds. 2004. *Dominican Migration: Transnational Perspectives*. Gainesville: University Press of Florida.

Sánchez, José Ramón. 2007. *Boricua Power: A Political History of Puerto Ricans in the United States*. New York: New York University Press.

Sánchez-Korrol, Virginia. 1994. *From Colonia to Community: The History of Puerto Ricans in New York City*. Berkeley: University of California Press.

Seelke, Clare Ribando. 2012. "Dominican Republic: Background and U.S. Relations." Washington, DC: Congressional Research Service.

Segura, Denise A. 2001. "Challenging the Chicano Text: Toward a More Inclusive Contemporary Causa," *Signs*, 26: 541–50.

Sheridan, Clare. 2003. "'Another White Race': Mexican Americans and the Paradox of Whiteness in Jury Selection," *Law and History Review*, 21: 109–44.

Skidmore, Thomas E., and Peter H. Smith. 1992. *Modern Latin America*, 3rd edn. New York: Oxford University Press.

Skrentny, John David. 2002. *The Minority Rights Revolution*. Cambridge, MA: Harvard University Press.

Smith, Rogers M. 2011. "Living in a Promised Land? Mexican Immigration and American Obligations," *Perspectives on Politics*, 9 (3): 545–57.

Tajfel, Henri, and J. Turner. 1986. "The Social Identity Theory of Intergroup Behavior," in Stephen Worchel and William Austin, eds., *Psychology of Intergroup Relations*. Chicago: Nelson-Hall, pp. 7–24.

Tate, Katherine. 1993. *From Protest to Politics: The New Black Voters in American Elections*. Cambridge, MA: Harvard University Press.

Terrazas, Aaron. "Central American Immigrants in the United States." Washington, DC: Migration Policy Institute, available at: www.migration-information.org/usfocus/display.cfm?ID=821 (last accessed July 23, 2013).

Tijerina, Reies López. 2001. *They Called Me "King Tiger": My Struggle for the Land and Our Rights*, trans. José Angel Gutiérrez. Houston, TX: Arte Público Press.

Torres, Andres, and José E. Velásquez, eds. 1998. *The Puerto Rican Movement: Voices from the Diaspora*. Philadelphia, PA: Temple University Press.

US Census Bureau. 2001. "The Hispanic Population: Census 2000 Brief," May.

Voss, Kim, and Irene Bloemraad, eds. 2010. *Rallying for Immigrant Rights: The*

Fight for Inclusion in 21st Century America. Berkeley: University of California Press.

Waibel, Michael. 2013. *Sovereign Debts before International Courts and Tribunals*. Cambridge: Cambridge University Press.

Wallach, Brett. 1989. "Puerto Rico: Growth, Change, Progress, Development," *Focus*, 39: 27–33.

Wang, Ted, and Robert C. Winn. 2006. "Groundswell Meets Groundwork: Preliminary Recommendations for Building on Immigrant Mobilizations." New York: Four Freedoms Fund.

Young, Iris Marion. 2000. "Structure, Difference and Hispanic/Latino Claims of Justice," in Jorge J. E. Gracia and Pablo De Greiff, eds., *Hispanics/ Latinos in the United States: Ethnicity, Race, and Rights*. New York: Routledge, pp. 147–65.

Zavella, Pat. 2011. *I'm Neither Here Nor There: Mexicans' Quotidian Struggles with Migration and Poverty*. Raleigh, NC: Duke University Press.

Index

Page numbers in **bold** type refer to a figure or table in the text.